Milestones on the Dover Road

John Dover Wilson, *c.* 1964

MILESTONES
ON
THE DOVER ROAD

by

John Dover Wilson

FABER AND FABER
24 Russell Square
London

First published in 1969
by Faber and Faber Limited
24 Russell Square London WC1
Printed in Great Britain by
Ebenezer Baylis and Son, Limited
The Trinity Press, Worcester, and London
All rights reserved

SBN 571 08775 2

TO MY DESCENDANTS

Contents

Contents

Illustrations

Acknowledgements

Acknowledgements are due to Sir John Gielgud and the Society of Authors as the literary representative of the Estate of the late John Masefield for the use of letters quoted in this book, and to Mr. C. B. Purdom for the use of quotations from his Life of Granville-Barker; to the British Academy and the British Museum for the photographs of W. W. Greg and Alfred Pollard and also to the executors of Sir William Rothenstein, Sir John Rothenstein and Mr. Michael Rothenstein, for the use of the portrait of Alfred Pollard; to the Radio Times Hulton Picture Library for the photograph of Field Marshal Wavell; to Barrie and Rockliff Ltd. for the photograph of Harley Granville-Barker; and to Professor and Mrs. R. A. Humphreys and the Clarendon Press for the photograph of Richard Pares.

This book, composed and written down over a considerable period of years, inevitably owes much to friends and relations. If, however, kind helpers do not find their names in the accompanying list, an old man with failing memory must ask their forgiveness.

Dr. Erasmus Barlow
Mr. Michael Black (Reader to the Cambridge University Press)
Professor Geoffrey Bullough
Mrs. Butt
Mr. Ernest Haddon
Professor and Mrs. R. A. Humphreys
Miss Khan (reader to Faber and Faber)
Professor Mustanoja
Mrs. Pares
Mr. W. H. Perkins
Miss Dorothy Pullinger
The Rev. David Stalker
Countess Wavell
My wife Elizabeth, my daughter Audrey, and above all my secretary, Miss C. A. M. Sym.

Preface

This is not an autobiography, though in the main it registers successive stages in my career and a lifelong self-education. After Chapter 1 there is little about home life and only a hint here and there of my religious beliefs and of the joys and sorrows that come to most men who live for eighty years.

Though I owe the title, suggested to me by my friend Professor Andrewes, to 'the inexorable and awful statement' of 'Mr. F's Aunt' in *Little Dorrit*,

'There's mile-stones on the Dover Road!'

I am thankful to feel none of her 'mortal hostility to the human race'. On the contrary, this book is a record of many friendships, some of them earned by my good fortune of having hitched my little wagon to a star, and all of them I think warm if not affectionate.

I

Childhood and Schooling

I was born on 13th July 1881 at Mortlake, near Putney, at which time my father, Edwin Wilson, was eking out a rather precarious living for himself and his young wife, whom he had married a year before, by drawing butterflies and other entomological specimens in the South Kensington Natural History Museum, for the illustrations of scientific books and the papers of scientists. At this time the Museum was infested with fleas, and one day when my father sat drawing, surrounded by a ring of Keating's Powder, the curator entered the room with an old man in gaiters looking like a farmer, whom he led up to one of the cases; he threw back the covering, at which the old gentleman, gazing before him, said, 'Lor, what a wonderful woman old Mother Nature is!' It was Charles Darwin. I never saw that great man but I was destined to have much to do with the members of his family who resided in Cambridge; and I still number Margaret Keynes, granddaughter of Charles Darwin, among my best friends. And I owe to Erasmus Barlow, grandson of Horace Darwin, a number of points in the following account, which he gleaned from the business records of the Cambridge Scientific Instrument Company.

My father's work at the South Kensington Museum brought him into general notice, and presently he received an invitation from Horace, youngest son of Charles Darwin, to join his company at Cambridge. At this date there were two sides to the Scientific Instrument Company; Darwin looked after the instrument-making and Dew-Smith, the well-known photographer, a wealthy amateur, had charge of the illustrations. But to complete this particular side, it was necessary to supplement Dew-Smith's photography with woodcuts, and my father came in for this purpose. Having no capital, he was never technically a partner; and

B   17

to the best of my recollection his relations with Dew-Smith were always of the best. Horace Darwin treated him as if he were a partner, and his wife, Lady Darwin, established very friendly relations with my mother. Indeed, I used to go about in a perambulator with a little boy of the same age called Erasmus Darwin who was, alas, killed in the First World War.

After joining the firm, my father had to supplement woodcuts by lithography. To master this technique he paid a visit of four months to Jena, where he could study the whole business from the Germans, who were the best lithographers in the world. From Jena he brought back G. Schneider, to work the lithographic printing machine.

It was in January 1884, while he was at Jena, that his young family made the move from Mortlake to Warkworth Terrace, Cambridge, overlooking Parker's Piece. My uncle, Walter Wilson, helped my mother to settle in the new home, himself standing godfather to her third child, born on 24th March 1884 and named after him. All in all, the family eventually comprised four boys and two girls, from myself as eldest to Winifred nine years younger.

One of the first-fruits of my father's visit to Jena was the lithographic reproduction in colour of successive phases of a sunset upon the Thames in 1883 that was created by the dust following the enormous eruption of the island of Krakatoa on the other side of the globe. This series of six lithographs reproducing sketches made by Mr. W. Ascroft made my father's name famous; it was indeed something of a miracle of skill, since it involved the use of several stones, each contributing one colour or shade in the total effect of a glorious sunset changing in colour from minute to minute. But even before he went abroad, I believe, he had provided illustrations for an elaborate edition of the scientific papers of Francis Maitland Balfour (brother of A. J.) who had just perished in the Alps.

The partnership between Darwin and Dew-Smith was dissolved in 1891, which meant that something had to be done about my father. The firm generously allowed him to retain the lithographic printing machine which he had worked for the past nine

or ten years. But now he had to set up on his own. For this purpose he secured the upper floor of a building in Post Office
Terrace, not far from the Scientific Instrument Company headquarters. And there he worked all day for over twenty years. I
was, as will appear, often away from home; but I have a vivid
recollection of seeing him at his drawing-table, sitting on a high
stool with a double-eyed microscope and the paper or whatever
he was drawing upon lying before him. His drawings, sometimes
on wood, sometimes on stone, were of a variety of objects, but
his chief work—exquisite and extraordinarily accurate—consisted of illustrations for different volumes of the Cambridge
Natural History, now of course long out of date. The type of
illustration now demanded for scientific papers being usually done
by photography, his plates in the C.N.H. are therefore I suppose
no longer considered of any value. Yet they were exquisite and
extraordinarily accurate, more accurate than any photograph
could be, since with his mastery of the microscope he had all
planes of an object, such as of a beetle, within his vision; and the
work is unique, for he had no serious rival. In short, it was
craftsmanship of the highest order.

Some of his clients, in particular Shipley, the Master of
Christ's, fully appreciated his genius. Under Shipley's aegis he
published an illustrated paper in the *Proceedings of the Royal
Society of Edinburgh* on the 'Stridulating Organ of the Mosquito'
in which the leg of the insect was shown, greatly magnified,
working across a ribbed portion of the body like the bow of a
violin.

Why was it that this wonderful work was, in general, finan-
cially so ill rewarded? Previous to 1891, my father had a fixed
salary from Horace Darwin of three hundred pounds per annum
—roughly equivalent in modern money to over one thousand
pounds, which was quite good for a young man. But after that
date, he had to make terms with his own individual clients. And
it was during this period that the family found it so difficult to
make ends meet. My father worked as hard as ever if not harder;
but he had now to put a price on each commission as it came
along. And like all genuine craftsmen, what mattered to him was

the work itself; and being a modest and retiring man he could never bring himself to put a price on his productions at all adequate to their real value. Indeed this was hard anyway to assess, since there was little market for illustrations of this kind. I have no doubt that many of his clients would willingly have paid more than he asked but thought that 'Wilson knew his own business best'. The trouble was he did not, and his income gradually dwindled. He struggled on until 1913, when he had to allow his business to be absorbed by the Cambridge University Press, and moved to a new office in Mill Lane. A sympathetic account of this absorption is given in an article on 'The Old Art Department' by Brooke Crutchley, now University Printer. By this date, my father was in failing health, and he died in 1915. There was, however, an even darker side to all this: the progressive mental disorder of my beloved and unhappy mother. But I shall speak of this later.

My father was one of the eleven children of Joseph Wilson, a civil engineer, who was much in demand as a consultant and founded the Crystal Palace School of Engineering; this was, I have always understood, the first engineering school in the country, preceding most of the engineering departments since established in technical colleges. The Wilsons, who sprang from farming stock in Derbyshire, were later a city family, mainly silk merchants. One member in the first half of the nineteenth century became Lord Mayor of London, Alderman Samuel Wilson. We were proud of him, but my pride became tempered with some amusement when I edited Matthew Arnold's *Culture and Anarchy* in 1932, and discovered in the forgotten first edition that the philistine Alderman Colonel of the City of London Militia, upon which Arnold expended some of his best witticisms, was the same Samuel, whose name, together with a number of other names, had been carefully removed in the second edition.

But the Wilsons were even prouder of their bishop than of their Lord Mayor. Daniel Wilson, at once cousin and brother-in-law of my great-grandfather, was a great builder of churches, not in England but in India. For he became Bishop of Calcutta, where he erected a cathedral together with a number of other churches in different parts of that great sub-continent. He was clearly a man of character. But, to me, the Bishop's greatest title to fame is that his name is linked in Newman's *Apologia* with that of Thomas Scott, author of the well-known commentary on the Bible and vicar in my mother's village of Aston Sandford. The reverence of a man like Newman for the extreme evangelical thinker that Daniel Wilson was, taken in conjunction with my own grandfather's reverence for the same man, suggests the kind of churchmanship which influenced the mind of my parents as they grew up.

My great-grandfather on my father's side, a very wealthy clergyman, had two livings; he was Vicar of Walthamstow in the winter months for sixteen years and of Worton near Woodstock in the summer months. And the story went that the migration from one to the other was a grand affair: a train of carriages and wagons to convey a large family, a number of servants and all sorts of household requisites, while I was even assured that a flock of geese formed part of the caravan. What an England it calls up in the imagination!

As one with a life-long interest in education, I like to remember too that this ancestor founded, in 1824, the Walthamstow-St. Mary's Infant Day School, which claimed at its centenary to be the oldest Church of England Infant school in the country. He also built the district churches of St. John, St. Mary, and St. James, so that he was a pluralist in a good as well as a less good sense.

My mother brought me a different background. Her father, John Dover, of Aston Sandford in Buckinghamshire was proud to call himself a yeoman farmer. He owned a thousand acres, and would say that if you stood above the White Cross on the hill overlooking the Vale of Aylesbury, the Dovers had cultivated most of the land within view at one time or other since the reign of King John. Aston Sandford was a cul-de-sac hamlet about a mile from Haddenham. It consisted of the manor in which my grandfather lived and my mother and her sisters grew up, a little church with a comfortable vicarage (my grandfather being the rector) and some dozen to fifteen cottages for the labourers on the farm. We were very Roundhead in those parts and the tradition went that Oliver himself had breakfasted at the manor on one occasion. As a child there I got to know the lovely Buckinghamshire countryside, before London stretched out its tentacles towards it.

My branch of the Dover family has died out, except, I think, for three second cousins and an unknown number of cousins of a sort somewhere in South America. And the ancestral manor has passed long since into the hands of strangers. My grandfather had five daughters and two sons; he also had a brother (a farmer like himself, with land in another part of Buckinghamshire) who died many years before I was born, leaving two young sons under the guardianship of my grandfather. He, being the soul of honour as I was always told, and so generous that his left hand knew not what his right hand did, took his guardianship very much in earnest: made a will to the effect that if the boys' land, which he was farming until they came of age, depreciated in value, they could instead take the equivalent in money according to the valuation at their father's death. In the meantime the agricultural depression intervened and the value of land fell greatly. After my grandfather died in 1880, the home farm of Aston Sandford, left to my mother and her sisters, was eventually sold up for the benefit of their younger cousin in compliance with the original will, the elder cousin having died. It was a family tragedy which overshadowed the life of my mother for many years and was the more difficult to bear in that my father's income declined so greatly after 1891. For a time her eldest sister with her husband lived at Aston and carried on the farm, until things became too difficult.

Res angusta domi would be an appropriate motto for our family life at Cambridge, or rather Chesterton, to which we soon moved from Warkworth Terrace. I can remember going to the village school at Chesterton, clutching a threepenny bit in a hot little fist. I suppose this was the fee one had to pay per week for education in a National School in those days. I later went on to a preparatory school in Kenley, where lived my Wilson grandparents, with whom I stayed during term-time for those years. At Kenley, I think I was more interested in butterflies and birds than in lessons—probably because the latter were not made interesting, whereas the former could not help being so. The Surrey fields, covered with the wild flowers that flourish on chalk, gave me a different country education from that of Buckinghamshire. At that date Surrey too was not yet a suburb of London. Kenley indeed was only approached by a branch line from Purley—or as it was then called, Caterham Junction. Coulsdon parish church beside which my grandparents now lie buried was within easy walking distance of Elmhurst, my grand-parents' house. We usually went there to church on Sunday, along a path leading through nut-woods full, in the spring, of primroses and bluebells. Those nut-woods—long since gone—seemed mysterious to a whipper-snapper; 'Enter these enchanted woods, Ye who dare.' But all things have an end, and when I got too old for the preparatory school (the fees of which I suspect were paid by my grandparents), I returned home and was sent, in 1894, to the Perse School, Cambridge. During that year, when I was about thirteen, we moved to Cherryhinton Road and became intimate with the Haddon family. Its head was the famous anthropologist A. C. Haddon, who, though residing at Cambridge, held a chair of zoology in Dublin at this time, and organized two separate expeditions to the Torres Straits. He had three children, his only son Ernest becoming my playmate and lifelong friend. We were fond of boxing, but though he was a year younger than me, my nose always bled first—which I never considered fair. Later when I came up to the university, I had the run of A. C. Haddon's study and many talks with him about anthropology; so that had I not gone in for university essay prizes, I might have become an anthropologist instead of an Elizabethan scholar. In point of fact, it was my son who became the anthro-pologist.

In the summer holidays after my first year at the Perse, I paid a visit to Sussex, at the invitation of my father's elder brother Ambrose J. Wilson. After being headmaster of the Melbourne Grammar School, he had recently returned to England as head-master of Lancing College. Like my father, he had six children, the eldest being about my age; so I had a great time, 'making one bathing of a summer's day', to say nothing of boating and careering across the Downs. Then one day at breakfast my uncle said, 'We've got a Scholarship Examination on today, Johnnie; would you like to go in?' As the sun was shining, I didn't much like; but with a rather bad grace I spent the day indoors, scribbling answers to questions, and thought no more about it. Shortly after my return home, my parents called me in from the garden with an open letter in their hands, telling them that I had been awarded a scholarship. I was surprised at the result, but expect I got it on the essay. Anyhow, I went to Lancing in September 1895 and was there for five years. Another wonderful period of country education, and a different variety altogether—the Downs, the sea, the tidal river, the combes full of primroses and sweet violets in the springtime. What more could a boy ask?

Public school education at the end of the nineteenth century, as far as my experience goes, would shock many public school masters and certainly all trained teachers today. French was taught by a mild native from France whom we used to tie to his desk; we afterwards decamped out of the window, returning before the hour's end to release him. As for the mathematics master, he was just a figure of fun upon whom we played as many practical jokes as our ingenuity could devise. The history—never any English history, at any rate in class—was Roman history from a horrid little green book packed with facts of which we were supposed to learn so many pages in prep. The history lesson consisted of questions shot at us by our form-master in early morning school, questions written on little slips of paper and only requiring a single word as answer. For example, 'Date of the Battle of Cannae?', 'Name of Julius Caesar's father?' and so on. The churchmanship was that of the Oxford Movement, and provision was made for the appointment of a school chaplain, who had charge of religious instruction. He was independent of the headmaster and was supposed to hear confessions from boys who so desired. As my uncle was Low Church, this gave rise to constant friction.

It was not until I reached the sixth form that I came across a real teacher, Ernest Crawley, still remembered, I believe, by anthropologists as author of *The Mystic Rose* and *The Tree of Life*—a strange man but extraordinarily stimulating to growing minds. His room was hung with Arundel reproductions (this was before the days of Medici prints); there they were, all the gods and goddesses of the ancient world—for I do not remember any Christian pictures—gloriously seen through the form and colour of the Renaissance imagination; and on the top of the bookshelves, running along the wall below them, were plaster casts. It was an experience thrilling beyond words for a lad growing up in a very Victorian atmosphere to visit that chamber of beauty once a week, to have his essay looked at. Crawley was a Hellenist through and through—his clerical orders were very incidental—and filled everyone in his sixth form with a passionate enthusiasm for the Greek way of life. The Greeks, I remember him once saying, had everything worth having that we have, except tobacco, and they had that in the Eleusinian Mysteries. When someone timidly asked how he knew, he replied, 'Why not?' It is one of the great regrets of my life that I never came under his full charge, for when I was in the fifth form, the form-master (who shall be nameless—*de mortuis* . . .) said to my uncle, the Head, 'This little nipper can write English; he ought to be crammed for a history scholarship.' I have never forgiven him, for though I got my history scholarship I was robbed of half my birthright. Instead of reading Homer and Aeschylus with Crawley, I sat alone in 'Big School' reading more or less ill-written history textbooks. But Crawley did look after my essays and my education generally in literature, elementary philosophy and so on. I have an essay still with marginal comments in red ink from a beautifully chased fountain pen—he had 'Everything handsome about him'. He disciplined my feeble attempts at style, and I owe him much, and not only for this. He opened the door of the world to many of the boys who came under his eye.

So far I have said little of my home life, but as I spent most of term-time away at school there is not much to retell. Yet my home-comings were always greeted as a kind of family festival, with my younger brothers and sisters learning to chant, 'When

Johnnie comes marching home again, hurrah, hurrah'—enough to undermine any native modesty I possessed.

It is the Sundays at home that I remember best; my mother seated at the piano on Sunday afternoon, while my father, who had a fine baritone, sang passages from Handel. I can hear him still, beginning 'He was despisèd and rejected'—memories that can never be lost, memories which taught me more religion than all the sermons I ever heard in church.

My father, being at work all day and coming home tired in the evening, could contribute very little directly to his boys' education. But to his close connection with the Cambridge scientific world and the minuteness and exactitude of his reproductions of natural life I must owe something of my interest in textual exactitude and the minutiae of bibliography. My brother Lance, who inherited something of the mechanical gifts of the Wilsons and even more of our father's artistic genius, shared with me our mother's instruction in literature and science.

Agnes Giberne was a first cousin of my father, and her popular book on astronomy was often conned by us both; while my mother, the gentle woman who had grown up on the farm at Aston Sandford, bequeathed to us a deep interest in flowers and wild birds and in nature generally. As we grew up she introduced us to various novelists, including Mrs. Ewing, Mrs. Gaskell, Charlotte Yonge and Charles Reade. Her favourite was George Eliot and the book she loved best *The Mill on the Floss*; on rereading *Adam Bede*, though, I suspect it probably lay nearer to her heart, as its descriptions of village life recall so many scenes at Aston Sandford.

My mother longed to be a novelist herself, was one indeed, though she could never get a publisher to accept any of her manuscripts. I believe quite a number were discovered under her bed when she fell ill and had to go away to a mental hospital. For in the end life became too difficult for her: the disappointment of being deprived of the financial help that she hoped to bring to my father; the daily effort to pay the bills and feed the mouths of a hungry family; the coming of the babies themselves, one after the other—after the three boys, twins arrived. They were a wonderful pair, the girl dark and very much like her mother, the boy a little archangel for fairness and beauty; and their birthday being Michaelmas Day, Michael and Angela had to be their names. Their birth, however, almost killed the frail mother. She struggled on for some years and gave me another sister, my beloved Winifred. The two sisters, coming at the end of the family, have ever since lived together and carried through in triumphant fashion a large school in Bexhill which they started shortly before our father's death some fifty years ago. During his last years, after my mother broke down, Angela had to leave school at the age of sixteen and step into the breach to keep house for him.

Meanwhile, I had arrived at the end of my school years. The time had come to enter for the history scholarship, for which this young colt had been fed and groomed. At that period, and it may still be the case, a group of colleges held a common examination for scholarships; a form arrived at Lancing, on which the candidate was asked to name the college of his preference. Growing up as I had done in Cambridge, King's College with its glorious chapel, its wonderful choir, its wide lawns stretching down to the river, looking across to the Backs, had always been the college of my dreams. So when my uncle said, 'Which college do you want to go to, Johnnie?' I answered without any hesitation. But he was deaf, and instead wrote down 'Caius'—and there it was. I was, of course, disconcerted when I found out what had happened, but I felt so lucky in getting a scholarship at all that I couldn't make a fuss about it. As it turned out I became luckier still through my uncle's mistake, for when the college adopted me as an Honorary Fellow in 1930, I became one of a band of brothers.

2

University and Marriage

I went up to Caius College, Cambridge, in 1900. The college, though I didn't realize it at the time, was very good to me from the beginning, for they allowed me to live at home while receiving the full total of the scholarship. My parents were so poor that this was indeed the only way I could have managed, and I didn't consume too large a share of the family larder since I ate my main meal of the day—and main I made it—in Hall. Yet it was a serious disability not to have rooms in college or even in lodgings near by; we lived some way out and I had no room at home in which I could conveniently entertain college friends. So I didn't get as much out of college during my undergraduate life as I ought to have done, yet when I asked at the office what I owed the college for three years, it came to only three shillings and sixpence.

As a history scholar I of course read for the History Tripos. Being at that stage much on the Left in my thinking, I had hoped to take the French Revolution as my special subject. I was unfortunate however in my supervisor, whose method of tutoring me was to put me in an easy chair in his room for one hour a week reading *The Times* and smoking cigarettes, both provided by him, while he copied out, in illegible handwriting, passages for me to read, mark and learn from textbooks which I already possessed. For this I understand he was paid a guinea a time by the college; his instruction also included the names of lecturers, all friends of his, whose lectures he expected me to attend. I, knowing nothing better, did as he said, being unaware that such giants as Lord Acton, Cunningham, Marshall and Maitland were all lecturing on subjects I had to read. And when he informed me that my special period was Frederick Barbarossa, for which he expected me to read a monkish Latin chronicle by Otto of

Freising, my heart sank; in the end I rebelled, for I never opened the chronicle and my examiners therefore could not give me a First Class in the Tripos. As time went on, however, I discovered some great men for myself, and began to attend lectures by George Trevelyan, Lowes Dickinson and Neville Figgis, all of whom became friends for life.

Trevelyan was five years older than myself at this time; a young don at Trinity, he had just finished his Fellowship thesis on the age of Wyclif. Though after he took to writing his great histories he seemed to lose the power of lecturing well, he was at this time brilliant and a joy to all the young men who flocked to hear him. He was also at his most iconoclastic period and one incident sticks firmly in my memory.

He was lecturing on the Counter-Reformation. Appearing suddenly to realize that a row of priests in minor orders sat beneath his nose, he turned directly to them. 'Gentlemen,' he said, 'do not misunderstand me. The Jesuits did not invent the art of assassination; they merely consecrated it to the service of God.'

His rooms in college were open to all who liked to drop in, and he delighted to read poetry aloud to us, Browning and Meredith being his favourites. He also organized tramps and would lead a party up to the Fleam Dyke on Sunday morning (so as to prevent us going to chapel), the party generally including some who afterwards became members of the Bloomsbury set. And I still have a picture in memory of George striding along the dyke shouting Meredith's verse at the top of his voice, while we trailed after, Lytton Strachey at the end of the pack, dragging weary steps along, quite out of earshot.

In any case the Sunday tramps did not continue long, since Trevelyan presently announced his intention of leaving Cambridge. And how well I remember the moment when he told a number of us gathered in his room that he was going! It was a catastrophe; what would Cambridge be like without George; or what would George do without Cambridge?

'I am going away,' he said, 'to write. It is impossible to write in Cambridge; the atmosphere is too critical, too negative.'

But there was another and more urgent reason, I suspect. Lord

Acton had recently been succeeded as Professor of Modern History by J. B. Bury, and Bury stood for a conception of history from which Trevelyan violently dissented. As it happened, I was present, like Trevelyan, at Bury's Inaugural Lecture in 1902. 'History is a science, nothing less and nothing more,' the professor insisted again and again; and all the while I watched the blood mounting in Trevelyan's face, and when it was over he flung out—to give us *Clio: a Muse*, and to spend the rest of his life writing history of another kind altogether.

He eventually returned to Cambridge, however, in 1940, as successor to J. J. Thomson, the Master of Trinity. One of his first acts was to take over an invitation to myself originally made by the college in 1935 to deliver the Clark Lectures. By then the war had begun and I was living in Edinburgh, so there was some difficulty in arranging dates. But the lectures were ultimately delivered at a lecture room in Mill Lane in May 1943 and I was put up in the Master's Lodge during that week. The title I chose was 'The Fortunes of Falstaff', based upon my study of *Henry IV Parts I and II*—plays I was then working on for the *New Cambridge Shakespeare* and ones I knew were favourites with Trevelyan.

It was a delightful renewal of friendship, the more delightful in that it extended to Trevelyan's wife, Janet. Daughter of Mrs. Humphry Ward, and niece of Matthew Arnold, she was endowed with Matthew's refusal to take things too seriously, however serious he might think them—the perfect wife for her serious-minded George with whom she had travelled all over Italy when he was writing his Garibaldi books. Alas, all tramping days were over, for when I first met her at Trinity she was already falling into the grip of the paralysis which was in the end to keep her chained immovable to her chair. But the spirit could never be in chains; it remained sweet and cheerful, even merry, as it must always have been. To her husband it was agony to watch the progress of the disease. He endured it with Meredithian stoicism, but there came moments when he could not help half-crying aloud. I was with them once in his room at the house in West Road on either Janet's eightieth birthday or just after; suddenly he uttered a terrible cry, so loud that it rang through the house,

'We ought to die when we are eighty! We ought to die when we are eighty!' And all the while there sat Janet, smiling in her chair.

'Oh life! how bitter and how hard when known.'

About a year before Trevelyan himself died, I found him stretched upon his sofa with a large book lying on the floor within reach of his hands. 'I see you have been reading,' I said. 'What is it?' 'The greatest book in the world,' he cried, lifting it up to show me. It was Carlyle's *French Revolution*.

My friendship with Trevelyan, so close that he always seemed to regard me as his son, covered a period of sixty years. My contacts with two other dons, Neville Figgis and Lowes Dickinson, who influenced me in ways scarcely less important, were cut short by death, one as soon as 1916, the other in 1932. I came to know both when I began to read political science for the Second Part of the Tripos, since this was a subject upon which they lectured and I found myself writing essays for each of them. That political theory and constitution-making have remained abiding interests was due, I believe, to the original stimulus of their excellent teaching. And to both I owed far more than this.

Neville Figgis was a tutor at St. Catharine's (commonly known as 'Cat's'), and had already, before I met him, published his still well-known book, *The Theory of the Divine Right of Kings*. He was in orders, acting as curate to Archdeacon Cunningham, the economic historian, Vicar of Great St. Mary's. Cunningham, by the way, delighted in controversy, especially with the economic theorists, followers of Alfred Marshall; he being a Tariff Reformer, they Free Traders. I once heard him remark from the pulpit, 'My brethren, there is one joy on earth we shall not have in Heaven, the joy of strife.'

It was a sentiment in which, at that time of life, I heartily concurred, being engaged in much controversy with fellow undergraduates provoked by my reading of Nietzsche. His writings, then very popular with the youthful intelligentsia, were available in Common's translation. His book entitled *Antichrist* I was amused to discover in a room of the original university library called 'The Old Divinity School'. What, then, was my

surprise and delight when at my first tutorial with Figgis, my eye
fell upon a row of Common's Nietzsche on a bookshelf by the
fireplace. 'This,' I said to myself, 'is the parson for me!' When
later on I plucked up courage to refer to the subject, I found he
was as ardent a Nietzschean as I was, though of a different com-
plexion. For, of course, he could see far deeper into him, being
able to view him as part of the panorama of political and theo-
logical thought that he could command. Only one thing, he
assured me, prevented Nietzsche from becoming one of the
greatest of Christian philosophers. 'If only he hadn't had that
aunt!'

On the more strictly academic side I came, under Figgis's
guidance, to obtain a pretty fair grasp of medieval political structure. Mastering Bryce's *Holy Roman Empire* as a start, I next
discovered that St. Augustine's *De Civitate Dei* was a great prophetic vision of the European system that was to follow. Of
Figgis's own writings on political theory I suppose it was his
Studies of Political Thought, from Gerson to Grotius which taught me
most; though he led me to appreciate Acton's *The History of
Freedom* which I might otherwise have missed. It was at his bidding
also that I came to read and admire Maitland's wonderful
Domesday Book and Beyond. Furthermore I eagerly devoured some
of Figgis's books on religion, of which *Churches in the Modern
State* and *Civilisation at the Cross Roads* made important contributions to political science; the second was the more personal in
that it was clearly written by a man at his own spiritual cross-
roads. In 1901, like Trevelyan, though in a very different mood,
he left Cambridge and took a college living in a remote country
village, Marnhull in Dorset (the Marncote of *Tess of the D'Urbervilles*) in order to wrestle with the problem, the solution of which
took him to the Community of the Resurrection at Mirfield in
1907. One April I paid him a visit at Marnhull, an experience I
can never forget. For being then deeply in love, I became
intoxicated with the beauty of Dorset in spring.

The last time I saw him was shortly after the First World War
broke out in August 1914. At the outset men were, on the whole,
optimistic. Sadler was then Vice-Chancellor at Leeds, where I

had moved in 1912, and knowing Figgis held a different opinion, had invited him to give a public lecture at the University. The large audience left the room appalled. For they had listened to a prophet, if ever there was one, who with his profound knowledge of history and his penetrating insight into the very springs of modern civilization, showed us as in some magic glass what was to come upon the world; and the vision, as can now be seen in retrospect, even extended down to the tyrannies of yesterday.

His 'war work', as the phrase ran, was to go to and fro across the Atlantic and preach in America, so as to rouse some people at any rate to the gravity of the situation. He was at the time nearing the completion of a book on Bossuet—he told me it was to be his masterpiece. On one of these voyages back to England his vessel was torpedoed, all his notes on Bossuet went to the bottom of the sea, and though he was himself picked up after being exposed for over a week in an open boat, he died soon after he got to land.

I once mentioned Neville Figgis to H. A. L. Fisher. 'A second-rate mind,' he loftily remarked. Fisher was in his way a great historian and I yield to no one in my admiration for *A History of Europe*. But his estimate of Figgis taught me how limited he was himself. He could not help despising a 'Mirfield monk'. And being unable to understand one half of Figgis's mind, there must needs be quite half of the spiritual and intellectual side of Europe beyond his comprehension.

My acquaintance with Lowes Dickinson covered a much longer period than that with Figgis, but never ripened into friendship. Dickinson was, however, most kind to me and I learned a good deal from him, in particular—as so many did—from his Platonic dialogue *The Meaning of Good* and his charming *Greek View of Life*. He was one of the judges who awarded me the Members' Prize in 1902 for an essay on Byron, which he urged me to publish. I did not comply because it contained what I felt were rather pretentious chapters on Byron's influence abroad; not very honest either, as they implied a knowledge of languages like Spanish and Russian of which I was then wholly ignorant.

I attended the small class at King's to which Dickinson lectured

C   33

upon the constitutional changes in France during the nineteenth
century and occasionally paid a visit to his rooms and showed him
essays from time to time. I was always made very welcome
whenever I called, whether it was to discuss a point or just to
have a chat, to find out what he thought about the latest turn in
English or foreign politics; for he was our Nestor.

The rooms in Gibbs's Building indeed were worth a visit for
themselves; one of their windows commanded what must still
be the loveliest park-view of any house in England, looking out
as it does across the great lawn of the college, stretching down
to the river, and then across another expanse of grass to the
towering trees along the Backs beyond. I still find the sheer
beauty of it almost overpowering. And I recall it now as the
perfect frame for my last memory of this lover of beauty. The
exact date of my visit escapes me; but it cannot have been long
before Dickinson's death in 1932, for we fell to talking of the
impending breakdown not only of the European system as established by the Versailles Treaty but, so it seemed, of civilization
as a whole—at any rate, such as we had known it since 1815, for
the dictators were abroad.

It was a bitter moment of history for the old humanist, having
seen mankind's hopes of an enduring peace and ever-widening
freedom disappointed by the 1914–1918 war. He had toiled since
then on behalf of the League of Nations, only to find all his hopes
once again overthrown. It was in a heartbroken voice, ill-
concealed by a smile, that he quoted,

> 'the time has been
> That, when the brains were out, the man would die
> And there an end; but now they rise again
> And push us from our stools.'

One can hardly imagine a more suitable epitaph for the dying
liberalism of the world.

Without any mention of Lytton Strachey this story of my life at
Cambridge would be sadly incomplete. I first got to know him,
not a don but my exact contemporary, through Elizabethan literature. John Lyly was the subject set for the Harness Prize Essay
in 1904 for which we were both competitors, though at that time

neither had ever heard of the other. He, I am sure, sent in a brilliant essay, but it appears that I had done more work for, as dons love diligence, the prize was awarded to me. When the result came out I received a letter from him saying, 'You've got the prize I wanted; do come and have coffee with me this evening', a letter which I have always regarded as a fine gesture of generosity.

His room, if I remember rightly, was second floor up in the corner turret to the left of the Great Court of Trinity. He liked being original, and he made his coffee as the alchemists conducted their experiments with a series of retorts, a structure of glass tubes, standing on a table. The process was striking; the coffee was cold. He was original also in the form he devised for a little society of King's and Trinity men into which he now introduced a Caius man. For it was conducted as follows: at the end of each meeting, cards were placed face downwards on the table and the member who drew the highest card became secretary of the meeting that had just finished, writing up the minutes in a book that was used by successive secretaries, and giving a name to the society that had now ceased. The man who drew the next highest card became the chairman of the society that came into being at the next meeting, it being also his duty to propose the subject for discussion—a subject which according to the rules had to be either absurd or indecent; the one I remember proposing when the lot fell to me was 'that immortality on this earth was desirable', an unconscious anticipation of Shaw's *Back to Methuselah*. From such a beginning the discussion at once developed in all sorts of directions, and I often found myself out of my depth. For this, in fact, was my introduction to moral philosophy. Though I never met G. E. Moore, his *Principia Ethica* was the gospel of the group of which I now found myself a member; and in hope to be sealed of the tribe I bought a copy which stood for many years on my shelves and was never understood, so that my infant intellect, not yet past teething, was cheerfully content to suck philosophy from the more digestible *Meaning of Good* by Lowes Dickinson. Nevertheless, the discussions of the group were the finest education I found at university. And when I note that besides Strachey its meetings were attended by

Maynard Keynes, who was a year junior to me, J. T. Sheppard (later Provost of King's), H. O. Meredith who was to keep the flag of poetry flying in Belfast where he became Professor of Economics, Leonard Woolf, and his future wife's two brothers (Leslie Stephen's sons), my reader should not be surprised at that statement; or that Lytton's friendly gesture to someone neither a Trinity nor a King's man was a far greater reward than the Harness Prize. I might have got more out of it, but unfortunately my membership only lasted for one session, as I had already taken my degree and had to go on to earn my living. But it was a real sorrow for me to lose touch with Lytton for several years, during which time he was publishing his beautiful little *Landmarks in French Literature* (1912) in the Home University Library, and his essays in denigration, the famous *Eminent Victorians* (1918).

As I have begun about Lytton, I may as well give an account here of later meetings. It was a later volume still, his *Queen Victoria*, that brought us together again. Soon after it was published, in 1921, I was staying with Quiller-Couch at Fowey, in connection with the early volumes of the *New Cambridge Shakespeare*, and at a rather protracted session the night before my departure he gave me, as a token of affection, a copy of the second series of his *Studies in Literature*. It was three o'clock when I left him, with various empty bottles on the floor, and took the book up to bed with me to pack it for the journey. But sleep did not come at once, and finding an essay on Strachey's *Victoria* in the contents, I couldn't resist reading it. So when I came down to breakfast (with a distinct hangover, to find Q as fresh as a daisy) I said, 'I have read your attack on Lytton Strachey—an old friend of mine—but as I haven't read his *Queen Victoria*, I can't tell you whether I agree with you or not.' 'Well,' he said, 'take it away with you to read in the train; it's all rubbish but you'd better return it.' Which I did, saying in my 'Collins' letter that I thought he had misunderstood the book, because being so much older than Lytton and myself, he could not bear a shade of criticism of the great Queen during whose reign he had spent most of his life; whereas Strachey and I, tired of everything Victorian, could not abide the old woman. 'Yet,' I added, 'you didn't notice that he was on his knees to her in the end.' No reply was expected—or received. But some eight or ten years later Q resigned the co-editorship of the *New Shakespeare*, and I got the consent of the Cambridge University Press to approach my old friend to write the Introductions. Lytton himself seemed quite attracted by the proposition and came—complete with the famous red beard, which I had not seen before—to discuss the matter with me. During our talk he said, in his high-pitched voice which I can still imitate but cannot reproduce on paper, 'Do you know you made it up between me and Q?' 'What!' I cried. 'Yes,' he said, 'he wrote me a most charming letter, telling me you had shown him the error of his ways. It's true,' he impishly continued, 'that he asked me in the same letter whether he might quote a passage from the *Victoria* in his *Oxford Book of English Prose*.' Alas, he and the Cambridge Press didn't hit it off on the question of copyright, so in the end I had myself to write the Introductions.

I never saw him again, for he died soon after. But his essays on Shakespeare show the world what it lost by losing his Introductions to the plays.

Among other fellow students with whom I made friends were members of my own college—in particular the Greek scholar, H. J. W. Tillyard, and Alexander Brown. Alexander Brown was a rather older man than the rest of us, who had already distinguished himself at Aberdeen before he came south. Indeed, he must have had all the mathematics he required for the Cambridge Tripos before he did so, since he never seemed to do any work at Caius; although he was far more interested in philosophy than anything else, he still, to the amazement of us all, was the Senior Wrangler of his year. I saw a lot of him and together we founded a vigorous if short-lived discussion club, anticipating Lytton Strachey's society, which we called the Gresham Society, after the distinguished sixteenth-century member of Caius. As I have mentioned, I had at this phase become enthralled by the works of Nietzsche, especially perhaps by his *Antichrist*. I read them, alas not in German, except for *Thus Spoke Zarathustra*, of which the German is as easy as it is lovely. I gave a paper on Nietzsche to the Greshamites which led to a discussion that went on all night, I was told, though as I lived out of college I had had to escape before twelve o'clock. Another meeting even more vividly remembered was our first, at which our president, William Ridgeway, Ulsterman, Professor of Archaeology, Fellow of Caius, and author of many books (e.g. *The Origin of Tragedy* and *The Horse*—an animal he closely resembled), had consented to read a paper. To 'read' is a euphemism, for he was so blind by this time that he could scarcely have read. At any rate he talked; his subject—a characteristic one—was 'The Disposal of the Dead'. It was a wonderful evening, for despite the ghoulish subject, he kept us in fits of laughter most of the time, no doubt helped by his Ulster accent and his odd trick of interjecting 'Eh? Eh?' every half-minute or so. But the most entertaining part of it was what happened before the meeting officially began; for being blind he never could read his watch exactly, so we counted ourselves fortunate that he arrived twenty minutes before the appointed hour and not twenty minutes after. Nothing abashed, he provided a curtain raiser for those already present by giving us an irreverent account of the exhumation and re-interment he had attended of a seventeenth-century Caius worthy, to wit William Harvey, who discovered the circulation of the blood.

So much for the Gresham Club. Ridgeway—and whatever the depth of his learning, its width is undeniable—was a figure never to be forgotten. He knew my father well and said to him once, 'When I came here, eh, nobody knew me. But I walked up and down the K.P. telling 'em stories; they soon knew me, eh?' I only knew one handwriting worse than his, George Saintsbury's; but whereas Saintsbury did make marks on the paper, Ridgeway might write half his letter on the table next to it, so that his voting papers in the Senate House were not always very effective. I last saw him at lunch one day many years later in the Combination Room at college. A number of us were seated at the table when he was brought in by one of the Fellows who, with his eye roving round, said to Ridgeway, 'Oh, there's Dover Wilson; you know him, I think?' 'Know him!' snorted the old man. 'Of course I do; put me next to him!' And next to me he sat, talking at the top of his voice while he shovelled the soup more into his lap than into his mouth (the college servants usually cleaned him up afterwards). 'You ought to have been a Fellow of this damned college but they wouldn't listen to me.' All this while the Fellow who was elected in my year, fortunately one of my best friends who was enjoying the joke more than I was, sat immediately opposite.

Incidentally, Ridgeway was a great collector of coins, and despite his lack of vision could, by shoving his hand into a tray of coins belonging to some dealer or other, detect at once what was worth his attention and possibly purchase. He was also something of an anthropologist and had a number of skulls in his library at Ditton. The legend goes that after his death one of them was found to bear the label, 'Skull of the priest shot by my father'.

Rupert Brooke came up to university in October 1906, after I had married and gone off to Finland, so we were never contemporary residents; yet he became one of my Cambridge friends because I was able to spend most of the Finnish university vacation from May to mid-September at my father-in-law's vicarage at Harston, whence I could easily keep in touch with Cambridge events. And if the professors nowadays tell their adolescent students that Rupert Brooke is the poet of adolescence, it was wonderful to be adolescent with him, for fifty years ago I was not his senior by much. Besides, Rupert-worship was catching, and only those who can recall the sight of his personal beauty can understand the spell he cast upon the Cambridge of his day. The Marlowe Society, which he helped to found in 1907, decided to celebrate the tercentenary of Milton's birth the following year by a performance of *Comus* in the New Theatre. In this, he played the Attendant Spirit and I can still hear the gasp of wonder that broke from the audience when he appeared before the curtain to speak the opening lines.

I cannot recall how or when I first came to know him, but feel pretty sure it was in connection with the writing of his fellowship thesis on Webster, which he began in 1910 and for which he wished to consult me about the puritan attitude to the stage early in the seventeenth century. And either then or probably in the following year I had tea with him in the Old Vicarage, Grantchester. In any case, of one thing I am sure: it was as his guest that I witnessed a special performance by the Marlowe Society of *Dr. Faustus* for the benefit of German students who were over in Cambridge in the summer of 1910. It was acted in the Victoria Rooms—now a cinema—in the Market Place, and Faustus was played by Francis Cornford. Who took the other parts I forgot afterwards, though Rupert, then busy with his thesis, at first refused and then agreed to play an angel, the bad one for preference. After it was all over, the players, still in costume and myself provided with tights so as to be of the company, repaired to the Cornfords' garden in Madingley Road for an al fresco supper under the starlight of a warm August midnight. And then, supper over, there being to my surprise some unlighted torches at hand, Rupert seized one, lighted it and crying, 'Now we will have a torch-light procession through the streets of Cambridge', led the way with his hair waving in the wind.

That was, I think, the last time I saw him and I took it as a vision of the youth of England, of ourselves marching to the victory of poetry and the spirit of beauty over ugliness, wrong and cruelty. For the heart of young England beat high in 1910. Frances Cornford, wife of Francis, had jestingly described Rupert as,

'Magnificently unprepared
For the long littleness of life.'

Tragic and poignant indeed; in less than five years Rupert was dying on his way to Gallipoli, while the youth of England and the youth of Germany were slaughtering each other like animals in the graves they had dug for themselves.

Two years after I entered Caius College, another Lancing boy, two years my junior, entered Hertford College, Oxford. This was Godfrey Theodore Baldwin, only son of the vicar of Harston, the Rev. E. C. Baldwin, Honorary Canon of Ely. About this time I began to see a good deal of Godfrey and we became fast friends.

During the long vacation, the vicarage at Harston became a meeting-place for Godfrey's Oxford friends whom I came to know through him. I would cycle over from Cambridge, six miles off, to join in their talk and the reading aloud of our favourite poets; in particular at this date (1902 or thereabouts) we read Meredith, Swinburne, Rossetti, Oscar Wilde, and of course Tennyson and Browning. Once or twice, when the Canon happened to be away, we would sit round the oil lamp in his study with the wooden shutters closed, talking and reading all through the night, until we threw open the shutters and dashed down to the river at the bottom of the garden for an early morning bathe.

A member of this reading party, who could not, of course, always be present was Godfrey's sister, Dorothy. About this time she reached eighteen and I celebrated the occasion by giving her a copy of *Tess of the D'Urbervilles* (which Godfrey thought a little advanced for a girl of her age); nevertheless I inscribed the copy with her name and this couplet,

> 'Eighteen you are, but were you eight years less,
> To score off Godfrey, I would give you *Tess.*'

Modern readers may smile, but Dorothy had to secrete the book very carefully, for the Canon and Mrs. Baldwin were very old-fashioned in their views on what was proper in literature.

In August 1904, after I had taken my degree, I was staying at my grandmother's at Kenley. One lovely morning I was walking with my aunt in the upper part of the garden—the whole scene stands out so vividly in my mind that it might have happened yesterday—when a telegraph boy appeared with a message for me. I opened it; it read, 'Godfrey drowned come Dorothy'. I realized not only that I must go, but something that had never before entered my head; I was deeply, profoundly, in love.

My friend was, of course, buried at Harston, and I stayed in the house until after the funeral. There was one great problem Dorothy and I had to face: the Canon, terribly bowed by the death of his only son, had this additional burden to bear, that he suspected the boy was not, as he understood it, a Christian. So it fell to my lot to try and calm his fears. Somehow I managed to do so, not entirely, I fear, within the strict limits of the truth. In point of fact my own religious position was not that of Godfrey, since I had never had to suffer the extremely rigid upbringing that he had. Nevertheless, when just before leaving I had an interview with Mrs. Baldwin asking that I might be allowed to consider myself engaged to Dorothy, she not only refused to agree, but demanded that I should break off all relations with her unless I promised a far stricter adherence to the doctrines of the Church of England than I could accept. There followed months of misery for Dorothy, only relieved by secret meetings on the river at the foot of the garden, which I could reach from my bicycle and she in her canoe, while my best friend, Ernest Haddon who knew Dorothy, carried messages between us. It was a Romeo and Juliet interlude as I now look back on it, full of rapturous meetings and agonized partings.

In the end, however, the parents realized that they had in any case lost their daughter to this young Cambridge graduate, and that I was not so far removed from them in opinion as I had seemed. The engagement was permitted, and we were married at the end of July 1906.

The parents were becoming proud of their son-in-law, especially as Canon Baldwin was an ardent admirer of Shakespeare, and indeed in Cambridge circles a much-admired reciter of scenes from his plays. In 1911, I dedicated *Life in Shakespeare's England* to him. Meanwhile Harston became my home whenever I was in England. My two elder children—Godfrey in 1908 and Audrey in 1911—were born there, and even our third child, Carol who arrived seventeen years later, was born in the house of Dr. Young at Harston who delivered all three children.

I owed all this happiness in the first place to my friend Godfrey and it is only fitting that I should conclude this story by quoting the verses that I wrote in his memory for the Lancing College Magazine of February 1905.

'AVE ATQUE VALE'

(In Memory of GODFREY BALDWIN)

1

'Hereunder lies a friend'.
Beside his grave what more is there to say,
For those who loved him in his shining day,
His smiling end?

2

What need hath he of tears
Whose eyes were heavens that held a dancing sun
Whose lips, a Bow that sped the shaft of fun,
Would curl at fears?

3

Naught but a sharp regret
We feel—that Beauty cannot reach his eyes,
That he who knew the larks in morning skies
Must now forget.

4

But even so, we err!
For ours is still the Beauty that he saw,
And from the Earth he loved he craved no more
Than love of her.

5

The dreams that in his brain,
Grew towards the good, like sweet, unopened flowers
Yet live to bear, since they are also ours,
Memorial grain.

6

Not here beneath this mound
He lies; but in the hearts of all who see
Fire in the rose and spirit in the tree
He may be found.

43

3

Schoolmaster and 'Lektor'

I got a Second in the History Tripos (I had certainly not deserved a First), and therefore could not expect the college to give me a fellowship; I tried for one nevertheless, and in 1906 submitted an elaborate thesis on the bibliography of Martin Marprelate. I had been busily engaged upon this subject for some time, since Adolphus Ward, Master of Peterhouse and one of the judges of the Harness Prize, had asked me, after reading my essay on John Lyly, to contribute a chapter on Martin Marprelate for Volume III of the Cambridge History of English Literature; this had led me on in time to a bibliographical enquiry into the printing of the Marprelate tracts. But the thesis was not successful. Fortunately for the college, the only fellowship that year was given to 'Chubby' Stratton, an astrophysicist, who became the best-known Caian of my day and one of my close friends.

I was not downhearted; but I was penniless, except for what I could earn by private tuition, and engaged to be married. Being at a loose end, I decided to try extension lecturing as a possible career. I was accordingly asked to give a specimen lecture at Homerton Training College. What the young girl teachers thought of it I shall never know, but the two solemn judges representing the Cambridge Extension Board, who sat at the back of the room, one of them Cranage, who afterwards became Dean of Norwich, thought nothing of it. They wrote me a scarcely polite letter telling me that I was not born to be a lecturer.

It is amusing to recall that my next meeting with Cranage was in wartime about a dozen years later when, quite by chance, we found ourselves in the same first-class railway carriage on our way to inspect the same W.E.A. lecturer. Cranage was acting, as before, on behalf of the Cambridge Extension Board and I as an H.M.I. visiting adult classes. Having recently returned from part of the Russian Empire, I had become a well-known public lecturer on our great eastern ally. Neither of us betrayed the faintest recollection of the events at Homerton in 1903. That first lecture of mine had been bad because it contained far too much, and it had been justly condemned.

And so I became a schoolmaster instead. I took the two fourth forms at the Whitgift Grammar School, Croydon, for a year and a half—one of the most fortunate things I ever did; for the head-master, a Lancashire man called S. O. Andrew, and his charming Lancashire wife, became my life-long friends.

The school had many attractions. For example, I already knew something of its founder, Archbishop Whitgift. For it was he who had suppressed the writers of the Marprelate tracts, hunting down one of them and having him hanged. He was also a patron of Thomas Nashe, in whose writings I was then deeply interested since he was an anti-Martinist pamphleteer. Again, the school was situated in that part of Surrey from which my grandparents had come—indeed one of my uncles had been a scholar there. What was even more attractive to me at this period was its proximity to London where, at the Court Theatre in Sloane Square, Vedrenne and Granville-Barker were producing, for the first time on the public stage, the plays of George Bernard Shaw. My correction of Latin exercises was I fear somewhat interrupted by my eagerness to see each new play as it came forward.

My job was to act as form-master, that is to say, to teach all the subjects except French and Mathematics to Forms IVa and IVb. I still have a photograph of the two forms with the master seated in the middle; but alas I never kept a record of the names of the boys. I fear, however, that they were just of the age to be slaughtered in the trenches of 1914–18. It is possible that one of the faces is that of a very famous soldier who afterwards became Air-Marshal Tedder and later Chancellor of the University of Cambridge.

My time at the Whitgift was limited to four terms, as I went off to Finland in January 1906. But in that brief time I acquired a deep affection for the school and especially for its headmaster. He remained there long enough to preside over the destiny of my own son who owing to—apart from mother-wit—the excellency of Andrew's teaching obtained a Senior Scholarship at Hertford College, Oxford. And when I add that two of my son's contemporaries were Professor Whitteridge (Fellow of the Royal Society) and Professor Kenneth Jackson (Fellow of the British Academy)—both professors at Edinburgh University—it is clear that the Whitgift was no ordinary grammar school in Andrew's day. He was indeed a very remarkable man; and after his retirement (when unhappily the school fell into the hands of a very inferior successor) he occupied his leisure with two interests: translating Homer into English verse with a metre of his own invention based on the stressed Anglo-Saxon metre—a portion of which, 'Hector's Ransoming', a translation of *Iliad* XXIV, I think deserves a high place among Homeric translations; and a discussion of textual points in *Beowulf*, including some on grammar. These were put forward in various learned journals, such as *Medium Aevum* (Vol. VIII) which includes his paper on 'Three Textual Cruxes in *Beowulf*'. They were at first ignored or treated with contempt by Old English scholars, until one day when my old friend was more or less on his deathbed, an eminent Anglo-Saxonist wrote a review of an article in which he roundly asserted, 'Mr. Andrew has been right all the time.' I well remember my delight as I left a copy of the journal with him so that he might enjoy his triumph. It was characteristic of him that there was no triumph when I went to see him next day: on the contrary, nothing but scorn. Pointing to a passage in the review, he exclaimed, 'Look! the fellow doesn't know his own business!'

Himself a product of the Manchester Grammar School when Rutherford, whose memory he revered, was High Master, Andrew was an outstanding representative in his day of the English grammar school tradition, which goes back to Colet and beyond; the tradition of the scholar-headmaster, who by a combination of learning and character in himself is able to endow his sixth-form boys with a like combination, and so prepare them to become the leaders of their generation. It will be a disastrous day, if it ever comes, that sees this tradition, this precious origin of our English education, impaired or destroyed by the monkeying of politicians.

While I was at the Whitgift, the poet Walter de la Mare was living at Anerley and his two sons attended the school. One summer evening, I think shortly before I was married, when my fiancée was staying with the Andrews, they invited two great men to dinner to meet us—de la Mare himself and Mrs. de la Mare, and Professor A. N. Whitehead and Mrs. Whitehead. I was just fresh from reading Whitehead's *Science and the Modern World* with its fine tribute to the value of poetry in human life, while, of course, I was an enthusiastic devourer of every new volume of verse that de la Mare issued. But what I wish to put on record here is the intense pleasure that each of the two men took in this their first meeting together. After dinner they walked round the headmaster's small garden with Andrew and myself just behind, close enough for me to observe how the poet deferred to the philosopher and the philosopher deferred to the poet—a scene I carry in my mind as a fine picture of the humility of true greatness.

During the summer of 1905, at the end of my first full year at the Whitgift, the Master of Peterhouse drew my attention to the advertised post of English 'Lektor' in Finland at the University of Helsingfors (now called by its Finnish name, Helsinki). I applied with his backing, and was appointed.

The post had hitherto been held by a Swedish-speaking Finn, and I believe I was the first Englishman to be appointed. It had several attractions for a young man of twenty-four: it was my first university post; it would compel me to study modern English with such science as I could muster; it was a great adventure; and, above all, it held out modest financial prospects which would enable me to marry.

Very few people in this country knew anything of Finland at that time, and it was part of the Russian Empire then boiling with partially suppressed revolution. The beginning of the year had seen Bloody Sunday, when a group of St. Petersburg workers petitioning the Tsar for reform had been fired on without provocation. Subsequent liberalizing reforms had been abandoned and Stolypin put in charge of new repressive measures. So that I promised myself interesting experiences, which indeed came my way.

It was only a month after Stolypin's appointment that, in January 1906, I went on board a Finnish steamer in Hull to proceed to Helsingfors. I travelled second class and there was only one other passenger with me—January is not an auspicious month to cross the Baltic. He called himself Professor Schmidt of Chicago, and as he spoke English with an American flavour I did not question this identity at first. But we soon fell to talking about events in Russia. I myself was young and a member of the Fabian Society at that time; Socialism in England was then stirring—a stirring which really led to the great Liberal triumph in the General Election of 1906. The professor on his side was evidently very much interested in the revolution in Russia, about which in the four and a half days we had together he told me a great deal.

And then, about eleven o'clock one morning, when the day was just beginning to dawn, we stood on deck together and saw the dim outline of the Finnish coast. I turned and looked at him and noticed that he was overcome with emotion, greatly to my surprise, because he had hitherto struck me as a man of austere reserve. I said, 'Now, tell me your name. You know me and can trust me.' He drew himself up and said, 'I am Tschaikowsky'; whereat I, knowing nothing of Russian history, said, 'You don't mean the musician!' He almost knocked me down, for Tschaikowsky the musician was despised by the revolutionaries since they regarded his saccharine music designed for Court consumption as so much dope. He was quite another person: he was Nicholas Tschaikowsky, a leader of the Social Revolutionaries in the eighties, known as the Kropotkin Circle, returning to Russia after twenty-five years of exile. 'I shall disappear when we get to land,' he said, 'but I shall put you in touch with my friends, and we may meet again.'

In Helsingfors itself the names of the streets at that time were written up in three languages, Russian, Finnish and Swedish, a trilingualism which graphically expressed the existing political situation. Previously an outlying province of Sweden, with a Swedish Governor, but allowed a good deal of power for internal self-government, Finland was annexed by Russia in 1809 during the Napoleonic Wars. When doing so, however, the Russian Tsar, absolute monarch in the rest of his dominion, solemnly promised to respect the constitutional rights and status of his Finnish subjects. The truth was that geography decreed Finland should be a buffer state between Russia and Sweden; that she should be loyal and content was always of first importance to whichever mighty neighbour exercised a suzerainty over her. Such was the basis of the freedom she had enjoyed under Sweden and as a Grand Duchy of Russia in the nineteenth century. But Russia was not always astute enough to see the wisdom of this flexibility. In 1906 the foolish Nicholas II, exasperated by revolutionary outrages in Russia itself and incited by a still more foolish wife, was attempting to withdraw one by one Finland's constitutional liberties and privileges, a process the Finnish Government was resisting with all its strength and its cunning. It managed indeed to maintain its position for the three years I was there. This meant incidentally that Tschaikowsky and his Social Revolutionaries found in Finland a base of operation more or less outside the reach of the Russian police.

But Finnish politics were conditioned not only by outside relations with Russia but by internal party differences, the most acute being those due to language differences among its people. The great majority of the population—all those indeed who inhabited the interior—spoke Finnish, a language akin to Magyar and Estonian. This, with its grammar containing fifteen cases, I decided it was best to pass by for the nonce and to devote myself in the first place to a study of Swedish, which with its complete absence of inflection was linguistically as close to English as Finnish was remote. Swedish had this additional advantage that in my day it was still the language of culture, and was spoken by my own professor and other professors at the University. But the use of the Finnish tongue was beginning even here, those who favoured it being labelled 'Jung Fennomans' or Young Finns. An outstanding example was Yrjö Hirn, a great scholar well known to English anthropologists for his book *The Sacred Shrine*. And when I paid a return visit to Finland in 1950 I found the professors all speaking Finnish—even those whose names had been Swedish had replaced them by Finnish ones—the street names were then in Finnish alone and the country itself called Suomi.

The professor under whom I had to work in 1906 was the well-known philologist, Uno Lindelöf. A bachelor, he lived in a flat overlooking one of the harbours of Helsingfors together with his father, sisters and another brother, a professor and bachelor like himself. He was very welcoming and indeed told me that one of my chief functions was to be his whetstone, so that he could polish up his own spoken English. And knowing that I was fond of exercise he soon arranged that we should skate together on a small swept surface in the harbour just in front of his flat.

I may add here that I continued to keep in touch with my kindly professor long after I had ceased to be a member of his staff and returned to England; for he would pay us a visit about once every two years, largely in order to increase his knowledge of spoken English. He also followed my doings with interest; and I had an enthusiastic post-card from him after the publication in 1914 of *The War and Democracy*, though he deprecated my article on Russia in that volume—a chapter which events have themselves since disproved.

My work at the university consisted mainly in coping with a large elementary class, so large indeed that it was impossible to deal with adequately until it had considerably diminished under the stress of discouragement. But there were other duties of a more advanced kind which gave more interest. For example, the English *lektor* was expected to examine all persons who presented themselves as able to read English aloud. And on one occasion a railway porter from the north of Finland offered himself. He professed never to have met an Englishman before or heard English spoken; he had taught himself English through the reading of phonetic transcripts. I could find no reason to doubt his statement and granted the certificate; the articulation was correct though the intonation was entirely mechanical. I should state here that these duties only took place in the winter months, since the university session ended at the beginning of May every year and reopened in September. This meant that my wife and I could spend our summer months in the Harston vicarage, where both my elder children were born.

The arrival of a real Englishman at the university was quite an event in Helsingfors, and presently Lindelöf proposed that I should give a course of popular lectures. 'Who,' he asked, 'is the writer most talked of just now in England?' 'Oh,' I said, 'Bernard Shaw.' And indeed, it was so; for all young London had recently been flocking to see the first public productions of these extraordinary and most exciting plays. So I gave a course to the Helsingfors public on Bernard Shaw, and was flattered to find that when I returned to Finland forty years later it was still remembered. Nevertheless I fancy that my original audience, or at any rate a good many of them, came for purposes other than an interest in G.B.S.; at the end of my first lecture an elaborate Helsingfors lady swam up to me, pressed my hand, and said, 'Ach, *Lektor* Vilson, it was scharming, scharming!' I felt duly elated, until she went on, 'You see, the bloom is on your speech, the bloom!'—I had not been in Finland many weeks. I understand that in Sweden English *lektors* were not engaged for longer than two years (at that date, at any rate), since by then the bloom would have worn off.

Lindelöf had found me rooms in a pension, which enabled me to live comfortably without having to think about buying my meals. Not long after I was established there I received a call from a tall, grey-haired man who spoke with an American accent, like Tschaikowsky, and introduced himself as Tschaikowsky's friend. He was in fact Konni Zilliacus, leader of a small political party in Finland calling themselves the Activists. A highly intelligent and indeed commanding person, he was home again now after a wandering life in different parts of the world (during which he claimed to have been even a cab-driver in Sydney), to take part in the Great Adventure. His party was in close alliance with the Social Revolutionary Party in Russia, of which Tschaikowsky was a member. The Social Revolutionaries themselves were not

Marxian Social Democrats, but corresponded in their brand of socialism fairly closely with the Fabians in Britain, though their methods differed. Instead of seeking to win power by a policy of 'gradualness', they advocated violence, since they held that nothing gradual would ever get rid of the Russian government.

When I first arrived in Finland, the Social Revolutionaries were up in the bows, the millennium was just round the corner—indeed all the progressive parties in Russia at that time felt the same. Bloody Sunday in 1905 had been followed by a general strike which frightened the Tsar; yet he had already promised liberal reforms including a Duma, which, however, took months to assemble. In May 1906 I myself attended a meeting of the first Duma, in company with Bernard Pares, who was able to translate all the languages of the speeches delivered that morning—an extraordinary feat. But when I asked him what it was all about, he said, 'The speakers all said the same thing' (which I later noticed was what happened at the first meeting of the Dail in Dublin). The leading party in the Duma were the Constitutional Democrats or Cadets (an abbreviation derived from the Russian letters C.D.) with Milyoukof at their head. But the liberalism for which the Cadets stood could not survive in Russia, since as Milyoukof put it to me when, in 1909 he passed through Finland on his way to America virtually in flight and certainly in despair, 'Russia lacks that social cement which in England you call snobbery.'

But in 1906, when I visited St. Petersburg, I couldn't help thinking of Wordsworth and the young Girondins in Paris at the halcyon period before the Terror. For Russia too then felt herself

'Standing on the top of golden hours
And human nature seeming born again.'

The Russian Terror was still a generation away, coming after the Bolshevik Revolution. What happened between 1905 and 1909 was something different—the return of reaction under Stolypin, and a general decay of the Revolution, the main symptom of which being—to judge from what I saw in Helsingfors—that the revolutionaries and the Secret Police seemed to get mixed up underground.

For example, around 1908, I might meet a member of Zilliacus's party in the street and perhaps enquire after so-and-so; he might reply, first looking round, 'So-and-so; you be careful, he's suspect.' Then, later in the morning, I might run across So-and-so and tell him I had just met the other man; and he might equally reply, 'You be careful of him, he's suspect.'

One day, not long after Zilliacus and I had first met, we ran across each other in the street—Helsingfors is a small place—and he said to me, 'Didn't you tell me you were going to get married soon?' 'Yes,' I replied. 'Now that I find that Finland is a place to bring a wife to, I'm going home to get married in the summer.'

'Where are you going for your honeymoon?' he asked, to which I answered we hadn't yet decided.

'Well, what about Archangel?'

'Archangel!' I was astonished. 'What about it?'

'You couldn't have a more delightful honeymoon trip in the summer than from Britain to Archangel.'

'Well?' I said.

He continued, 'There are fifty revolutionaries who have escaped from Siberia and are hiding in the woods round Archangel. You go home to England my boy; charter a steam-yacht (we'll pay all expenses)'—It was part of my political education to learn that revolutionaries were never at a loss for money— 'marry your good lady and go off for a trip from Hull. And one night when you're in the White Sea and fast asleep, the revolutionaries will be taken aboard and stowed away under deck, so that you won't see them or even know they're there if you don't want to. They'll go back with you to Hull, train across from there to Liverpool, and within a short time will be sailing past the Statue of Liberty into New York.' (Hull, by the by, was the Russian escape-port at this time in our country, and innumerable emigrants from Russia, mostly, I believe, Jews from southern Russia, would pass across the country to take ship from Liverpool to the States. There was actually a junction at a small station in Yorkshire where these emigrant trains were shunted or stopped, and where the names of the various offices were written in Russian characters.)

'It all sounds very nice,' I said to my friend. 'But of course I have to ask the girl.' Which I did. She replied at once, without consulting her parents, that she was all for it. Alas, this story comes to a dead end: long before we were married the revolutionaries escaped in some other way, and one day I shall have to write an ode to Archangel Unvisited.

My next encounter with Zilliacus was more fruitful. One Sunday morning I received a telephone call from him, which began, 'Didn't you tell me that you were a correspondent for the *Manchester Guardian*?' 'Hardly,' I replied, 'a regular correspondent.' Dr. Ward, who had been Vice-Chancellor of the University of Manchester before becoming known to me as Master of Peterhouse, had put me in touch with the paper before I left England, and they had promised to print anything of interest I liked to send them from time to time, though so far I had done nothing for them.

'What I have to tell you,' he said, 'will certainly be of interest. But we can't talk of such things over the telephone.' So I took the next train to a little station about twenty minutes from Helsingfors and was presently sitting in a very comfortable chair drinking coffee with him. He introduced me to his American wife and two young sons, both since famous, one as an educationist, the other (bearing his father's name) as the well-known leftist Member of Parliament until his death in 1967.

The year before I had arrived, the reader will remember, His Sacred Majesty Nicholas II had had a deputation of working men mown down with grapeshot in the square in front of his palace. The leader of this deputation on Bloody Sunday was a priest in minor orders, called Father Gapon, who had escaped at the time. He had been very much written up in English newspapers, while a serial life of him was appearing in the *Strand Magazine* when I left. Imagine, then, my astonishment when Zilliacus opened by saying, 'My news is that I had dinner last night in Helsingfors with the man who has just had Gapon executed.'

'Good God!' I exclaimed. 'But you must tell me more: the *Manchester Guardian* would never print it just like that.'

'No,' he replied, 'I want your paper to know the whole story.'

54

The story he then related—and I want to make it clear that it was *his* story—ran as follows:

The Secret Police in St. Petersburg decided, in order to get underground among the revolutionaries, to float a sham revolutionary organization, and they hired Gapon, since he had 'the gift of the gab', to make the sham revolutionary speeches. For many weeks Gapon spoke eloquently at street corners or in drink-shops, and managed to collect quite a following among the working classes; indeed, his eloquence was so persuasive that after a month or so he had enlisted no less a convert than himself. And so he turned his sham revolutionary organization into a real one and, escaping on Bloody Sunday by the help of a friend of his called Rutenberg, made his way to Paris. There for the first time he met the Central Executive Committee of the Russian Social Revolutionary Party, who had not hitherto recognized his followers. The interview was stormy. They were highly suspicious of him and he, an exceedingly vain man who saw himself as the Savonarola of Russia, told them that though they sat in Paris and deliberated they knew nothing of what was really going on inside Russia. From Paris he went on to Switzerland, where he spent some weeks and the little money that he had with him getting his photograph taken and amusing himself with actresses. But presently starvation began to stare him in the face, and in the end he decided that since he must live he had better rejoin the Secret Police. He wrote to them offering his services once more, putting up his price, since he was now a famous man. They accepted, but insisted on the promise of a *quid pro quo*. He returned to St. Petersburg, where he was received with joy by his old comrades, and took up his former revolutionary activities.

Presently, however, the Party began to notice that their members were disappearing into Siberia with a rather ominous frequency, and it became apparent that there was a traitor in the camp. It dawned gradually on Rutenberg that the man might even be his friend, Gapon. To test these suspicions he began to throw out hints to him that he himself might like to make the best of both worlds. The bait was swallowed. They agreed to meet and discuss terms in an empty wooden *dacha* deserted in winter at a little place called Terioki, a suburb of St. Petersburg just inside the then Finnish frontier. Rutenberg arrived before Gapon and brought with him four other leaders of the Party, all working men. These he placed in an inner room. Gapon came, and it was not long before the talk had incriminated him beyond any possibility of doubt in the ears of the four listeners. At this Rutenberg denounced him. Gapon laughed. 'Who'll believe your word against mine?' he said. 'I am Gapon.' Rutenberg answered by throwing open the door. Within a few minutes Gapon was hanging from a beam in the ceiling. Rutenberg fled St. Petersburg and had dinner with Zilliacus in Helsingfors on his way to Paris.

Such was the story, which I sent to the *Manchester Guardian*, and which the editor, C. P. Scott, had the pluck to publish *in extenso*. For weeks it became one of the main topics of the European newspapers, and I amused myself in the university reading-room trying to make out what the various journalists were saying about it. One verdict I can well remember. It was of a man called Soskice (another name since familiar in British politics) who was Russian correspondent of the *Tribune* and dismissed the whole thing as 'a cock-and-bull story of some irresponsible journalist'. Six weeks later, however, two things happened with striking simultaneity: the police discovered the body of Gapon in an empty *dacha* (I had not mentioned the name of the place in my article); and the Social Revolutionary Party published a brochure in Paris confirming the story in all detail. The *Manchester Guardian* was jubilant; they published a leading article on the excellence of their foreign service, and C. P. Scott sent me a cheque for £10.

That wasn't the end, however, for the story has a sequel even more remarkable than itself. I had at one point been asked by one of my revolutionary acquaintances to meet a 'very important friend' from Russia, a man called Azev. I had spent one evening in his company, though as his English was far to seek and I had no Russian, I couldn't get on intimate terms with him. I am glad to remember this, for I didn't like him at the time. 'What wonderful eyes he had,' said my hostess to me later. It was his eyes I hadn't liked. Yet of his importance there could be no doubt. He was, I was informed, Chairman of the Central Executive Committee of the Social Revolutionary Party, the committee, in fact, with whom Gapon had had that stormy interview in 1905, which suggests that he thought Gapon a dangerous man who ought to be got rid of.

Imagine, therefore, the effect of the subsequent discovery, appalling beyond words to the revolutionaries, that their leader, Azev himself, had been for years in close touch with the Secret Police. How he was unmasked and the details of the unmasking are unknown to me, but somehow he escaped the vengeance that would have fallen upon him. Plenty of stories of his past, however, came out. The astonishing thing, I was told, was his activity as a revolutionary. 'Others talked,' they said, 'but he did things.' How he did them may be illustrated by one tale which sticks in my mind.

At one time he proposed to the Committee in Paris that Dournovo, Prefect of Police in Moscow, should be got rid of. Dournovo, as we now know, was in fact one of his chiefs. Nevertheless, his execution was organized in the usual way. The job was advertised in the underground revolutionary papers. A large number of applicants sent in their names, among them not a few girl students. A short list was made, and those on it were interviewed in Paris, Azev taking the chair. One of the girls was picked out and Azev took her to a hotel in Interlaken where his friend Dournovo was staying on holiday. He led her into the *salle a manger* and pointed to an innocent German merchant. She fired the pistol, killed the German, was at once seized and thrown into prison, while Azev returned to Paris and told the Committee that the girl had lost her nerve at the last moment.

Such was Azev. Such was the man, in fact, who interviewed Gapon immediately after Bloody Sunday; and Azev I strongly suspect was the real source of the story about Gapon which I sent to the *Manchester Guardian*. Was Gapon a genuine revolutionary after all—the person, in fact, whose existence and party was a nuisance to Azev? Or was he really a police spy? I leave the problem to the historians who, as an eminent historian once said to

me, *never* guess. As for Azev, he died peacefully in his bed some
years later, having made, I was told, something of a small fortune
on the Berlin Stock Exchange.

But to return to the upper surface of my life in Finland—I was
married in July 1906, and after our honeymoon (very far from
Archangel) brought my wife to Helsingfors. We came to the
same pension where I had been living before—a convenient little
sort of flat where she could begin to adjust herself gradually to the
habits and language of the country. She actually memorized
enough Finnish to enable her to shop in the market-place—an
entrancing experience for a newly-married lady.

The pension was useful too, occasionally, for our friends of the
underworld. Tschaikowsky spent a few nights there in disguise;
I remember my wife hissing to him across the breakfast table,
'You've got some dye on your cheek!' Another 'friend', like
Tschaikowsky a former member of the Kropotkin Circle, had
returned after a twenty-four-year exile. He was Felix Volkovsky.
He looked far older than Tschaikowsky, since he had been for
some years chained in a dungeon of the fortress of St. Peter and
St. Paul below the water-line of the Neva. He had managed to
escape to England and was now returning with a daughter who
had grown up there. But she was not interested in the Russian
social revolution and soon went back to England, leaving my wife
to darn his socks for him. We both grew fond of Volkovsky; he
was the gentlest of spirits, and wouldn't have hurt a fly. Yet he
believed fervently in the virtue of blowing up policemen and
grand-dukes.

Meanwhile the new *Lektor* and his wife (who was entitled
Lektorska) were fêted by kind friends in Helsingfors, anxious of
course to practise the English language. One of the most interesting houses we visited was the Donners'. Our hosts were the very
tall, wealthy, Swedish-speaking Finn, Ossian Donner, who later
became Finnish Ambassador to Great Britain, and his little
Scottish wife. There we enjoyed many evenings, the family
providing a quartet, followed by a very elaborate dinner which
began about midnight. Patrick Donner, then only an infant,
afterwards became a British subject, a Conservative Member of

Parliament and a well-known public servant; he was knighted in
1953.

Our lives were very busy, since I was able, with my wife's
help, to give enough private lessons to double my official university salary. My most famous pupil (if I may call him so) was
Mannerheim, made Marshal of Finland in 1942 and still the
country's hero. At that time he was an officer in the Finnish
regiment of the Russian Army, and had rooms in the large hotel
facing the market-place. There I visited him for a series of conversation lessons, just to polish up the English of which he already
had a pretty good command.

In my day, Finland offered two sources of enjoyment independent of all internal differences. First of all, music and art. The
genius of Sibelius was already becoming recognized. I was able to
hear his second symphony, conducted by the composer himself,
in the lovely assembly room of the university. Its semi-circular
background had been made resplendent by a triptych painted in
1904 by the Finnish artist, Albert Edelfelt, since destroyed by
a Russian bomb. It represented an imagined academic procession
at the founding of the university in 1640, but showing the figures
of professors familiar to me; among them was a green-cloaked
aide-de-camp depicting Sibelius at that date.

Sibelius' Second Symphony is an intensely mournful work, and,
to my uneducated ear, can only be understood by those who have
experienced the profound and melancholy mystery of this
country of illimitable forests and a thousand lakes. Through
Finlandia Sibelius voiced the patriotism of his country, breathing
a hatred of Russia so unmistakable that public performance was
forbidden by the Russian authorities.

The other source of keen pleasure the country provided for a
young couple was the sea and islands that lay about the city.
Helsingfors is built on a peninsula which juts out into the Gulf
of Finland like a hand with its fingers spread out, with stretches
of water between them. Soon after Christmas all this water
freezes up and, if the weather remains clear enough for no snow
to fall, there is a chance of ice-yachting, a highly exciting if
somewhat dangerous sport. You sit in a small sailing boat, with a

steel keel, like the base of a skate, attached to an outrigger also with a steel keel. The whole is controlled by a rudder on some kind of swivel so that swift turns can be accomplished. The speed can become very fast; the danger points are the turns, which if unskilfully managed may lead to the complete collapse of the craft, with its occupants thrown violently onto the ice with the risk of cracked skulls or broken hips.

But snow-free ice never lasts long and in some years does not come at all, so that we only tried ice-yachting once or twice. The sea well covered, however, with thick snow, so deep and impacted as to make it impossible to slip about on the ice beneath, afforded the greatest sport of all. I am not thinking of ski-ing— this is the normal mode of getting about in winter in Finland, since it is out of the question to walk in boots alone on ground that is almost everywhere knee-deep in snow. I speak rather of riding on horseback across the frozen sea, either at a straight gallop for a mile or so at a time, or on a drag-hunt across one of the islands that lie dotted over these inlets.

Among our friends were an engineer and his wife who had English horses which they lent us to ride. Early in January the shoes were taken off the horses so that they could enjoy the galloping as much as we did. Neither my wife nor I had ever ridden before, or indeed rode again after we left Finland. But when mounted and flying across an illimitable waste of snow on a bright morning at minus ten degrees centigrade, a young married couple were for a while as gods.

The same friends asked us to spend Christmas Day with them; and having made enquiries from my wife, produced a plum pudding according to her recipe—as they thought. But, alas, in place of sweet almonds—they had used *bitter* almonds. The pudding was accordingly a disaster. Both sides went through with it valiantly, our hosts receiving the impression of an extraordinary taste among the British, and we unwilling to suggest that something had gone wrong in the kitchen.

But departure was in the end inevitable. Children had begun to arrive and my wife, who was a very bad sailor, could not manage to look after more than one on the four days' voyage from

England. So in 1909, after leaving as usual in May, I transferred my loyalty, with many regrets, from the University of Helsingfors to that of London, only returning for a week in the summer to arrange for the removal of our furniture. I returned by sea, sailing at night-time from Åbo (Turku, as it is called in Finnish) to Stockholm across the Gulf of Bothnia, watching the midnight sun as the ship threaded its path amid the hundreds of pine-covered islets that lie like beads scattered about the gulf. It was a vision that induced a mood of profound and mysterious melancholy, well suited to my farewell to that enchanting land in which I had spent the happiest three years of my life.

POSTSCRIPT

As confessed above, I made no attempt to learn Finnish; and the Swedish literature I read consisted mainly of books written in Sweden. But Finland had its own literature, in particular Runeberg who was acclaimed as its great native poet. Nor could I altogether escape the influence of the *Kalevala* stories, some of which I could read in a wooden English translation in the World's Classics, and the magic of which I could feel in the music of Sibelius and on the canvases of Akseli Gallén-Kallela.

When I paid my return visit to Finland forty years after I had left, the Professor of English who now sat in the chair formerly occupied by Uno Lindelöf was Professor Mustanoja, whom I am happy to name among my friends. (I suspect that it is thanks to him that in 1963 I received the honour of becoming a Member of the Finnish Academy of Science and Letters.)

On one occasion he consulted me about the Minutes of the Finnish Literary Society for 1906 in which it is noted that two bards singing *runos* of the *Kalevala* had paid a visit to the capital. These were the last bards of whose existence there was any record, and my presence at that meeting was also noted in the Minutes. It appeared, he went on, that at this date no one else was alive who had seen them. Could I supply him with any recollection?

In reply I sent him the following notes. Calling down upon me the scorn thereby of the Professor of Greek in Edinburgh, to whom I submitted the notes, I riskily headed them *Pre-Homeric Bards*.

'Soon after my arrival as English *lektor* at Helsingfors my Professor, Uno Lindelöf, told me that two bards from the interior were to sing *runos* before a special meeting of the Finnish Literature Society, and offered to take me. It is now over fifty years ago, so I cannot guarantee that the following account is exact in all details: but this is how it stands in my mind. The bards were old men, bearded I think, and dressed in a special costume, the only features of which I remember were a peaked cap made of plaited birch-bark, and shoes plaited of the same material, together with a kind of apron. They sat opposite each other, their knees touching, and on the lap of each of them rested a Kantele, a rude musical instrument, little more than a closed box with a hole in the lid and strings across it. What the strings were made of I don't know. The bards held each other by the right hand, while their left hands rested on the instruments. Thus the *runo*—an episode or story from the *Kalevala* cycle—was sung antiphonally, one bard intoning a line, strumming the while with his left hand, the other bard doing the like with the next line. And so it went on, a monotonous chant, but not in the least wearisome. And so, I was assured, they could have gone on for days; for apparently their heads were full of *runos*, and as they had long ceased to read, their invention had not been destroyed or even contaminated by printed matter, as is that of all civilized persons. It was from such bards that Lönnrot collected the material which he pieced together in the middle of the nineteenth century as the *Kalevala*. The metre is in fact familiar to most English readers, since Longfellow borrowed it and a good deal of the story of his *Hiawatha* from a German translation of the *Kalevala*.

'No doubt the old men had once been able to read a little from the Bible; for you could not be married until you were confirmed and you could not be confirmed unless you could read to the pastor. Indeed, the Swedish for "to be confirmed" is "gå att läsa", which means "to go and read". But it is not to be supposed that the priest was very exacting in this preliminary examination. And what was true of the old men was also true of many old Finnish women who at that date carried in their heads hundreds of embroidery patterns.

'I wish I could remember more about the old men, but, alas, my memory is a civilized one. I know, however, that after an evening of listening to *runo* after *runo*, though of course I could not follow the Finnish, I came away with the strong impression that Homer may have listened to just such bards.'

4

Goldsmiths' College and H.M.I.

My life in Finland was succeeded by fifteen years' service in the cause of public education, first as a lecturer in a London training college for elementary teachers, and later as an inspector of evening classes in the North of England.

For the first three years of this period I lectured in English Literature at Goldsmiths' College, New Cross, an experience which, though brief, profoundly influenced my later career in more senses than one. I found, for example, that I could make the most unlikely types of students listen to poetry with attention. The success of my popular lecture courses in Finland had given me confidence; my failure as a university extension lecturer at Cambridge was a thing of the past. I also learnt how to draft examination papers in collaboration with other lecturers; for while other two-year training colleges for elementary school teachers were examined at this time by inspectors of the Board of Education, Goldsmiths' was unique in conducting its examinations internally.

When I joined its staff in 1909, the College had only recently come into existence; the building, which had previously housed the Royal Naval School, had been presented by the Worshipful Company of Goldsmiths to the University of London, together with the land surrounding it. This remarkable institution was at that time a combination of training college in the day-time for four to five hundred elementary school teachers (both men and women) and art college which occupied the building in the evenings. The day training college was itself two-sided; or rather was two colleges, one for either sex, each with its own vice-principal (in my day Mr. Raymont and Miss Graveson, both of whom I knew and liked very much) and staff of lecturers. These two sides met only once a day for prayers and a brief address by the

64

Warden who presided over the whole college for all purposes. I never got to know William Loring, the Warden in my day, personally. He was bound to be a somewhat remote figure. But clearly he had a strong sense of duty, both to the college as a whole, which kept him labouring at his desk for a good part of twenty-four hours a day, and, especially, to the large body of young men and women in the training department. He was unable, however, by his very nature to understand much of theirs, as was shown by his complete failure to communicate with them in the morning assembly, the only moment of the day when he had the chance. He was indeed the typical Cambridge don, a keen and learned classical scholar, but somewhat formal in manner. Nor is he the only great scholar and administrator that I have known to prove himself a failure in communicating with young people.

In addition to the ordinary run of students, we had a small group reading for University of London degrees. Those wishing to qualify in English were obliged to take one paper on Anglo-Saxon, and I, in order to learn the language myself, volunteered for the job; I managed to push the whole group through, first by devoting a hard-working vacation to an attempt to master the grammar and metre as expounded by Sweet, and then by keeping a fortnight ahead in the close study of passages from Sweet's *Anglo-Saxon Reader*. I need hardly say that I also read round the subject, in particular Chadwick's *Heroic Age*, and W. P. Ker's wonderful books on the literature of the Middle Ages. Of all the extant poems of pre-Norman England, I set myself to master the greatest: namely the fragmentary but fine *Battle of Malden*.

Anglo-Saxon, however, was but a minor duty, the bulk of the work being lecturing on literature to the men students not doing a degree course. But their numbers were in fact so great and the two-year course (which at that date was general in elementary training colleges) covered so wide a field, that two English lecturers were needed. My colleague—who rapidly became a friend—was W. T. Young, a former student of Professor Elton at Liverpool. The work kept Young and myself very busy, for besides teaching at the college we had to visit students doing their

E   65

teaching practice in local elementary schools. This taught me a great deal about elementary schools which proved useful in the work in which I was later to be engaged.

When Young and I first met, we had to plan a division of labour and the details of our courses. When we were informed that one of our classes consisted mainly of Welsh international football players, we felt we were in for some excitement. 'What's to be done with those fellows?' asked Young. 'They think all poetry is cissy.' I suggested Browning, thinking of Shackleton reading him to his mates in the Antarctic, and declaring that Browning never failed with men of action. So I tried Browning on the Welshmen—and scored a goal straight off by selecting 'A Soliloquy in a Spanish Cloister' as the *pièce de résistance*. I read it aloud—by way of introducing myself, so to speak; when I had finished with 'Grrrrr, you swine!', I knew, looking round the class, that I had them for good. Indeed, I still possess a selected volume of Browning presented to me by the group at the end of the session.

Young and I were dissatisfied with the selection of poetry and prose chosen for training colleges by educational publishers. So we planned a series, 'Cambridge Anthologies' (to be published by the Cambridge University Press), which illustrated the main features of poetry and prose during the major periods of English literature. Four of the volumes were published before war broke out, two in the Shakespearian period and two on the early nineteenth-century Romantics. Of the former, Young undertook the poetry volume, while I made myself responsible for the prose. My anthology later became a bestseller under the new title *Life in Shakespeare's England*.

It so happened that at this point both Young and I, unknown to each other, set to work writing a short outline history of English literature, as a kind of framework for our anthologies. When Young showed me his I thought it the better and got him to offer it to Cambridge and they accepted it. Though this left my draft on my hands, it came in very useful later on as the basis for lectures I was to give at Edinburgh.

Young also wrote an admirable chapter on George Meredith

for the *Cambridge History of English Literature*. What sort of future would have come to this brilliant and promising scholar, my delightful colleague, no one will ever know. He died in the trenches in 1914, two years after I had left Goldsmiths'.

I cannot leave this period of my life without mentioning the annual college dramatic productions. I cooperated in these with a pleasant lecturer on the women's side who cast the female parts from her students. Two of the plays we did were Shakespeare, *The Taming of the Shrew* in 1911—my second year—and *Hamlet* in my last year. *Hamlet* was aiming high, but the experiment proved successful—so successful that we hired a small West End theatre and played *Hamlet* there for two or three nights, earning about twenty-five pounds for charity.

A few weeks later I moved to Leeds and plunged into a new life as an H.M.I. for adult classes and into a hitherto undreamed-of country, the industrial North. This move opened the second and longer chapter in my service of public education. In effect, I had been unconsciously prepared for it six years earlier. For in 1906 my wife and I spent our honeymoon near Douglas on the Isle of Man with our friends the Andrews and Mrs. Andrew's brother, Frank Pullinger.

Pullinger was assistant to Robert Morant, the Permanent Secretary to the Board of Education, and as we lay on the cliffs near Douglas looking over the sunlit sea, he had poured into my ears Morant's dream of an industrial democracy. In such a democracy, young persons would find that part-time day continuation schools could provide meaning for the work they did with their hands. This idea was not confined to Morant and Pullinger, since some kind of continuation schools for adolescents were then under discussion.

Such schools, Pullinger had explained to me, would be a type of education provided by the Technical Branch which would give back to the people what they had begun to lose when the industrial revolution had created a schism between culture and crafts. The industrial democracy that Morant dreamed of would welcome and understand the results of technical achievement, face them boldly, and declare that the works of man's hands, even in these grimy days, deserved the blessing which poetry, art and culture had previously conferred. It was a vision that both he and Morant believed in passionately; and it was Pullinger under whom I was now to serve as an inspector from 1912 to 1920.

Pullinger himself was a first-rate administrator, prepared to ride roughshod over anything and anybody who might jeopardize projects he considered vital in the public interest. In this he resembled Morant, who was busy constructing the first English state system of education, a system he had himself helped to found in the Act of 1902; for as Balfour's secretary he had virtually drafted the Act behind the scenes, though Sidney Webb is also reputed to have had a hand in it.

The Education Act of 1902 transferred control of the elementary schools, hitherto provided by local school boards working under the Education Department at Whitehall, to the new local authorities elected for all public services as well as education. The Education Department became the Board of Education which gave 'Grants in Aid' to the local education committees and employed a large number of inspectors who replaced the inspectors of the earlier National Board Schools. Moreover, the Act empowered the local authorities to supply education higher than the public elementary schools, e.g. secondary schools, technical schools and evening classes of all kinds. The Act in short meant a complete revolution in English public education.

Morant, the principal architect of the state system, seems to have communicated some of his temper to two of his chief officials, under whom it was my good fortune to work—Pullinger and Edmund Chambers. Both were devoted to the cause of education, in particular the cause of post-primary education.

Morant's own character is still a matter of debate; his passionate and disinterested enthusiasm for education involved a certain unscrupulousness. Yet we must distinguish very carefully between the sort of intrigue adopted by Morant and Pullinger for purely public ends and that prompted by personal ambition. Valuable testimony to Morant's character has recently reached me from Sir Henry Bunbury, one of the Commissioners of Lloyd George's Health Service of which Morant became Secretary in 1911 upon leaving the Board of Education. Bunbury recalls him as a man of genius gifted with almost prophetic fervour, 'an Elijah in Whitehall'. To Morant's admirers in the Board of Education his character seemed rather that of a general, with powers of imagination, of improvisation, and of strategic foresight comparable with those displayed by a military genius. I myself never had any talk at all with him and only saw him once. But on that occasion I heard him make a (to me) surprisingly emotional speech delivered at Toynbee Hall in praise of Albert Mansbridge, the founder of the Workers' Educational Association, who was just leaving for a holiday in Australia; a speech which could only have been given by a man with enthusiasm for the cause of adult education.

When I first met Pullinger in 1906, he had recently been appointed an inspector by Morant. It is, moreover, clear that Morant had already marked him out for technical education, since in 1908 he appointed him Chief Inspector in the Technical Branch of the Board of Education.

When Pullinger came to offer me an inspectorship in 1912, Morant was no longer his chief, having fallen from power in 1911. The reason would have been ridiculous if the result had not been so tragic. A thoroughly competent all-round well-educated inspectorate was essential for building up the new system. There had been inspectors, of course, of the Board Schools—Matthew Arnold had been one—with underlings called sub-inspectors who went round and examined the 'three R's' for the damnable system called 'Payment by Results'. But after 1902 most local authorities appointed their own inspectors from among the ranks of public elementary schoolmasters, often at that time men of inferior intellectual ability. Morant naturally regarded their influence on schools with extreme disfavour; one of the officers of the Board, E. G. A. Holmes, sent round a confidential memorandum commonly known as the 'Holmes Circular', among the Board's Inspectorate, condemning these inspectors in no measured terms, and urging that future appointments should be made from men with a university education. Unhappily a copy of the document got into the hands of a Member of Parliament and was quoted in the Commons in a question put by Sir Samuel Hoare. This gave rise to an unholy row. Morant's head was demanded, and both the President of the Board and Morant, its secretary, were forced to resign. Nevertheless, as we shall see, his vision of day continuation schools reached the Statute Book in 1918.

The inspectorship offered me was in Pullinger's Technical Branch, which we inspectors called the 'T' branch for short, because it was concerned with everything that happened after tea. There were three other branches of the Board, each with its inspectorate—Secondary, Elementary and (a very shadowy one) University—the four initials conveniently grouped as the word SUET.

By 1911 Pullinger was ready with plans for furnishing his department with a full staff of technical inspectors. The large sum of money necessary had become available through the disbanding of the inspectorate which had for many years existed under the Department of Science and Art.

The 'T' inspectorate was so arranged as to cover, as far as possible, all types of technical education and evening work. In general, each subject had at least two inspectors, a staff inspector based on London and a colleague; most of these colleagues functioned in the North of England. For example, the Staff Inspector of Commerce was a Mr. Kahn (father of the economist) whose colleague in the north was Frederick Spencer. There were inspectors also of building, mining, textiles and agriculture and there were a couple of women inspectors of domestic subjects. I came in as an inspector of English, History and Economics. Adult classes for working people (which, as they met in the evening, came for administrative purposes within the purview of the 'T' branch) were also my concern—at first, as will be explained, my chief concern.

The organization of the new inspectorate had been most carefully thought out and proved admirable. There were frequent 'full inspections' of important technical institutes in large industrial centres and also reports upon whole areas under different local authorities. These 'full inspections' generally meant a varied group of us staying there for, perhaps, inside of a week.

As the business end of our duties took place in the evenings we spent a good many of our morning hours visiting mines, factories and other places of employment connected with the particular area. This was a great step forward in my education. I had studied Economic Theory for the History Tripos at Cambridge; now for the first time I was brought in touch with its realities. Indeed, in a way I had a better chance than most of my colleagues to comprehend practical economics because of my connection with adult classes, the majority of which were studying economics.

My chief friend among the northern band of inspectors was Frederick Spencer, an inspector for commerce. With W. H. Perkins, the Director of Education for Warwickshire, the best equilateral triangle of friendship I have known came into being. But 'Spen' was our leader, the wittiest and wisest of the three; the best read too, in economics and politics. Early on in his career he had been recommended by that great man, Graham Wallas, to Sidney Webb and became research assistant to the Webbs. (He thus met another of Webb's assistants whom he eventually married.) To anticipate the conclusion of this chapter, had the Board appointed him in 1921 as Pullinger's successor, day continuation schools might have been saved. All his colleagues in the North, I believe, knew him to be the right man to become their chief. After the betrayal of the day continuation schools we both left the Board, he to become Chief Inspector of Schools under the L.C.C., and I to become a Professor of Education in London. He has left us his autobiography in *An Inspector's Testament*, a beautifully written, witty book, full of good tales.

One feature of the 'T' inspectorate was that every specialist had in addition to his area a small district for which he was administratively responsible. Thus my area as specialist was the six northern counties and Cheshire; and Leeds was assigned to me as my headquarters because it was the best railway centre in the north of England; while my small purely administrative district was a section of the West Riding round about Batley and Dewsbury. Incidentally, this small district close to Leeds provided a number of ordinary evening schools within easy reach.

Shortly after I was appointed, Pullinger sent for me urgently.

'A very awkward thing has occurred,' he said. 'I've had to give the district next to yours to another John Wilson. What does that damned "D" stand for in your signature?'

'Oh, that's my mother's maiden name, Dover.'

'Well then, you are Dover Wilson; and let's have no more nonsense about it!' And so I have been called Dover Wilson (without a hyphen, please) ever since.

To complete the picture of the administrative side of our activities, something must be said of the office in Whitehall—an important function of inspectors being to answer questions and deal with enquiries sent down from London. These questions came to us in 'jackets', which often contained a series of minutes ending with the question one had to answer. Further, the accountant's department in the office scrutinized the 'diaries' which we had to send in every week through the Chief Inspector, to see whether the travelling or hotel expenses were legitimate and necessary. These diaries were single sheets, with compartments marked off for six days in the week and three periods for each day—morning, afternoon and evening. The inspector who wrote his name at the head of the sheet was required to record his occupation during a minimum of two periods for each day.

In Whitehall Pullinger's opposite number was Edmund Chambers, whom Morant had found in the office of the Education Department when he got there—a man after his own heart and withal a friend of Pullinger's since they had been exact contemporaries at Corpus Christi College, Oxford. Under Morant, Chambers moved round the office, organizing all the different branches at Morant's suggestion. He may be justly regarded as the main builder of that particular side of Morant's administrative machine; while he was even more interested in the adult education work than was Pullinger himself.

It must be noted here that before Morant's arrival Chambers had at least sketched out most of his monumental work, *The Elizabethan Stage*; for, as an official before 1902 in the Education Department, he once told me, he only found a few letters to deal with when he reached the office, dictated replies to his secretary,

Goldsmiths' College and H.M.I.

spent the rest of the day at the British Museum, and returned on his way home just to sign the letters. Morant changed all this; for Chambers threw himself wholeheartedly behind his chief in his work for the Board. And this accounts, I am sure, for the fact that the four volumes of *The Elizabethan Stage*, published in 1923, give the impression of a vast amount of material thrown together, often apparently haphazard and never welded into a single book. It was only after he left the Board in 1926 that he could get down to his invaluable *William Shakespeare: a Study of Facts and Problems*, and give it the form of unity. The date of *The Mediaeval Stage*—1903—speaks for itself.

Pullinger's invitation to me to join the inspectorate had taken me entirely by surprise and it was some time before I found my feet. I had never before, for example, heard of the Workers' Educational Association, founded in 1903 by Albert Mansbridge, a clerk in the Cooperative Movement. The new association was to be strictly non-vocational and non-sectarian, and its aim was to promote free higher education among working people. The old type of university extension classes, originally started in 1850 for working people, had long since developed into courses of lectures delivered to large fee-paying, mainly middle-class, audiences.

The new classes were set on foot by enthusiasts, who were called district secretaries. They travelled about their area holding meetings, expounding the objects of the W.E.A. and enrolling students. It was their duty to enlist appropriate teachers from a university, secondary school or elsewhere.

In 1907 the W.E.A. begat as its eldest child the University Tutorial Class Movement, one of the purposes of which was to bring reality into scholarship by associating the universities closely with the workaday world. As will be explained later, the tutorial class involved a much more severe discipline than the ordinary W.E.A. class; in fact it aimed at university Honours. In taking this step Mansbridge enlisted the help of Oxford and in particular he succeeded in securing the ardent support of a Fellow of New College, Alfred Zimmern. Author of *The Greek Commonwealth*, Zimmern had arrived by way of Greece at something near

Morant's dream of our industrial democracy. He was on fire with the conviction, partly inspired by Mansbridge, I believe, that Oxford should give the benefit of its learning and instruction to the community at large and of course especially to the workers who were ready to grasp with both hands what Oxford had to give them. This faith was proclaimed in an historic appeal to Oxford entitled *Oxford and Working Class Education* (1909). At Mansbridge's suggestion he later became one of Pullinger's staff inspectors, in fact the man who worked with me.

In Edmund Chambers, Mansbridge secured another great ally, for it was Chambers who drew up the special regulations for university tutorial classes (which I was later to administer). The ultimate purpose of these regulations was to make universities responsible for advanced classes of adult education and thereby to secure a special grant direct from the Treasury without having to go through the local education authorities, who were often served at this stage by unenlightened officials who might have suspected such gatherings of working men as 'hotbeds of socialism'. With regard to grants and inspection, non-tutorial W.E.A. classes were treated on the same footing as any other evening classes.

The regulations for the university tutorial classes laid down that a class should consist of not more than thirty-two students; that the sessions should extend over at least two terms and the course over three years; that the meetings should be for at least two hours every week, half the time devoted to a lecture by a tutor approved by the university and the other half to discussion by the class; that there should be a library at the disposal of the class for reading about the subject; and that a student could not be registered for the grant at the end of the course unless he had written essays to the satisfaction of the tutor. Mansbridge rightly insisted on the discussion hour, his point being that what the class was after was the truth, and the truth can only be arrived at, as Plato exemplified, through discussion.

As to the libraries—at the beginning they just didn't exist, though the universities, who were responsible through a joint committee of W.E.A. and university, were supposed to supply the books. One of my principal functions in the early days was to bully vice-chancellors to supply this need of their extra-mural classes. It was soon evident, however, that something more was required; and Mansbridge, proceeding on one of his principles— 'Why not?'—established a central library for students which has now become the National Central Library in Store Street, London. It acts *inter alia* as a clearing house for public libraries all over the country. Anyone who can prove himself to be a genuine student can, by applying to his local public library, borrow almost any book he may require for the pursuit of his studies.

Of course these regulations did not spring like Athene from the head of a Zeus sitting in Whitehall. They represented Mansbridge's ideals, and were a formulation of the practice of a few tutorial classes already in existence, being carried on by R. H. Tawney and one or two others. The best known of these experimental tutorial classes were those located at Rochdale and at Longton in the Potteries.

My appointment, as I soon became aware, was designed by Pullinger partly to deal with evening and technical schools and partly to have his own man, so to speak, as a colleague of Zimmern, then enlisted as a Staff Inspector. How well I remember my first meeting with Zimmern over a lunch at that extraordinary marble palace, the National Liberal Club. Rather taken aback at first by the sight of this rotund little Hebrew, I soon fell beneath his charm. And if Pullinger thought that I should maintain an independent point of view, he was mistaken. I was then not long back from Finland and my contact with the revolutionary movement that had recently failed in Russia; and I had not known Zimmern an hour before I jumped at the idea that *here* was a sounder revolution.

After this meeting there followed many journeys together. It was a halcyon period before the war. Zimmern seemed to have a high hand with—to use Spencer's phrase—'the little black man in Whitehall' who checked the diaries, for our travelling expenses were lavish. At times Zimmern stayed with my wife and me. It is characteristic of his ebullience that on one occasion he leapt into bed and alighting on the top of the rubber hot water bottle, burst it. But ashamed to rouse the family, he slept under a blanket on the floor.

To return to the earlier tutorial classes, it is a mistake to imagine that the artisans attending them were ignorant of the kind of literature that middle-class readers are familiar with. For example, I happened to call unexpectedly one day on a class secretary who was a Durham miner. He was off shift, washed, of course, and in his Sunday suit, reading aloud Butcher and Lang's translation of the *Odyssey* to his children.

But, even so, how pitiably and pathetically ill-equipped were some students, thirsting for the rudiments of knowledge. It was my business to see that the classes complied with the regulations in the matter of essay writing. And I tried the experiment in a class at Middlesbrough, mostly composed of heavy-iron workers, of seeing what progress they had made with their essays during the three years. So I asked the tutor to let me have all the essays he could recover from the students towards the end of the course. I don't remember anything which convinced me more completely of the value of this great movement than what I found at Middlesbrough. One student in particular had obviously never handled a tool as small as a pen since he left the elementary school at twelve years of age. The tutor therefore started by making him copy out passages from a textbook (Townsend-Warner, *Outlines of Industrial History*) which was used in the first year. At the end of the year this student was beginning to set down his own ideas on paper, and by the middle of the third year he was expressing himself freely and in quite good English. And as I read with growing excitement I turned over the page; the essay broke off short with the words, 'It's three o'clock; I've got to be at the forge at six. Can't write any more.' Those were apostolic days.

Let me tell you the tale of a different kind of working man, one who got his intellectual food by his own effort not in order to 'get on' but to get knowledge. After the end of the First World War, I moved south for a few years and visited classes in the Midlands and the West, often in rural areas. One of these classes, which from my list I found began early in the session, was in Shaftesbury in Dorset, and the subject was Shakespeare. I marked that down for an early visit, in the hope that I should see the harvest moon rising above the valley. It was a lovely September evening and a nice walk from the station, about half a mile, I think. The class was held in a room in one of the inns, and I found the members already assembling—very disappointing: the local curate, a local chemist, etc.; not a horny-handed son of toil among them. The time was almost up, but we sat waiting for the arrival of the tutor who I learned upon enquiry came by a local bus which was then due. As we spoke, the door opened and the only peasant in the class entered the room and, being a little late, began his lecture before he got to the desk, therefore I could not introduce myself. He was an old man, well over seventy, I should say, dressed in the corduroy of his class. His subject was *Romeo and Juliet*. It was a lovely lecture, well expressed and making all the important points. But at the end he said, 'Now, my young friends, I've had to take this play, you know, as an example of Shakespeare's early tragedies; but this love business, don't take it too seriously. It all passes away; it all passes away!' I then had to reveal my presence, at which he started back as if I had been the devil. 'Oh sir,' he said, 'if only I had known you were coming, I would have prepared the lecture properly. I'm afraid I haven't given as much time to my preparation lately as I should. You see, I've got so engrossed in some translation I'm trying to make from Greek epigrams.' H.M.I. that night went to bed a much humbler man.

Let me complete this section with a few more anecdotes of visits to W.E.A. and tutorial classes. The very first tutor I ever inspected (though he didn't know it) was the real founder of the tutorial class movement, R. H. Tawney (who took the famous class at Longton in the Potteries already mentioned). He is well known to scholars as author of *The Agrarian Problem in the Sixteenth Century*, the more popular *Religion and the Rise of Capitalism* and other books. He was a friend of William Temple who was for many years president of the W.E.A.; and though I never had an opportunity of being on intimate terms with him, yet I always revered him as something of a saint as well as the greatest scholar who gave himself to the movement.

I had arrived at Roundhay, a suburb of Leeds, to take up my duties in the autumn of 1912. There I received a friendly welcome from the well-known writer F. S. Marvin, a secondary school inspector who was to be a neighbour. Almost at once, in the course of conversation, he told me that if I wanted to know anything about the W.E.A., Tawney was holding a public meeting that very evening for the formation of a W.E.A. branch at a small town called Castleford, some twelve miles away. The meeting was to be held in the town hall, and the brass band of Castleford had been engaged to play through the town and bring the audience to the door—which they did. Marvin and I arrived early and found a few people inside waiting to hear Tawney who was already seated on the platform. Presently the brass band approached and was soon very audible through the open doors. Most of Castleford appeared to have followed it; and most of Castleford remained outside to listen to it. But the band, having begun, couldn't stop, and went on playing; so that in the end Tawney's brief inaugural address was barely audible to the small group more anxious to hear him than the music without.

Another branch of adult education was set on foot after the First World War by Charles Douie, an official working under Chambers in the office of the Board of Education. He was particularly interested in education in prisons, and whenever an opportunity occurred on my travels persuaded me to come and lecture on Shakespeare at these institutions. Accordingly, happening on one occasion to be in Lincoln to inspect an evening class, I spent the next morning, by arrangement with the Chaplain, on a visit to the gaol. 'I think I ought to explain, sir,' he said on my arrival, 'that of the two hundred and sixty-five male prisoners here at least two hundred are quite illiterate.'

'But how can I lecture to them, then, on Shakespeare,' I said to him, 'as has been arranged?'

'I really don't know,' he replied.

But I had a volume of Shakespeare in my bag, and hoping for the best I proceeded to the only lecture room in the place, which was the chapel. There, standing on the steps of the altar, I found myself faced with rows and rows of the most unmitigated scoundrels I had ever seen, with the warders standing round the walls to quell any disturbance. Happily the sight of the last gave me my clue. I turned to *Much Ado About Nothing* and after a word or two read aloud the Dogberry and Verges scenes. And every point that Shakespeare made about those worthy constables was taken up with alacrity by the prisoners, who kept pointing and jeering at the warders standing round. The whole thing proved a great success. Shakespeare never fails, if you can find him the right audience, and my visit to Lincoln told me a good deal, I thought, about the groundlings who had stood round the platform at the Globe Theatre.

Many tutorial classes had one or two women in them; but it was not often that one came on an exclusively feminine class. One of these, however, I well remember. It was provided by a Co-op in Liverpool or Birkenhead (I forget which) and consisted entirely of Co-op women. The tutor was that young novelist Olaf Stapleton, well known in his day but cut short in his prime. He was lecturing on Shelley and Keats, if I remember rightly, and illustrated his talk by reading aloud—which he did very well. At the end of one impassioned reading which I can never forget, one stout dame exclaimed, 'Oh, dearie! doo 'ee read it again! *Do* 'ee read it again!'

That class, being provided by a Co-op, was somewhat unusual in its origin, most of them being organized by the local W.E.A. secretaries. I was full of admiration for the eagerness and untiring hard work these men put into the task. The tutors were in early days mostly university lecturers in economics, or good secondary school masters, approved by the University Joint Committees as qualified to take on teaching of a university standard. And the class would grow so fond of their tutor and the knowledge he had to give them that they usually followed him to the station as he went off by train at some late hour in the evening—if they didn't persuade him to stop the night so that the discussion could be indefinitely prolonged. D. H. Macgregor, at this time Professor of Economics at Leeds and later translated to Oxford, took one of these classes in the West Riding. And the awe which he inspired may be gauged by the question which the secretary's little son put to his father, who passed it on to me, 'Daddy, is Professor Macgregor God?'

Many a class consisting wholly or in part of industrial workers had asked for economics as their subject in order that they might discover something about the world in which they had their being (well or ill). After all, it was rare that a member of the class could not provide some experience, either from the factory or in connection with his trade union, which would throw light upon economic theory. The lecture on the theory would help the members of the class to get their bearings, while the discussion which followed would often help the tutor to understand the realities of the industrial world. Indeed, I believe that these classes, and the fact that a fair proportion of their teachers were academic lecturers, had some not inconsiderable influence upon the study of economics in England. Certainly, the inspection of such classes added incalculably to my own education.

But not all subjects lent themselves so readily to discussion by the students. Philosophy would naturally lead on, and so might psychology, to the views and experiences of individual members. The skilful tutor moreover would leave loose threads here and there in the course of his lecture for the class to get hold of. But some subjects—for example political history—lay so far outside the knowledge of most working men of that time that discussion tended to fall dead. I remember hearing a lecture by that brilliant historian A. J. Grant, Professor of History at Leeds, which was so perfect, so beautifully rounded, that there was nothing more to be said about the subject when it was finished.

I may add that it was not uncommon to find a member of the Labour College, a Marxist rival of the W.E.A., in one of their classes. And I was always pleased when it happened, since he with his rather crude Marxism was apt to call the class back to fundamentals. He acted like the garlic in the salad.

In August 1914, of course, the First World War broke out. Realizing from our knowledge of even serious-minded members of the W.E.A. and the tutorial class movement, that British working men knew nothing of modern history or of the political set-up of Europe and the world in general, Zimmern and I made up our minds to produce a textbook (which came to be called *The War and Democracy*) designed especially for this public. It was conceived, planned and its chapters allocated immediately after war broke out, in a canoe on the river at the foot of the vicarage garden at Harston where my father-in-law was vicar. Zimmern elected to write chapters on the war, the British Empire and on Germany. I wrote a historical introduction outlining the political history of Europe from Napoleon up to 1914 entitled 'The National Idea in Europe' and, also being recently back from that part of the world, a chapter on Russia. If ever there was false prophecy written, this last was a good example; but there was some excuse, as what I had seen in Russia was the failure of the Social Revolutionary Party, which convinced me that there was no middle class strong enough or large enough to succeed in transforming the state as the Parliamentarians had done in seventeenth-century England or the Girondins at the end of the eighteenth century in France. I could not prophesy a portent like Lenin who arrived in 1917. But before that, the defeat of the Russian Army seemed likely to be followed by a disintegration of the whole empire into a number of separate states; indeed, my old friend Nicholas Tschaikowsky actually reappeared as President of the North Russian Republic.

Arthur Greenwood, then a tutor at Leeds University, wrote on economics; there was a chapter on foreign policy by a young official in the Foreign Office who signed himself 'P'—a letter which was later revealed to stand for Lord Eustace Percy. But perhaps the most prescient and influential chapter of all was that on the Austro-Hungarian Empire by Professor Seton-Watson. This forecast the break-up of that 'ramshackle' twin-monarchy, Austria-Hungary, into a number of independent states. And indeed Seton-Watson, who was a friend of Masaryk's and wrote much more about this subject than was contained in our little volume, came to be described as the creator of Czechoslovakia. Our book answered a need beyond our dreams. I forget how many editions it went through or into how many languages it was translated. The proceeds, allocated from the beginning to the W.E.A., made quite a useful addition to their funds for a time.

I ought to add that we received an official reprimand from the Permanent Secretary of the Board; we had overlooked the fact that before proceeding to publish the volume, full of a great deal of implicitly contentious doctrine, we should have asked permission. Zimmern was summoned to the presence of Sir Amherst Selby-Bigge, who had succeeded Morant as Permanent Secretary; as Zimmern's fag, as I called myself, I could take shelter behind his superior rank and therefore was not to enter the presence until I did so to take my leave in 1924.

Although I saw much of Zimmern in later years, he had to leave the Board soon after the war broke out. His knowledge of Germany and his first-rate personal abilities made his presence at the Foreign Office necessary. Indeed, he is said to have had a good deal to do later with framing the Treaty of Versailles. Zimmern's post as Staff Inspector was taken by Joseph Owen, like Zimmern an Oxford man but of working-class origin; he therefore naturally found it a little difficult to go all the way towards accepting the W.E.A. ideal—viz. to raise the intellectual standard of the working class as a whole rather than to give individual students an opportunity to climb out of their own class. I must confess that I was disappointed not to be named Staff Inspector as Zimmern's successor; but Owen was very amiable and we got on excellently together. I ought to have realized that Pullinger had designed me, ever since he first met me at Douglas, as a special instrument for carrying through his and Morant's dream of day continuation schools and was reserving me for the Act of 1918.

The W.E.A.'s ideal of raising the intellectual standard of the whole working class was to some extent realized. I venture to suggest that but for the leaven of these students throughout the country, with their three years of instruction in economics and history—non-political, non-sectarian, under tutors of university standing—the abysmal disillusion that followed the end of the First World War, which had been supposed to create a land fit for heroes, might well have resulted in revolution.

The war threatened to wipe out the whole W.E.A. movement but for one bright spot, Yorkshire, where a moribund district was rejuvenated, largely owing to the genius of George Thompson. A joiner from Halifax and a product of a tutorial class there, he was a man whose memory I revere above that of most of these early apostles. He was not a very prepossessing person; he could be harsh and even ruthless if he thought it necessary, but I never knew anyone who worked harder or thought less of himself. His scorn for self-seekers is illustrated by an incident in his career. I never knew the exact details, but some member of one of his committees insinuated that the W.E.A. money which he was spending on visits to centres all over Yorkshire was being used to feather his own nest. Thompson resigned, and got someone to lend him enough money to travel steerage with his family to New Zealand. When there he resumed his work as a joiner and at once began to earn three times as much as he had ever earned in England. I forget how long it lasted, but the disconsolate Yorkshire district was very soon on its knees begging him to return; which of course he did, because his heart was there.

I knew Thompson very well; we trusted each other. He said to me one day, 'I wish you would not call me Thompson.' I asked why not. 'Only the boss calls us by our surnames,' he replied. 'Call me George, or Mr. Thompson if you like.' One learned things about working-class etiquette that members of other social groups could not even begin to suspect.

As H.M.I. responsible for the inspection of tutorial classes in the North of England, I was often brought officially into touch with the vice-chancellors of the universities in that part of the world. The tutorial classes were, as stated above, conducted under the authority of the universities, working through a joint committee consisting of representatives of the universities on one hand and those of the W.E.A. on the other.

Living in Leeds, I was a neighbour of Sir Michael Sadler who was then Vice-Chancellor of the university. He naturally got into touch with me soon after I arrived, since he had formerly been concerned with the administration of education, though he had left the board after quarrelling with Morant. I found him most charming; and when later he became Master of University

College, Oxford, he proved himself exceedingly kind to my son, at that time an undergraduate.

I only once saw Sadler and Chambers together; but the meeting well illustrates the attitude of the hard-boiled officials at Whitehall (especially those who like Chambers had been inspired by Morant) to Sadler's notions on education. The occasion was a dinner at Sheffield University following a session of the Central Joint Advisory Committee for Tutorial Classes. (This was a kind of upper deck invented by the fertile brain of Mansbridge to bring different university joint committees together.) The time was late in 1916, during the interval between the fall of Asquith's government and the announcement by Lloyd George of the names of his new ministers. Sadler sat at the foot of the table, with Chambers (representing the office of the Board) and myself (the local inspector of tutorial classes) on either side of him. H. A. L. Fisher, the host of the evening, presided at the other end, but moved down to join us after the King's health had been drunk. Who was to be the new President of the Board, was the question in the minds of all present. And Sadler, eager and charming as ever, began telling us what he would do if the choice fell upon him. 'Education is a science,' he asserted. 'For science one needs *research* and experiment. We ought to set aside some administrative county or county borough as our laboratory, and carry out there all sorts of experiments in teaching and organization and so on—for only so can we hope to arrive at positive results.' Chambers's face as this went on was an interesting study. At last he could stand it no longer. 'What would the *parents* say?' he blurted out, and the question brought the topic to an end. Fisher kept silence, smiling his Chinese smile, and a few days later we read in the newspapers that it was he whom Lloyd George had chosen as President of the Board—as he must have known when we sat there.

Meanwhile the war went on, and having two brothers at the Front I grew more and more impatient with being 'reserved' by the Board of Education. I minuted Pullinger from time to time, begging for my release, but it was not granted. As a kind of salve for my conscience, however, I was instructed to supplement my official Board of Education work by doing additional inspectorial work on behalf of the Ministry of Munitions. And accordingly I found myself a Munitions Area Dilution Officer (M.A.D.O.).

After Lloyd George had taken over from Asquith, he insisted on a great increase in munitions. But since it was important that the production of munitions should not impede the flow of recruits into the army, joint offices were set up in all the large munitions centres, especially of course in the North of England and in the Midlands. One of the two offices, known as a Munitions Area Recruiting Office, was under an army officer, and existed to recruit from among the munition workers those who were not doing essential work and were of age to join the army. On the other hand, its twin, the Munitions Area Dilution Office, was there to protect essential munition workers from being drafted into the army. My new job was to visit these Dilution Offices and to see that they were being conducted properly and that the right men were being released. I found it a piece of war work well worth doing; these offices I had to inspect were presided over by managers and sub-managers of engineering works who, supplied with schedules of employees and their occupations, were supposed to distinguish between the essential and the non-essential occupations. But in many cases these presiding officials, for all their knowledge of engineering, were semi-literate and had little or no office experience. On the other hand they had been supplied with a clerical staff among whom I could sometimes discover one or two far more competent for the job than the boss who ruled over them.

I think I visited over half a dozen of these offices in England. My calls were not announced beforehand. My procedure was as follows: I entered the office, presented my credentials to its head, who generally asked, 'You are an engineer, sir?', to which I replied, 'I know nothing about engineering. I have come to look at your schedules.' I would then sit down with the lists and go through them to see how he had been carrying on his duties. After an hour or two I generally found that the thing was full of mistakes, that the wrong people were being recruited, and vice versa. If so, I said good-bye; and a day or two later the engineer might find himself replaced—perhaps by a member of his own staff. It was an exciting phase of my life; I suppose the one occasion on which I could feel I was moving along what C. P. Snow calls 'the corridors of power', though I couldn't help feeling also double-faced in the exercise of these powers.

My chief in the Ministry was a friend of mine, Alan Barlow, son-in-law of Horace Darwin, with whom my father had worked. Hearing that the Scottish M.A.D.O. wished to know how the work was being carried on in England, Barlow suggested that I should pay them a visit which I proceeded to do, spending a week there. This was my first visit to Scotland. I little realized that eighteen years later I should be returning to spend the rest of my life there.

When the war drew to its close, I went up to London to see Pullinger and asked to be moved south in order to send my own son to the Whitgift Grammar School of which Andrew was still headmaster. And when he replied that he couldn't see his way to such a change I took my courage in both hands and threatened that if so I must seek for a post as a professor or lecturer in English literature and leave the Board. At this he yielded. So in early 1919 I was building a small house in Purley for myself and my family, while I continued my inspection work in the Midlands and the West, leaving London to be looked after by the new Staff Inspector, Joseph Owen.

The Purley house was situated in a large garden, in which I had a tennis court laid. And on one occasion Pullinger's daughter Dorothy, who was then I believe at Oxford, came over to play tennis, bringing with her her college friend Joanna Perry-Keene. The latter I came to know very well after she married F. P. Wilson, Merton Professor of English at Oxford—no relation but a great friend; indeed, at the very time she was playing tennis at Purley, 'F.P.' was waiting for her at Victoria Station.

To turn to more weighty matters, I was then much occupied with the problem of the teaching of English, as in May 1919 I was appointed by the President of the Board of Education as a member of the Departmental Committee to enquire into the position of English in the educational system of England. This committee occupied the best part of my time for nearly two years, as will appear in the next chapter. I had also been giving more and more attention to the problem of the continuation schools, to deal with which Pullinger had originally appointed me. For the Board at that time was preparing for a new Education Act, which was ultimately passed in 1918.

This Act, known as the Fisher Act because it was introduced while H. A. L. Fisher was President of the Board, marked the first great advance in English education since 1902. Its timing was of particular interest, for the Commons first debated it in the spring of 1918 when the Germans were breaking through on the Western Front and the nation was even more, I will not say panic-stricken, but at any rate conscious of extreme peril, than it was during the Battle of Britain twenty-two years later. In this country, war has often seemed to be the parent of educational acts. In 1870, 1902, 1918 and again in 1944 the two have been closely connected. And when the 1944 Act was introduced as the Bill of 1943 we were by no means yet sure of victory. It is when the nation finds itself in peril that it thinks most about the children.

But the 1918 Act did not become law until later in the year, just before or just after the signing of the Armistice. By that time all danger had disappeared and the businessmen of the community were tugging at the reins in order to turn once more from national interests to individual profit—a reaction which shortly after gave cause for the wielding of the Geddes Axe.

I once asked Fisher, after he had retired, what he considered his greatest contribution to education during his presidency, expecting him to say, 'The Act of 1918'. 'Without a doubt,' he replied, 'what I was able to do to increase the salaries of elementary school teachers, thus making it possible for the first time for women teachers, at any rate, to travel; for I cannot imagine a more educative experience or one more likely to influence education as a whole.'

Morant would have approved of this, and in other respects the Act carried further the great work he had begun. His successor as Permanent Secretary, Selby-Bigge, though an official of far less force of character, had agreed with his ideas and was prepared to develop them on lines he might have approved. For example, the Act abolished all fees in state elementary schools; and though difficulties remained in making the leaving age of fourteen compulsory at the time, this was the age specified in the Act, and even fifteen was hinted at, though that had to wait till 1947. As to secondary schools, the great advance of 1902 was consolidated. This was the era in which the new local education authorities were building secondary schools all over the country. An eminent employer, a friend of mine, who called himself 'Chairman of the 'Igher' (i.e. of the Higher Education Committee) of the West Riding, built more secondary schools than Colet ever dreamed of.

What was new to the public was Section 10 of the Act, which introduced compulsory part-time day and continuation schools for all boys and girls between fourteen and eighteen who had not gone on to secondary school or to full-time education in technical schools. But this, I believe, had long been the kernel of Morant's educational philosophy. For it was his faith that this type of school would ultimately bridge the fatal gap between education and industry, since its pupils would be at factory, workshop or mine for half the working week, and during the other half would be learning at school what their working life meant.

It was proposed in the Act to make a beginning with the establishment of part-time continuation schools, one day or two half-days a week. In these the instruction, as in their evening forerunners, was to consist on the one hand of such elementary scientific or mathematical principles as would help the pupils to understand the processes of the industry they were especially concerned with, or the main industries of the district in which they lived; and on the other hand, of simple courses in industrial history and economic geography, similarly related to the local industrial conditions—in a word, to the work that occupied them on the other days of the week. It was expected that persons with the requisite knowledge would plan such courses, whether semi-technical or humanistic, for each local authority. And from 1916 onwards, at Pullinger's suggestion I was preparing a memorandum for the Board, entitled *Humanism in the Continuation School*. This would, in general terms, suggest to the authorities and their teachers the kind of history, geography and literature the Board had in mind, and the way these subjects might be dealt with.

At the age of fourteen, I argued, the wage-earner, having just left elementary school, would be eager for adult life and employment; he would be ready to turn to a fresh curriculum, specially designed to prepare him for the life of the factory and workshop he is just entering. He should also learn to appreciate non-technical subjects that would help him to understand the adult world at the threshold of which he was standing. But if he found these subjects taught by the same kind of teachers previously encountered in the elementary school he now looked back upon with some contempt, he might be choked off. The continuation school teacher, whether technical or humanistic, I argued, needed a special training. Even more important, he must be at once well acquainted and sympathetic with the industrial life around his pupils. It had been my experience that the elementary teacher was rarely this; he generally felt he belonged to a class apart from and superior to that of the ordinary working man. And I was often shocked, when I visited evening classes, to find that the teacher, who was usually an elementary teacher earning a little extra pay, knew nothing and cared nothing about the sort of work his pupils were occupied with in the day.

In addition to the discussion of those problems of the class-room, the memorandum contained a long chapter entitled 'Humanism and Industrial Citizenship', in which, premising that since the industrial revolution civilization had become inevitably and forever based upon machine production, I looked forward to the day when industry would beget its own culture, just as commerce had done in the Athens of Pericles and in the Florence of the Medici. This was a culture that Walt Whitman had prophesied for the teeming industrial cities of nineteenth-century America,

'A song for occupations!
In the labour of engines and trades, and the labour of fields
I find the developments,
And find the eternal meanings.'

Morant, who was fond of quoting Whitman, must often have had these lines in mind; he must also have had Burke's profound statement of the only sound basis for the social life of a great people,

'To be attached to the sub-division, to love the little platoon we belong to in society, is the first principle (the germ as it were) of public affections. It is the first link in the series by which we proceed towards a love of our country and of mankind.'

But, as the memorandum implied, the most suggestive anticipation of 'industrial democracy' Morant envisaged was St. Augustine's dream of the City of God which found partial fulfilment in the medieval Church. There the priesthood provided a ladder of education which was open to boys in every rank of society, so that the peasant's son might even climb up onto the Papal throne. At the same time, the civil service of the State could only be run by the clerics, alias clerks, educated by the Church.

But even more to the present point was what the Church did for the labouring classes. For those in the towns and cities there were the miracle plays in which each urban craft was represented in the stories of Holy Writ and was thus given eternal significance and the divine blessing. And for the far larger number of labourers in the fields, everything was done in the parish church to add meaning and beauty to their lives. All the arts contributed to this culture, a culture popular in origin as well as in its appeal; for the artists were the sons of the people themselves. It was their son, too, as the parson of the village, who related or read aloud to his illiterate congregation stories from the Bible, lives of the saints and other edifying tales such as we can ourselves read in the *Gesta Romanorum*.

Alas for dreams! Section 10 appeared on the statute book and is still there, but it was followed by a proviso stating that the section would not become law until the Board 'named the appointed day'—a proviso ensuring a temporary postponement until local authorities generally had become accustomed to the notion and had secured properly trained teachers. But the day has never been appointed for the nation as a whole.

Nevertheless, a number of authorities precipitately set on foot day continuation schools in different parts of the country. There were, for example, many in the London institutes and a few in Lancashire. But unexpected difficulties soon began to emerge. For instance, these schools to be successful needed specially trained teachers; and in too many cases the teachers recruited from industry, commerce and elsewhere, and of course untrained, were viewed with disfavour by certificated elementary school teachers—all the more so because they were paid on the secondary scale whereas the teachers in the elementary schools had about thirty per cent less.

And there was another and even stronger reason for the hesitation of the Board to 'name the appointed day' nationally. When it came to the point, there was no one at the Board with guts enough to withstand the clamour raised by mill-managers and the like, especially in Lancashire, and by those in charge of shops and offices in London, at the prospect of being obliged to release successive batches of young people day by day for schooling. Yet in the end a few schools that had secured the right kind of teachers managed to survive—perhaps the best known of all being one at Rugby, the success of which was partly due to the fact that by far the most important industry of the place was favourable, and partly to the enthusiasm of P. I. Kitchen, the founding headmaster. He had been a headmaster in my own special district of Yorkshire, and I naturally took an interest in him. He published a short book which shows us what might have been adopted in the country at large.[1] And I am persuaded that even had it been postponed for a year or two, the enactment would have become law had Frank Pullinger, its champion and principal author (who would have fought for it like a wild cat) not been suddenly stricken down with a rapidly developing cancer which eventually killed him on 23rd December 1920.

It was just about this time too, when Fisher was producing his estimates, that hostility among teachers was voiced in Parliament. Thus the elementary school teachers were among those who killed the day continuation schools.

[1] From *Learning to Earning*, P. I. Kitchen, Faber 1944.

Yet that there were other officials at Whitehall who were hoping the postponement would be only temporary, seemed indicated by the fact that Chambers had taken over control of continuation schools as late as January 1919, evidently as the head of a new branch or department. Two years later, however, he had ceased to harbour such schemes, for he dropped the title. And he did so on 9th January 1921, that is to say within three weeks of Pullinger's death. This means, I take it, that he had made up his mind that Section 10 was dead. He would hardly have done this had he not known that the Secretary (Selby-Bigge) and Fisher himself were of that opinion or at least were bound to arrive at it. I must assume also that this conclusion was to some extent based upon reports about the feeling of the country, then being received by Pullinger's successor as Chief Inspector, another Lancashire man, though one of a very different type, and strongly influenced by the cotton magnates.

On the other hand, I could only guess at what was going on in the office, until in 1954 when I was able to establish the stages and dates of Chambers's career in the old Board by the help of officials at the Ministry, as it had now become. I had to do this for the obituary of Chambers which I helped to write for the Proceedings of the British Academy.

Pullinger's death filled me with gloomy forebodings. For a while my hopes rose a little with the publication in the following September (1921) through the Office of Special Enquiries and Reports, of my memorandum on *Humanism in the Continuation School* as Educational Pamphlet No. 43. It contained a preface, I suspect from the pen of Chambers, which stated that I had written the pamphlet 'at the request of the late Mr. Frank Pullinger, Chief Inspector of Technical and Continuation Schools, who was greatly interested in the matter'. It was in fact its official epitaph; for the day continuation school was by that time dead. Chambers, the last of Morant's disciples, was given the barren title of Second Secretary and a K.C.B. as a consolation for his disappointment.

As for myself, the Board that had engrossed my energies for ten years and given me a faith to live by—a double faith, the one expounded by Pullinger, the other by Mansbridge—had now nothing for me. Zimmern had left it and Pullinger was dead. I determined to get out at the earliest possible moment. That was not likely to come soon, as for a man with a family it is seldom easy to leave a government department, since this involves the sacrifice not only of a salary but also of a pension. And though I had recently begun to make a name as a student of Shakespeare, I had not yet done enough to deserve a chair. It is noteworthy indeed that the first volume of the *New Cambridge Shakespeare* was published in 1921, the year after Pullinger's death. So I continued to eat my heart out in the day-by-day duties of an inspector in the hope that sooner or later escape would come. It eventually came in 1924, when I was appointed Professor of Education at King's College, London.

Before transferring my loyalty from Whitehall to King's I looked in one morning at the Board to say good-bye to a few of my friends. Among these was, of course, Chambers, now Second Secretary of the Board; that is to say, he was very much on the shelf, with little to do but such odd jobs as Selby-Bigge found for him. Certainly when I stuck my head round his door to see if he was disengaged, he looked more than usually bored, sitting behind a desk without a paper on it. Seeing who it was, he wearily enquired, 'What do *you* want?'

'I've come to say good-bye,' I said.

'Oh, where are you off to?'

'London University.'

'London University; humph. English I suppose?'

'No,' I answered, hoping it would please him, 'Education.'

At this he almost leapt from his chair, all lethargy gone. 'Education!' he snorted. 'A *disgusting* subject!' Such was the opinion then of the second in command at the Board of Education!

My final call was, as in duty bound, upon Selby-Bigge, a man I hardly knew personally, since the heads of government departments have little time for any but their assistants who rule the branches immediately below them. But he was a genial gentleman and received me affably, even with some curiosity, for he had no doubt seen something of Pamphlet No. 43. 'I am afraid,' he began, motioning me to a chair, 'you are rather disappointed at the fate of those unhappy day continuation schools.'

'I am, sir,' I said bluntly.

'But when we went into it,' he continued, 'they were found to be impossible. I told Mr. Fisher that if we kept them in the Act we should all be hanging from lamp-posts.'

I at once saw what had happened in the office after Pullinger's death. And at his words which revealed, it seemed, a cowardly betrayal of the country's future, the bottled-up anxieties and indignation of the last three years boiled over. I looked straight at him, then without a word turned and left the room.

POSTSCRIPT

I cannot conclude this account without expressing my deep gratitude to my friend Mr. W. H. Perkins, formerly Director of Education for Warwickshire, who has read through this chapter more than once, has made many corrections, and supplied me with valuable information. He has been good enough to give me the following notes by way of bringing the matter up to date.

'It must surely be unique for a statutory provision requiring an "appointed day" to remain ineffective for more than fifty years. The Day Continuation schools of the 1918 Education Act or the County Colleges of the 1944 Act are still represented by only one small venture—that at Rugby. The failure was at first the result of economic depression, lack of vision and the opposition of vested interests.

'Since 1924, the spearhead of all reform has been provided by those who wished to raise the age of full-time education. Even this change has come slowly; the leaving age went up to fifteen in 1947, and will be sixteen in 1970–71. This last step was urged by the Crowther Report (1959) which hoped that it would be taken between 1966–1968, and be followed in the early 1970s by the introduction, area by area, of County College and compulsory continued full-time education. There is as yet no sign of the County Colleges in their statutory form.

'In the meantime, however, a kind of compulsion is being approached in a different way under the system known as "day release". Some employers already make attendance at further education classes in the day-time a privilege or even a condition of employment for certain groups of workers. Recent figures show that rather less than one-third of employed boys and not quite one in twelve of employed girls aged 15–18 are attending such classes. The scope of day release is being extended by the operation of the Industrial Training Act of 1964. Approved training schemes for young persons will generally have to include an appropriate element of education in Colleges of Further Education. The Minister of Labour is making good progress in setting up Industrial Training Boards and some of the Boards are already active. It is not yet clear whether the educational authorities will have access to the resources which will be required if the Training Boards do their work adequately. There is some danger that in this gradual operation those acquiring the higher levels of skill will benefit first and that a selection process will leave a residue of much less than average ability. For this group low industrial status may lead to inferior educational provision, or even to none at all.'

To these valuable notes by Mr. Perkins I must add my strong impression that if in 1918 compulsory day continuation schools had been established for all young persons between the ages of 14 and 18 in the manner outlined above, the nation would have been spared the worst features of the deplorable teenage problem that has plagued us for many years past. But I shall enlarge upon this later.

Before leaving the Board of Education and moving on to King's College (in fact during the period when I was hoping to escape), I had gained an insight into another aspect of education through a committee on the teaching of English. After the great Education Act of 1918 had become law, the subject that principally engaged the Board of Education was the teaching of English language and literature in schools. Accordingly a departmental committee for the investigation of this subject was appointed in May 1919 by the President of the Board, with the following terms of reference:

'To inquire into the position occupied by English (Language and Literature) in the educational system of England, and to

95

3. John Dover Wilson with his family, 1912

committee's session published at the Cambridge University Press an excellently written and popular book, *English for the English.* This last, however, disconcerted some of us on the committee who were devoting strenuous hours in the public service to a report which would follow much the same lines as his book, a book that could hardly have been written without the evidence which a member of the committee had at his disposal.

The proceedings throughout were dominated by our chairman, Sir Henry Newbolt, the poet, a personal friend of mine— charming, suave, delighting to discuss at length the problems that confronted us. But he possessed little knowledge or sympathy with English scholarship and the teaching of the history of English literature in universities. And though about the time the committee was sitting, he had himself seen through the press a book on the history of English literature (to which I had been asked to contribute certain chapters) brought out by Nelson, his true attitude was well revealed in the fact that he insisted, despite my protests, on placing all the Old and Middle English literature chapters in a sort of appendix to the volume. This, I told him, was literally preposterous, but he would not retract.

This prepossession of the Chairman helps to explain the attitude of two important university witnesses. It was unfortunate that a morning had been set aside for evidence from the professors of the two principal colleges of the University of London. University College was represented by W. P. Ker, and King's College by Sir Israel Gollancz—it being apparently unknown to our organizers that the two professors were not on the best terms. Ker, perhaps the greatest scholar who has ever taught English literature in a university, with all the austerity and acerbity of a learned Scot, had little but contempt for his rather garrulous colleague at King's. Gollancz, a keen Shakespearian, thought his main duty was to impress upon the committee the importance of keeping Shakespeare's Day in the schools of England. Newbolt found this an engaging topic, and the two went on talking about it for some time, until suddenly our chairman realized that he had not yet heard anything from Ker. He therefore turned to him and asked him something about the teaching of English at

University College. To this Ker tight-lipped replied, 'That is a domestic question.' These words constituted the whole body of evidence which he presented to the committee. Newbolt had him to dinner afterwards, we learned, but he refused to add anything more to the evidence or to countenance the committee in any way whatever; and when the Report appeared in print, he had it burned publicly in the courtyard of University College.

Thus an entirely erroneous conception of the aims and purpose of the committee became traditional in University College. Indeed, in a relatively recent controversy in the correspondence columns of *The Times* (on 18th November 1965), concerning the teaching of Anglo-Saxon, the then principal of University College clearly showed himself under the impression that the report of the committee (which incidentally sold like a novel when it appeared in print) was an attack on the teaching of Anglo-Saxon in universities.

Another university witness, Professor Saintsbury, had obviously been made suspicious by Ker. He had been succeeded in Edinburgh by Professor Grierson and had retired to Bath, but he was willing to appear before the committee. His purpose became clear almost immediately after he entered the room, for he began at once to harangue us on the importance of Anglo-Saxon. He continued this theme so persistently that at last I ventured to interrupt. 'Excuse me, Professor Saintsbury,' I said, 'but the committee is mainly concerned with children—the English of boys and girls in the elementary schools and the lower forms of the secondary schools. At what age,' I asked, 'ought one to begin to learn Anglo-Saxon?' He turned that extraordinary face of his full upon me and, raising his fist, thumped the table. 'Sir,' he thundered, 'you cannot begin Anglo-Saxon too early!'

Fifteen years later I was occupying his Chair at Edinburgh, where the memory of Saintsbury is ever-green. One of my staff had been a member of his and when I told this story, looked at me quizzically and said, 'That's a funny story, Professor; because, you see, Professor Saintsbury didn't know Anglo-Saxon himself.' *Know* is a relative term, and I expect my great predecessor knew as much as I ever did, probably much more. At any rate he could write learnedly about Anglo-Saxon alliterative metre. But perhaps his outburst at the committee was prompted by the knowledge that he himself ought to have begun earlier.

Another witness who provided entertainment of a different kind was Daniel Jones the phonetician, who was at that time a keen advocate of the reform of English spelling. He had recently published parallel passages in traditional spelling and the international phonetic script. And I was astonished to find that not a single member of the committee then present except myself, who had been forced to master Sweet's phonetics in order to teach English in Finland, had any idea of what Daniel Jones was talking about. So the 'evidence' developed into a seminar with Jones as the tutor and the committee as the class—our chairman, I recollect, posing as a polite but sceptical pupil. It followed that Daniel Jones left little influence on what the report had to say about the teaching of spelling; this was treated in a commonsense fashion as an obstacle to be made as little of as possible.

Despite the disapproval of W. P. Ker and a few other academic witnesses at the committee, the Report when published in 1921, two years after the first meeting, was at once welcomed by teachers in general. It sold, as I have said, like a 'best seller', being widely read in business as well as educational circles. This was partly due to the fact that, unlike most official publications, it was well written. Newbolt led off with a very attractive and persuasive introduction (stress being laid on the point that 'every teacher is a teacher of English'). Other chapters or sections were contributed by Bailey, Boas, Fowler and myself. I added a passage here and there to the general chapters on the elementary school and training college; while being mainly responsible for most of Chapters V and VIII, 'English in Commercial and Industrial Life' and 'Literature and Adult Education', together with the section on 'The Problem of Grammar' in Chapter IX; I must sadly admit that this section, upon which I spent much time and pains, was almost entirely ignored. I also compiled the index and lent assistance generally to J. E. Hales, an admirable and good-tempered Secretary who wrote the bulk of the Report and whose lucid and straightforward style was itself a model of the kind of written English that the Report advocated (see especially pp. 71 ff.). I believe our recommendations on this head exercised a wide influence upon the schools.

I cannot do better than quote Hales himself on 'The Writing of English',

'Our witnesses emphasize the great importance of the writing of English, or "Composition", as the climax of the school work. They agree in making a claim for it which puts it in a new place as a factor in education. They feel that in teaching Composition they are concerned directly and immediately with the growth of the mind. Dr. Ballard, for instance, told us that investigation showed proficiency in Composition to be the surest sign of a high degree of mental intelligence, and that it was the most valuable exercise in the school for the purpose of developing the specific abilities which enter most largely into our lives. Mr. Hartog claimed that the teaching of Composition develops individuality, that it has, indeed, a transforming influence on the children, on their whole outlook, on their whole judgement, on their sense of responsibility. We ourselves fully endorse these views. Composition cannot be regarded merely as a subject. It is the measure of all that has been truly learnt, and of the habits of mind which have been formed. In fact, the capacity for self-expression is essentially the measure of the success or failure of a school, at any rate on the intellectual side. If the habit of merely perfunctory or artificial writing is allowed to usurp its place the avenue to mental development will have been partly closed.'

Another important undertaking more or less contemporaneous with the Report of the English Committee should be noted at this point—the Society for Pure English. It was set on foot in 1919, the founders all being Oxford men—Henry Bradley, one of the principal editors of the Oxford Dictionary, Robert Bridges, the Poet Laureate, and R. W. Chapman, Secretary of the Oxford University Press. Though not in the list of founding members, I joined the society and became a subscriber shortly after its inception—prompted, I believe, originally by my friend S. O. Andrew of the Whitgift Grammar School who was one of the original members.

Goldsmiths' College and H.M.I.

Robert Bridges, deeply deploring several modern tendencies of the English language, was anxious to enlist the help of all those who wished to preserve what was of value in written, spoken, and even printed English. The title of one of his elaborate pamphlets was *A Tract on the Present State of English Pronunciation* and in it he advocated a new system of spelling which should be at once euphonic and beautiful to look at. I say euphonic to distinguish it from phonetic spelling as exemplified in the phonetic texts of Daniel Jones. Bridges regarded these with horror as an attempt to set up cockney pronunciation as standard speech.

Because of this attitude, a debate was arranged by the English Association between Bridges and Professor Ripman, the latter being a fervent believer in phonetics. Bridges, who was not accustomed to public debate, did not show up very brilliantly on the occasion; but when he had finished, and Ripman had, as he fancied, demolished him, the chairman announced to the audience, 'We have in the room Mr. George Bernard Shaw, who has offered to contribute to the discussion in defence of his friend, Dr. Bridges.' At the back of the platform, where he had concealed himself up to that moment, there arose that familiar figure, who proceeded to tear Ripman's speech to bits. As he did so, the professor presumably lost his temper and kept on 'rising to points of order', Shaw politely sitting down whenever he rose. Eventually this looked like two Dutch dolls bobbing up and down on opposite sides of the platform; and as the audience rocked with laughter I could not help feeling that he was tolling Ripman's leg like a bell!

Bridges was living at that time on Boar's Hill, overlooking Oxford. Owing to my work on Newbolt's committee, and I think at Newbolt's suggestion, Bridges invited me to stay with him a night or two to talk matters over. I cannot hope that my visit was of much help to him, since I could do little more than register my agreement with most of the causes he had at heart. But it was to me a great experience, and I felt it an honour to be in the presence of that majestic lion-headed figure. Though the course of English poetry has run in a very different direction from his, I still regard him as one of the major poets of my time. Bridges showed me over his house and took me in particular to his music room which was a connected but separate structure from the rest. As he went into it he said, 'This place was burned down a few years ago.'

'How dreadful,' I exclaimed.

'Well, no,' he replied, 'not really. I have plenty of architects in the family.' He was the son-in-law of Alfred Waterhouse.

I well remember getting up before breakfast and standing on the hill gazing down at Oxford with its 'dreaming spires' peeping through the mist. Later, Bridges walked down with me to Oxford and we paid a call on Henry Bradley. On the way he explained to me that Bradley had a photographic memory which was rather a nuisance than otherwise to him because the photograph faded within a few hours. When we got to his room, Bridges said, 'Bradley, have you read the leading article in *The Times* today?'

'Yes,' answered Bradley.

'Well then, write it out for Dover Wilson to see'—which he forthwith began to do, though twelve hours later he could not have done it. Bradley was so conscious of his embarrassing gift that I don't think he ever allowed it to lead him astray, as Macaulay, who had a memory of the same kind, certainly did at times.

I fear I ceased to subscribe to S.P.E. soon after I left London in 1935 after eleven years at King's College. But the pamphlets continued to appear, and R. W. Chapman printed a concluding Retrospect in 1948.

5

An Apprenticeship as Professor
of Education

I had been anxious to leave the Board of Education after the failure of Section 10, but it was not until 1924 that I discovered an escape in the form of an announcement by the University of London, King's College, that its Professorship of Education had become vacant.

I remained at King's until 1935—eleven years of great happiness during which I learned a good deal about London's secondary schools which supplemented my knowledge of elementary education acquired at Goldsmiths' College. For the students in my department were Honours graduates training to become secondary school teachers after securing the diploma at the end of our one-year course. I enjoyed too the friendship of two excellent principals in Ernest Barker and W. R. Halliday. When I add that I had among my colleagues on the professorial board Julian Huxley and Edward Appleton, who was then actively climbing up into the astronomical sphere which has been named after him, it should be obvious that I was very fortunate to be joining such company. And I must mention one other who was not a member of the professorial board, the witty and philosophical dean of the college, W. R. Matthews, later Dean of St. Paul's. And this reference to him leads me to explain to the unenlightened reader, if there be such, the peculiar constitution of King's College.

University College in Gower Street, at first calling itself the University of London, was founded in 1828 by Jeremy Bentham and other Radicals of that period, in order that London might have a university which was strictly undenominational, with no religious tests of any kind. It was intended to offset, of course, those antiquated and at that date over-clericalized universities on the banks of the Cam and the Isis. But Bentham and his radical brethren had reckoned without the Duke of Wellington. He played a king in answer to what he regarded as a knave among universities, and so founded in 1831, upon the bank of the Thames, King's College, for Church and King, to 'huff the godless institution in Gower Street'. It followed that the college (in its building a kind of east wing to Somerset House) had a clerical principal, a Faculty of Divinity and a chapel with a dean to conduct its daily service; and that though it was furnished with the secular faculties corresponding with those at universities elsewhere, when its professors signed a book recording their attendance at the professorial board they registered *ipso facto* their adherence to the Thirty-Nine Articles which stood at the beginning of the book they signed.

Universities, however, do not stand still, and at the bidding of commissions, royal or otherwise, they assume new formations. Thus on 1st January 1910, in accordance with an Act of Parliament passed in 1908, King's College became incorporated with University College to become legally part of the University of London. But the enlarged university, a non-sectarian institution both in origin and conception, could not possibly include the dean and chapel. The former was not of course expelled nor the latter demolished; that is not the English way. Private negotiations lay behind the Act, the result of which was that an invisible line was drawn as it were through the college, on one side of which was the purely secular incorporated portion, and on the other the dean carrying on his daily service as before in the chapel, together with an Anglican Faculty of Divinity—though the principal of the college was to be a layman. And I often enjoyed listening to the Lessons in Chapel read aloud in the broad Cheshire of Ernest Barker.

Owing, I suspect, to the diplomatic skill of the Dean, the process of incorporation appeared to have left no trace of bitterness when I reached King's. Yet my predecessor had not welcomed it and the last clerical principal, A. C. Headlam (1903–1912), who became Bishop of Gloucester, had heartily detested it.

An Apprenticeship as Professor of Education

When Barker resigned in 1927, to become Professor of Political Science at Cambridge, and was succeeded by W. R. Halliday, the college got a principal whose name became associated with a great deal of ingenious additional building: a suitable site was found, for example, for a much-needed Department of Anatomy on the roof of the chapel; while equally brilliant was the acquisition of a far more extensive site by negotiations with the London Transport authorities which resulted in the purchase of the air above Aldwych Underground Station to the east of King's College. There a whole new wing was erected, including very welcome rooms for the professors and lecturers, previously housed in what had been the most narrowly circumscribed academic building in Great Britain. And it must be added that since those days, the college has extended even further east, across to the other side of Surrey Street. A movement westwards absorbing Somerset House, which would have given us a noble frontage on the Strand, was forbidden by public authorities.

Among those benefiting by Halliday's building was the staff of the Education Department. Incidentally the Professor of History profited also. For when I first came to the college in 1924 I asked to be shown my room. I was taken down into the basement and shown a room below ground with a sky-light. 'No,' I said, 'that is not the Professor's room. I don't wish to grow like a potato in a cellar! And education needs fresh air and the sun.' But there was no other room in the building available. Hearing of my plight, however, F. J. C. Hearnshaw, the Professor of History, kindly offered me a desk in the corner of his room, and from that desk I managed to rule my department for five years. It was a gesture of extreme generosity on Hearnshaw's part, since he was the tidiest and most meticulous man whom I have ever known. Over his fireplace hung a green baize board to which he would pin the engagements for the day, one of which I remember as characteristic, '12:59 with ——'. And yet he endured with the greatest self-restraint one of the most untidy men in the world at the other end of the room.

In its education department, as in other ways, King's stood somewhat outside the rest of the university. It had, for example, been in existence as a training department many years before the University Institute of Education at which a large proportion of students from other colleges were trained for secondary schools. My predecessor, J. W. Adamson, who thought of this Institute as an upstart and despised what he considered the superficiality of its teaching, made no effort to disguise those opinions. Adamson was a true scholar; his *Pioneers of Modern Education* (1905) and *A Short History of Education* (1919) are remarkable pieces of historical learning in a little explored field. But he had been head of the teachers' training department of King's College for over twenty-five years and had grown rigid both in mind and temper. He probably did not notice that the hours of his lectures at King's did not allow time for the students of the Institute, at that date stationed in a building at the other end of Kingsway, to make the necessary journey to attend them.

When I arrived at King's I managed, however, to come to an agreement with Percy Nunn, the Institute's genial principal. We signed an unwritten treaty of complete good will whereby I should lecture at his Institute on the history of education in England, the lectures being attended by trainee secondary school teachers from all London colleges, including of course both his students and mine; while my students were free to attend any other lectures at the Institute.

And to my lectures I later added, with his agreement, another course on a new subject, called 'The Educational System in England and Wales'. In this, drawing upon my experience as an H.M.I., I briefly described the character of the local and central authorities under which most of my students would be carrying on their work, and also the different types of schools and universities.

There was a third Professor of Education at that time attached to the Institute, the well-known psychologist Cyril Burt whose great book, *The Young Delinquent*, was already available for my instruction as well as for that of the world at large. According to my agreement with Nunn, King's students would attend Burt's lectures on psychology and also his own on the principles of education.

As to the course on the history of education, this on consideration resolved itself into a history of education in the nineteenth century in the light of social developments in England. To take a few examples: I gave a lecture on the population question, another on the origin and development of public health; while I laid particular emphasis on the great minds who had originated these developments—Jeremy Bentham and his disciples, such as Dr. James Kay Shuttleworth, the first secretary of the Committee of the Privy Council on Education, and Edwin Chadwick, the architect of public health. To Bentham I always gave a whole lecture which had special relevance to a large body of students in the audience, the graduates of his University College. For the great man had bequeathed his embalmed body to the college, stipulating that it should be seated, suitably dressed, at all the meetings of the Council. This led up to my peroration, 'It still is,' I remarked, 'since there he sits in a glass case in his early nineteenth-century clothes and even his skull in the corner of the case, the whole being enclosed in a cupboard, the door of which is opened when the Council sits in the next room, so that the terms of his will are duly observed. In fact, University College is the tomb of Jeremy Bentham!' Upon this I fled, leaving the whole audience in an uproar.

At the same time King's students remained *my* students. Their school practice, or teaching practice, was organized by my staff, who also gave most of the lectures on the various subjects they would later have to teach. The teaching of science in particular was in the excellent hands of Dr. Titley, a delightful little hunchback whom it was a joy to know. And he was succeeded after his early death by J. C. Hill, a tower of strength in many ways. We were allowed, if we wished, to send our students up Kingsway to the Institute for lectures by members of Nunn's staff, for example those on geography by that first-rate teacher, Fairgrieve. I myself lectured at King's on the teaching of English to my own and any other students who cared to attend.

Meanwhile, a word must be said here of the education course

as a whole, seen in retrospect. In 1924 I was feeling my way and in particular was very vague about the subject called 'Principles of Education' which I had handed over to Nunn. My students had to learn how to handle a class; that was their first need and this we could help them in by school practice. Masters in the public schools boasted that they had not been trained—which means that they had to learn to teach by experience, the way I had learned at the Whitgift. But it is for most a painful method, the method of sink or swim, and too often the result is a miserable existence of vain efforts to keep discipline. But school practice, with the help of advice from the form-masters and occasionally inspection by members of the Education Department, meant learning to swim by getting in at the shallow end of the bath. After the year's training, if the student showed little sign of coping with a class, I would first watch his attempts myself, and if I felt the case was hopeless would advise him to become an assistant in a local public library. In the course of the years I made quite a number of librarians, and I hope they found happiness; certain I am that I saved them from a life of hell.

After class-management we had to help the students to understand children, the mental and moral character of the pupils they would have to teach. And here we were very fortunate in being able to draw upon the science and wisdom of Burt. From him my students gained both psychology and wisdom. Psychology was essential, since it provided the scientific element in a sound course of education. For unless the young teacher acquires a knowledge of the mental development of the children he has to teach, he may fall into grievous error. Those were heady times in the teaching world, since the revelations of Freud and Jung were still new and being hotly debated. The subliminal sexual life of the child, Freud discovered, is balanced, and in many cases more than balanced, by the child's imagination, which it is, in my judgement, the teacher's primary duty to feed.

But this brings me back to the question of 'Principles', designed as the crown of the whole course. Delightful man and colleague as Nunn was, when I read the little book on 'Principles' he had written for the students at the Institute I was much disappointed. For it assumed education to be an applied science— a view still held by most professors of education, I fear; but a view which I consider wholly misconceived. Education is an art, whatever aspect of civilized knowledge is to be passed on, even mathematics and the pure sciences themselves. It was indeed a great mathematician of our times who taught us this, A. N. Whitehead, our *wisest* philosopher. His pregnant book of essays, *The Aims of Education*, was not published till 1929, a little late for me to make much use of it while at King's. But there was always Plato's *Republic* at hand; I made an advanced class at King's study it with me and neglected no opportunity of reminding the ordinary diploma students that they were 'guardians' and must educate the imagination by the means Plato suggested. Above all, I attempted to make them realize that they were entering a profession not unlike that of a secular priesthood, dedicated to serve, and by their service to lift humanity onto a higher level. 'As the ape is to man, so man must be to the super-man,' wrote my old favourite, Nietzsche. A band of teachers with the right aims might fulfil Nietzsche's dream in three generations.

When I note that we refused to accept any students for training who had not first qualified with first or second class honours, it would seem that the King's College Education Department contained something like the cream of students. Yet if it were so, I found that their university honours had left some of them uneducated in one important particular. I had not been long working in the Strand when I received a visit from one of my previous colleagues, the Chief Inspector of Training Colleges, We greeted each other affably, and when I had given him a nice chair by my desk—one of Hearnshaw's chairs—I said, 'Now, before you tell me what I ought to do here, which I suppose is what you've come for, let me tell you what I *have* to do. First of all I have to teach them how to read, and then I have to teach them how to write. Now you can go on.' He did go on, though not quite in the way he had intended. For I was not exaggerating. Nearly all the students were receiving state grants, and before entering the department had to read aloud a declaration, provided by the Board of Education, that they intended to remain in the teaching profession for a certain number of years. I would hand this paper to one of the applicants, would tell him or her to sit down and read it to himself quietly and make sure he understood what he was reading, and then read it aloud to me. In many cases they failed to do so without stumbling. To give the student a second chance, lest he should complain that official English was difficult, I would hand him a passage from Macaulay or some other prose writer, and ask him to read that, generally with the same result.

As to writing, I doubt whether any had received instruction in writing English at university or at school either, except perhaps for the perfunctory essay the form-master asked for now and then. For it was too early yet for teachers in schools to show that they had profited from the excellent advice on the writing of English in the 1921 Report of the Departmental Committee. Most of the students had no idea how to use a metaphor. A writer must learn to hear what he writes as well, to avoid what is harsh and unrhythmical, obscure, confused. And here much can be learned by listening to passages from the English classics read aloud and analysing their style.

Finally, and above all, the good writer *thinks* what he writes and never stops thinking. For it is only by so doing that he avoids the cliché, the ready-made, reach-me-down phrase which is the stock-in-trade of those who write for the daily press and all forms of cheap literature. And because my students, because we all, grew up reading these publications, their tawdry, commonplace phraseology becomes part of our consciousness, so that it is these mouldy second-rate expressions that first offer themselves when we sit down to write. Mental habits of a lifetime are very hard to get rid of or suppress. And I found that teaching my graduates to write was one of the principal things to be done with them. The precept I kept insisting upon was, 'See what you write; hear what you write; think (or mean) what you write.' Plato's famous aims of education for the 'guardians' were easy to attain in Greek days, when the very stuff of

Athenian thought was conditioned by the beauty of poetry and of the religious drama performed in the supreme temple in which they worshipped their goddess. Plato tells us,

'. . . a musical education is a more potent instrument than any other, because rhythm and harmony find their way into the inward places of the soul on which they mightily fasten, imparting grace, and making the soul of him who is rightly educated graceful . . . now in the days of his youth, even before he is able to know the reason why: and when reason comes he will recognise and salute the friend with whom his education had made him long familiar.'

But we today have first of all to cleanse our thought of the filth and rubbish that has become part of it.

But we are fortunate to possess in the word of a great poet an account of the development of childhood and youth quite untouched by any of these deleterious influences of industrial civilization. And I found passages from Wordsworth's *Prelude or Growth of a Poet's Mind*, where he describes his boyhood in the Lake District, especially that beginning (in the 1850 text, line 301),

'Fair seed-time had my soul, and I grew up
    Fostered alike by beauty and by fear:'

followed by:

'Dust as we are, the immortal spirit grows
    Like harmony in music; there is a dark
    Inscrutable workmanship that reconciles
    Discordant elements, makes them cling together
    In one society. How strange that all
    The terrors, pains, and early miseries,
    Regrets, vexations, lassitudes interfused
    Within my mind, should e'er have borne a part,
    And that a needful part, in making up
    The calm existence that is mine when I
    Am worthy of myself!'   (340–350)

This passage forms an essential supplement to the incomplete picture of the growth of the child mind—helpful, of course, as many of these findings are—for example in the writings of Piaget.

An Apprenticeship as Professor of Education

The course for the Teacher's Diploma, the prize for which my hundred students (fifty men and fifty women) worked, lasted only a year. One of the difficulties of the whole department was to create some bond of unity between the students, and still more between students and staff, in such a short course. I therefore instituted a series of weekends, hiring a large building on the seashore at Hythe, and inviting all the students to come and spend Friday evening to Monday morning with me and some of the staff that we might get to know each other there. The visit was, of course, voluntary and each was expected to provide a small fee to cover expenses. Most of them availed themselves of it, and the country round—if the weather was fine—gave us excellent walks, while there were sing-songs and games in the hall of the building in the evenings. 'NO LECTURES' was written in large letters at the head of the invitation to each individual.

When I was appointed professor in 1924, my work on the *New Cambridge Shakespeare* had been under way for some five years. But a professor who does his duty should publish contributions to his own subject; and I took this duty seriously. King's College, with its habit of throwing open its doors to audiences at public lectures, facilitated this. For example, the Professor of Physiology, R. J. S. McDowall, projected a series of lectures on 'The Mind as Viewed from Several Academic Standpoints'. After Julian Huxley on 'The Mind from the Biological Point of View', McDowall himself delivered a lecture in which the cranium and its contents were distributed upon his desk as he spoke, so that there was much 'throwing about of brains'. And when it came to my turn to speak on 'The Mind Considered from the Point of View of the Study of Education', I was able to develop my own ideas of child and adolescent psychology; these were derived to a large extent from Plato, though I attempted to give them a modern aspect in the light of psychology as expounded by psychologists such as Burt and Aveling, the professor of that subject at King's.

Another course to which I contributed had been arranged by Professor Hearnshaw on the subject of the social and political ideas of some representative thinkers of the Victorian Age; and here I took as my subject Matthew Arnold's political ideas. This lecture, I believe, is the only serious attempt that has been made to work out this side of Matthew Arnold. It was actually, in a sense, a development of work that I was doing for the Cambridge University Press. They had undertaken to publish a series of texts entitled 'Landmarks in the History of Education', and my edition of Arnold's *Culture and Anarchy* (the first reprint to appear of the first edition) was the earliest in the series. Further texts, edited by other educational writers, included a volume containing what James Mill wrote on education in the *Encyclopaedia Britannica*, John Stuart Mill's inaugural address at the University of St. Andrews, edited by F. A. Cavenagh, and Cardinal Newman's *Idea of a University* edited by May Yardley, a member of my staff.

But I also had my own series of public lectures under the general title of 'The Schools of England'. This dealt with a description of all the various types of schools and universities in England from the elementary school upwards, each type being considered by an authority on the subject. The elementary school, for example, was the theme of my old friend Frederick Spencer, a colleague in the Board of Education and by now Chief Inspector of Schools under the L.C.C. I myself contributed an introduction, mainly historical in character, entitled 'The Schools and the Nation'. These ambitious lectures were published as *The Schools of England: A Study in Renaissance* and provided, I believe, a complete picture in miniature of the whole subject, though legislation soon made it out of date. In addition to all this, I wrote an article, 'Adult Education in England', which appeared in *The Nineteenth Century and After* in 1929.

Finally, in a series of lectures given for public school masters at Harrow in 1935, just before I left for Edinburgh, I tried to elaborate some principles that should guide teachers in instructing their pupils in the writing of their mother tongue.

Soon after I had arrived at King's College, Barker had said to me, 'Don't you think it would be a good thing to take women

H   113

into the department?' I could see what he was after: to double
the fees from the students by increasing the work of the staff.
So I replied, 'A very good thing; if you will provide me with
a very good woman to look after them.' My stipulation was
granted; we opened the door to fifty women students. This
would be a very incomplete account if I did not say something
about the woman lecturer brought in to preside over them, a
Lancashire lady, Miss Betsy Farrow. She had a good degree,
the women all adored her, and she also got on excellently with
the headmistresses of secondary schools whom it was her duty
to persuade into taking our students for school practice. She
eventually married one of Professor Hearnshaw's lecturers, a
genial Yorkshireman in orders called Norman Sykes, who later
became Dixie Professor of Ecclesiastical History at Cambridge,
and after that Dean of Winchester.

The happiness which I enjoyed in my eleven years at King's
was largely due to the delightful staff, both men and women,
which I was able to gather round me. And if any of them happen
to read these words, let me assure them that I often think of
them and that one of the pictures they gave me when I left
hangs over the fire in my library. Among these colleagues was
Mrs. Sykes's successor, Dr. Chaplyn; her appointment began
a long friendship, as she later became Headmistress of the Mary
Erskine School in Edinburgh.

But the last word of this account must be one of appreciation
for the remarkable principal of the college, W. R. Halliday.
His gifts of diplomacy were put to the proof from the start in
his relations with other colleges of the university, the two
principal ones being University College and the London School
of Economics, just across the road from King's. The heads of
both institutions were by no means friendly to King's when
Halliday came there from Liverpool University; Barker, excellent
man though he was, had lacked that peculiar gift which enables
a man to get his way on a committee without offending the
people from whom he gets it. One difficulty was happily soon
removed, when Allen Mawer who, like Halliday, had been a
professor at Liverpool, became Provost of University College.

4. Dorothy Wilson, 1904

5. John Dover Wilson
   c. 1904

6. Frank Pullinger

7. Harley Granville-Barker

8. W. W. Greg

As for the London School of Economics, I once asked Halliday how he got on with Beveridge, his opposite number there. 'Oh, that's easy,' he said. 'I always tell him the truth, and he disbelieves it, of course.'

The only fault with Halliday was that he was unable to spare himself, and I soon found that he was working a willing horse much too hard; nor could his friend Allen Mawer spare himself either. So I regarded it as my duty as Professor of Education to attempt to do something for the health of the two university principals by taking a leaf out of Trevelyan's book and organizing Sunday tramps, which I called 'airing the Principals'. But my greatest success was when I succeeded in inducing Halliday to take up golf. I have known many university principals, both in England and Scotland, but he was the finest of them all.

He retired in 1952 to his family home, a country house at Lynton, where he died in November 1966. I had carried on a fitful correspondence with him but do not know whether he was able in failing health to keep up those Classical researches which he had been forced to put aside during his Principalship. He once said to me, 'If I hadn't taken up this old college, I should have spent my life hewing down the Golden Bough.'

I left King's partly because a voice sounded louder and louder in my ears—that of William Shakespeare. For many years I had been working at and thinking about *Hamlet*—ever since 1917—and had accumulated a good deal of material. In 1933, I had the chance of gathering it together during a year of complete freedom from teaching. That year enabled me to produce three books on *Hamlet*—the bibliography, an edition of the text and an essay on the dramatic problems. All this was made possible by the grant of a Leverhulme Fellowship, the first that was awarded. The chairman of the committee that made the grant was Sir Hector Hetherington, at that time Vice-Chancellor of Liverpool University. The Fellowship stipulated that I found someone to take my place at King's during my absence, and I was fortunate enough to secure one to my complete satisfaction in my friend F. A. Cavenagh.

What I may call my Leverhulme year was spent at my home in

Purley. However, soon after I returned to King's, the Regius Professorship in Rhetoric and English Literature at Edinburgh was advertised as vacant, and I saw that as a further opportunity of getting on with my Shakespeare. I made application and was appointed in October 1935, but was unable to take up my duties at Edinburgh until January 1936 when Cavenagh, who was now accepted as my successor, could detach himself once again from Swansea.

Cavenagh was an ideal professor of education, as I had discovered when I came to know him as his External Examiner at Swansea, a few years earlier. Although he died in 1946, a comparatively young man, his memory and the educational principles he stood for, I am happy to say, live on at King's; for he brought with him from Swansea A. C. F. Beales who overlapped with me for a term before I left. He has recently (1964) been appointed Professor of Education, after Cavenagh's excellent successor, A. V. Judges.

I took up my duties at Edinburgh in January 1936. My coming to Edinburgh University meant almost a complete change of life for me, and though I have never regretted it, I have often felt it as a kind of desertion. For as a professor at King's, I was continuing the task of training the 'guardians' of England. Yet during that whole period I could never forget that I had come there because the nation had refused to establish day continuation schools; and in so doing it had turned its back upon its duty towards the vast majority of boys and girls of the country who had to be 'guarded'. And though successive Acts were passed raising the school leaving age bit by bit, it was evident that they meant retaining young persons of twelve and upwards who could not pass examinations qualifying them to enter secondary or central schools and so had to remain in their primary schools. There they became increasingly bored under the same kind of teachers that they had endured for many years, at that very time of life when they were straining at the leash to get out into the world and lead the life of wage-earners. In a word, the teenage problem, as we have come to think of it, might have been avoided almost entirely, in my view, had Morant's marriage of industry and education been recorded in the state registry office known as the Ministry of Education.

As a matter of fact, there was one Minister of Education after 1918 whose plans, had he been able to carry them into effect, might have come very near to realizing Morant's dream. This was Lord Eustace Percy, of whom a word must be said at this point. I first heard of him when Zimmern secured him as a contributor to *The War and Democracy* in 1914, at which time he was a young official in the Diplomatic Service. But I first came to know him personally in connection with the *Journal of Adult Education*. This, much to the disgust of my wife who thought I had already more than enough on board, I was induced by Harold Laski to found in 1926 and to edit for the first three years of its existence. For this work Eustace Percy, with his unrivalled knowledge of education on the Continent as well as in Great Britain, proved of the utmost assistance. By 1926 he was President of the Board of Education in Baldwin's Ministry. But it so happened that during his tenure of that office, the Chancellor of the Exchequer was Winston Churchill who regarded all public education of very minor importance and never let him have enough money to promote his own educational ideas.

These ideas were revealed in 1930, the year after Percy ceased to be President of the Board, in a remarkable book entitled *Education at the Crossroads*—a book which apparently owing nothing to Morant was inspired by a conception of industrial democracy similar to that I have tried to expound in the previous chapter. But Percy enlarged it by insisting upon the vital part which technical education at a university level must play in it.

In Baldwin's later government, the Prime Minister offered him a seat in the Cabinet—this time without portfolio—that he might have someone to talk to, it seems, for Percy clearly understood Baldwin (as his fascinating book *Some Memories* shows). But, like Hotspur, Percy never could endure inaction, and having nothing to do he soon resigned, to become Rector of King's College, Newcastle, in 1937. His tenure of office there will long be remembered and talked about; and when a new wing to Newcastle University (as it had now become) was opened to house the Faculty of Arts, it was named the Percy Building in his honour. And nothing in my career gave me greater pleasure or did me greater honour than when I was asked to open it on 19th October 1958.

6

Edinburgh

One of the chief attractions for me of the Chair of Rhetoric and English Literature at Edinburgh had been the chance it seemed to offer of getting on with my edition of Shakespeare. This, I was to discover, was quite illusory, partly because the Second World War broke out three years after I arrived, but chiefly because I found the work of a professor—including his own self-education—so absorbing that there was time between 1936 and 1946 for the publication of only one play (*Richard II*) and the delivery of the lectures on 'The Fortunes of Falstaff'.

The term 'Rhetoric' had attracted me also, since it suggested that my interest in the teaching and encouragement of good writing would find full scope. Lastly, I compared the Honours system in English and Scottish universities, much to the advantage of the latter. In England, the students were free from the beginning of their course to decide to read for Honours, with the result that at the end of the three years the final examination turned out a large proportion of them in the third class, a class I refused to admit at King's as qualifying for the course for the teacher's diploma. But it is otherwise in Scotland, where the student for Honours must be accepted by the professor at the end of the first two years of a four-year course.

It is amusing to recall the circumstances of my appointment and the way in which it was announced to me. The first intimation I received was a telephone message at Purley from the *Glasgow Herald* congratulating me on becoming the Regius Professor at Edinburgh—to which I said that I was not at that moment aware that His Majesty himself knew of the appointment. Next followed from the Scottish Office a request for seven shillings and sixpence for the purchase of the seal to be attached to the document with the royal signature necessary for a Regius professor. And it was only some days later that the postman brought me an official notification of the appointment from the same office.

Behind these rather strange proceedings lay an irregularity on the university's side of which I only became aware ten years later, when I was discussing with Sir Thomas Holland, the Principal, and the Dean, Sir William Calder, the circumstances of my resignation. When this business was concluded, the Principal said, 'Well, Dover Wilson, you may like to know now how you came to be appointed.' And then, with his eye on the Dean, he proceeded to tell me in words something like these, 'Officially, of course, the appointment to a Regius Chair is made by the Scottish Office, who advises the King. But it is our practice to set up an official committee to survey the field and to offer advice to the Scottish Office. Well, Grierson had resigned; and this wretched committee went mucking about until I lost all patience. So I went round to the Scottish Office and said, "Let me see these applications". It didn't take me long to pick you out, and I said, "That's the man".' After we had left the room, Calder, who was of course the chairman of the committee referred to, looked at me and said, 'Now I know how it was that I first saw your appointment in *The Scotsman*.' Thomas Holland had pulled, as the saying is, a fast one over the Dean.

Of course, the fact that Thomas Holland had practically imposed me on the Faculty of Arts was not a happy introduction to the university. Tommy, as we called him, was an Englishman; so was I. This was an invasion indeed, though there was a precedent in Saintsbury (whom I myself met only once). Furthermore, there was no love lost between Holland and Grierson. The story goes that soon after Holland's appointment he was expatiating at a dinner table (I believe at Grierson's own house) on the unexpectedness of his coming to Edinburgh. He didn't say that he had never *heard* of Edinburgh; but he rather implied that it was an Ultima Thule that had never crossed his mind as a possible scene for his activities. 'And yet,' he concluded, 'I was somewhere in South America, and it was offered me on a plate.' At which Grierson, concerned in all innocence with getting the facts right, interrupted, 'Yes; but ye see, Principal, first of all it was offered to So-and-so, and then to So-and-so, and then to So-and-so, and then . . .' Holland never forgave him. 'Grierson,' he said to me one day scornfully, 'his subject's Milton! Milton's *dead*!' I was so taken aback that I hadn't the wit to reply to this eminent geologist, 'Not as dead as the stones.'

I have perhaps rather over-emphasized the roughness of Holland's manner. He never disguised his contempt for the Scots, so that his reign did not tend to increase the friendship between the university and the city. He was seen at his best, however, at home, where Lady Holland presided, as gracious in manner as he was the reverse, and withal interested in things of the mind—literature, music and art. But, alas, she was chained to her chair by acute arthritis, so that she was never able to act as hostess for the university. Had it been otherwise, she could have gone far to soften the rugged edges of the Principal.

Since I could not disentangle myself from the Chair in London at once, I was unable to arrive in Edinburgh before the beginning of the Easter term in 1936. Before this, however, rumours had reached me that I was proposing to reconstruct the whole course. As if to repudiate such a notion, I let it be known that I intended to follow the procedure which my predecessor had followed—namely, that I should lecture to the First Ordinary class both on the history of literature and on rhetoric, while the others, of course, would remain unaltered.

In point of fact, the First Ordinary class was one of the features which had specially attracted me, both because it was here that the subject of rhetoric was dealt with, and also because the class contained the majority of arts students in their first year. In other words, I should be lecturing not only to my own potential Honours candidates but also to those of the other departments, e.g. Modern Languages, Philosophy, History, Classics, etc., not to mention the students taking the three-year course for the Ordinary degree. And as the best entrants had sometimes not made up their minds as to the subject they wished to follow up to the Honours standard, a professor in whatever subject could, as it were, advertise his subject and win students over.

At the same time I encouraged students in the literature course of the First Ordinary to specialize as much as possible by setting papers at the end of the year which allowed a generous variety of choice. Moreover, at my first lecture I made two announcements; one, 'These lectures will be of no use to you in any examination, and I don't wish to see anyone taking notes. You would attend to me much better if you didn't; and I remember how little I could recollect of what my professors at Cambridge really wished to convey because I concentrated on trying to set down every word they uttered.' And two, 'I shall waste no time in having a register checked at the beginning of lectures. At the end of term you will come up with D.P. (Duly Performed) cards; I shall know a good deal about you from the tutors you'll meet with in smaller classes. And if I do not, I shall look you in the face, and say *"Did you?"* and shall know whether you did or not.'

When I asked Grierson what he took with the First Ordinary apart from the lectures on rhetoric, he had replied, 'We take the history of English literature from *Beowulf* to Virginia Woolf. But it's true,' he went on, 'that we don't often get past the Pre-Raphaelites!' This programme suited my book excellently— and suited it literally; for I had among my papers the draft history of English literature which had been written for the Cambridge University Press when I was at Goldsmiths' College, and which I had laid aside in favour of one by my friend, W. T. Young. Of course it needed a good deal of both filling out and excision. Indeed, in the course of two or three years with the First Ordinary class, it became almost completely overlaid with additions and insertions. But I don't know how I could have started off without that typescript basis.

I always began my course with a lecture, not on *Beowulf*, but on the Old English poem which I regarded as far more characteristic of the enduring spirit of heroism that runs through English poetry: I mean that fragmentary epic *The Battle of Malden*, 991. After translating the climax of the whole poem, I would read aloud a few lines in the original so that the students might hear what Old English sounded like, and would write the same lines on the board so that they might see what it looked like. For the rest, I hurried on to Chaucer, to Spenser, gave them three or four lectures on Shakespeare, and as many on Milton, while I took some trouble over Dryden and Pope, of which poets most members of the class knew nothing, having been nourished on *The Golden Treasury*. Wordsworth and the other Romantics, followed by the Pre-Raphaelites, concluded the course. But all was illustrated throughout by copious readings aloud, and these readings were, I believe, what the students best remembered; perhaps the most exciting of all being the description of the expulsion of Satan and his angels from Heaven at the end of Book VI of *Paradise Lost*.

When I took over the First Ordinary, I found that one of my staff took a special interest in the lectures on rhetoric in the traditional interpretation of that science; and I allowed him to continue his lectures for a time. In a year or two, however, I made arrangements to take it over myself, and set formal rhetoric aside, in order to indoctrinate the students with at least the elements of simple composition—instruction which I discovered at once they sadly needed. To my horror, indeed, I found, arriving in mid-session, that my staff were intending to award First Class Honours to a student who couldn't write the King's English.

Furthermore, I was astonished that apart from firing lectures at them, the professor had no personal contact with his class at all. The class itself was sub-divided into three large, so-called tutorials, to which lectures on the set books were delivered by members of the professor's staff—again accompanied by little or no personal contact. I therefore went to the Principal and asked to have a number of assistant lecturers added to my staff, who should split the First Ordinary into small groups of not more than ten, each assistant taking two or more groups each week, getting them to write for him about the set books and correcting their essays, while conducting discussions at the group meetings. This request the Principal readily granted. I applied to him, following the procedure I had always adopted when a professor at King's, though of course (as Holland should have told me, and as I soon learned), I ought to have applied first of all to the Dean of the Faculty of Arts, namely William Calder.

When the latter discovered what had happened (too late for him to alter it), he was furious; and I received a letter marked 'Confidential' beginning, 'Do you think this is a bloody secondary school?' To which I replied, 'No, but I think it ought to be', explaining at the same time that I had gone behind him in all ignorance that the Edinburgh procedure differed from that of London University. We soon made friends and he proved one of the best I had.

Calder had first become aware of my existence in 1931 when he was elected a Fellow of the British Academy. Flattering himself that he was the youngest of all the Fellows, he found to his disgust that another, called John Dover Wilson, ten days younger, had been elected at the same time. Calder was incidentally a very good dean, and remained dean during the whole of my occupation of the Chair. He never lost his temper, and no one could ever quarrel with him; while when he had to deal with students, he was extremely just and took infinite pains to understand the point of view put before him.

He was a Greek scholar of an unusual type with a somewhat peculiar field of study, namely the inscriptions on the tombstones, mainly early Christian, in Asia Minor. Having to employ labourers, mostly Greeks, in his work among the graveyards, he had learned to speak modern Greek fluently; and he once assured me, pulling my leg, that he found *Hamlet* in modern Greek far more interesting than in the original. He was in effect an archaeologist and had got his scholarship by digging—a not inapt course of study for one who, had he remained in Morayshire where he came from, might have been a farmer, as his brother still was. He was indeed to be seen at his best on his native heath. Staying a few days at Forres some years ago, I visited him at his house and there drank the best whisky I have ever tasted. Morayshire, Calder explained to me, was not part of Scotland. 'We're all Picts here; and the Picts knew how to distil whisky.' And since Macbeth was a Morayshire man, and was, as the play tells us, on his way to Forres when he encountered the Witches, Calder asserted that this had taken place just outside his house; and he even contributed a page to the guide to Forres on this subject, illustrated by a woodcut of the encounter on the 'blasted heath', borrowed from Holinshed's first edition. All great fun, of course; and I told him I supposed it was in preparation for setting up a tea-garden for American visitors. But there was another side to him. He could write quite delightful lyrics; and I wish I had kept a copy of some of those he showed me.

His accusation that I was turning the large First Ordinary class into a secondary school was prompted by a feeling that I was offending against the whole tradition of a Scottish university which was in fact a lecture-shop, culminating in examinations for throwing out those who had not properly absorbed the wisdom of their professors.

But that was not the end of the matter, to return to the deplorable standard of written English in Scottish universities. As leader of a deputation from the English Association, I made an attempt, through the Advisory Council on Scottish Education whose chairman was Principal Fyfe, to get the Secretary of State to appoint a special committee. Its briefing would be to enquire into 'what steps should be taken to secure an effective training in habits of clear thought and clear expression in the English language among the boys and girls of Scotland, with special reference to instruction in secondary schools'. Fyfe was sympathetic but had to plead that the Advisory Council's plate was already overfull.

At much the same time I made a similar attempt through the Dean; he, like other deans, had been requested by the University Committee on the Educational System of Scotland to report to the Advisory Council on what the heads of various departments expected or desired their students to have studied before entering honours or pass degree courses. In looking up my records, I have discovered that they include not only my answers to the Dean but also the answers of other heads of departments—among them

Kemp Smith, James Drever, A. E. Taylor, A. J. D. Porteous, A. F. Giles, Alexander Gray and Gordon Childe—a truly historic collection! For the English department, under the heading 'The Reading and Writing of English', I replied, 'One of the most serious blots upon our educational system is that a large proportion of boys and girls who knock at the doors of the universities can neither read well and with understanding, nor express themselves on paper simply and to the point.'

These attempts upon the educational system of the Scottish people proved futile. I might have been kicking at the base of one of the pyramids. But I had got my small tutorials well established for the large class in the Arts Faculty at Edinburgh. It still remains a valued feature of university education in Edinburgh, and has now been adopted in Aberdeen where the late Professor of English was an old student of mine. And if it is copied in still other Scottish universities I may have reached my objective after all by working from within and not from without the pyramid.

One of my first duties at Edinburgh—which was at the same time a great pleasure—came when Grierson retired; it was to get together a volume of essays in his honour for his seventieth birthday which took place the term after I arrived. It was celebrated with a small dinner party held at the Roxburghe Hotel on 15th December 1937 at which the following were present: W. D. Paterson (in the chair), Herbert Grierson, J. Purves, D. Tovey, A. M. Clark, A. J. D. Porteous, H. H. Wood, J. C. Smith, G. Kitchin, N. Kemp Smith, and J.D.W.

These Festschrifts are often something of a ragbag in which the scholar to be honoured is greeted by his fellow-scholars with any odd bits of learning that they find at the back of their filing cabinets. I was determined it should not be so with my great predecessor, and that the proper offering would be a volume of contributions on different aspects of the seventeenth century which he had himself so signally illuminated. The result was a handsome volume in the familiar Oxford blue entitled 'Seventeenth-Century Studies', prefaced with a delightful picture of Grierson sitting with a book on his knee, leaning back in a characteristic attitude. It opened with a long poem specially written by his friend, the Dutch poet, P. C. Boutens, which was followed by articles from writers such as C. S. Lewis, T. S. Eliot, A. E. Taylor, Laurence Binyon, Mario Praz, L. C. Martin, F. E. Hutchinson, Sir Donald Tovey, Basil Willey and H. S. Goodhart-Rendel—the last-named, who as a schoolboy had been a pupil of my own, had since become Slade Professor of Fine Art at Oxford and was later appointed President of the Royal Society of Architects. Practically all the articles had been written for the occasion.

A special word must be devoted to the name of John Purves, who edited the whole volume and, in conjunction with Dr. Melville Clark, one of Sir Herbert's staff, saw it through the press; while it was Purves too, I understand, who read the proofs and checked all the references in Grierson's famous edition of Donne's poems. A sound classical scholar, Purves was Reader in Italian at Edinburgh, and had at one time been a professor of English in South Africa. He was at once the most modest and in my judgment the most learned member of the Faculty of Arts at the university—so unassuming, moreover, that when I insisted on mentioning him in my brief preface, he was so angry as almost to lead to a quarrel. As I have mentioned him, I must also relate that, finding neither the Regius Professor of English Literature nor the Professor of British History well seen in the Italian language, he offered to conduct tutorials during which Professor Vivian Galbraith and myself were enabled to gain some acquaintance with Dante's *Inferno*.

Soon after I got to Edinburgh, I had a ring from Sir David Wilkie, the Professor of Surgery, telling me that Sir James Barrie, then Chancellor of the University, was staying with him. Wilkie was arranging a little 'bachelor party' for him, and asking whether I would join it. I accepted with alacrity, but to my consternation found myself seated next to this formidable person at the table, guessing (rightly, I think) that he wanted to find out what sort of stuffing there was in this Sassenach who was now sitting in the Chair that Masson had graced. I was lucky, however. I had just been moving in and, arranging my volumes of Meredith on the shelf, had found among them a tiny little booklet by Barrie—to wit, a fantasia occasioned by Meredith's funeral. Anyhow, I opened the ball by reminding him of it, and it started him off talking about Meredith for the rest of the dinner.

He told us that when he got to London as a young journalist, he took the first opportunity to run down to Box Hill, hoping to catch a glimpse of the great man whom he almost worshipped at that time. Meredith's house was on the side of the hill, with the garden sloping downwards at the back, at the foot of which was a small iron gate. At this gate Barrie stationed himself, looking up along a straight path leading to a flight of steps going up to a door in the house. And to his delight it was not long before the familiar figure with a red tie and silver hair appeared. Meredith came out, walked down the steps, and down the path, growing nearer and nearer to him. 'I can still feel,' Barrie said, 'the iron gateposts in my hands as I clutched them in my excitement—until I could stand it no longer. I turned and fled!'

Barrie died in 1937, and when a Chancellor dies a tribute to him is recorded in the Proceedings of the Senatus of the University. The evening before the meeting of the Senatus at which this should have been read, I received a telephone call from the Secretary, W. A. Fleming. Grierson, who had promised to write the tribute, had apparently just told him that he had not been well and was not able to manage it. Could I supply what was needed? 'My dear Secretary,' I exclaimed, 'I'm afraid I'm not a Barrie fan. I don't think I've got any of his plays on my shelves. But you can't be in a worse position than you are. If I turn up tomorrow with something, your face will be saved, though mine may be for ever disgraced. If I don't, you must make your own apologies.' Yet by good luck I did find one other volume of Barrie's among my books, *An Edinburgh Eleven*, which contained portraits of several professors of his day. And as it gave me a vision of little Jimmie listening enthralled to Masson delivering his annual lecture on Chatterton the wonderful boy who never grew up, clearly the original inspiration for Peter Pan, it gave me all I wanted for my Minute.

In W. A. Fleming, the secretary, I found a very good friend, not only when I visited him in his office, but also when he partnered me at golf. What days they were when we motored out to Muirfield, the finest of all the courses round Edinburgh (and which claims indeed to be more ancient if less royal than the course at St. Andrews itself). We were met there at about ten by Croft Dickinson, Professor of Scottish History and another great friend of mine, and Brash, Professor of Anatomy. We played a four-ball match before lunch, then repaired to the clubhouse for a magnificent meal, with plenty to drink too, after which we played a foursome and reached home in the evening tired out but entirely happy.

I said to Fleming once, 'I don't understand how you get along by yourself. You have of course your assistant, but there are universities like Sheffield and Leeds which require for their administration a staff three or four times the size of yours. What's to happen when you retire?'

'Oh,' he said, 'they'll only get another W.S. in.' (For English readers, I had better explain that W.S. stands for Writer to the Signet, that is the highest grade of solicitor.)

I don't know what the size of the administrative staff is now at the university; perhaps it's better not to enquire. All I am aware of is that there are quite a number of charming persons about, called administrators. And yet Fleming never seemed to be over-driven.

In the matter of salary there was no financial gain in making the move to Scotland. Yet the Regius Professor possessed a perquisite which was both interesting and added to the salary in such a way as to appeal to my economical wife as a small recompense for digging her up by the roots. Under the terms of the will of the late James Tait Black, the Professor received a fee for awarding two prizes per annum, one for the best novel and another for the best biography published in the current year. Appalling as this task appeared at first sight, I found it far less onerous in fact, inasmuch as the fee included a special sum for an assistant who might share the burden. At the beginning much help of this kind came from one of my staff; and when he was no longer available I was doubly fortunate in finding in Edwin Muir, previously unknown to me and at that time hardly recognized as the great poet that he really was, ready to step in. Nor was it difficult for him since he was at this period writing short reviews for *The Listener* on the novels that appeared week by week. I therefore relied on him—and what better judge could I have found—to pick out those which he thought I ought to consider. In the end it meant for me having to read no more than about twenty novels a year—a light employment which made me acquainted with what was going on in modern novel writing, an acquaintance I have almost entirely lost since my retirement.

But above all the benefits I received from this work was the friendship with Edwin Muir. When I lost my only son in the Second World War, among the letters I received from my friends, none was more tender and understanding than the one he wrote.

The task of deciding on the biography for the James Tait Black was not so difficult, as there were usually not more than two or three biographies in one year which I regarded as likely to need careful study. I made it my practice, when a prizewinner had acknowledged the receipt of the award, to write a personal letter suggesting that he or she might care to visit the university and talk to the students—making it clear of course that there was no obligation to do so. Most were too shy or too busy to accept; but some did, a notable instance being Joyce Cary who stayed with me at our home in Balerno—and, being Irish, sat up most of the night talking. And what talk it was! The book of the award was *A House of Children*—not at all typical, but excellent in its way. But it was clear that he normally had three or four and even at times five different books on the stocks or partially in his head. And, as he explained to me, they got in each other's way; if he wanted to finish off one, he had so to speak to lock up the others, stamp on them, shove them to the back of his mind. He spoke as if it was almost a physical process. Cary may not have been a heaven-sent genius; but he was certainly a very remarkable writer, and my conversations with him were the nearest I ever got to looking into the imaginative fury (to use a classical word), or should I say furnace, from which bubbled forth the forms of things unknown, *The Horse's Mouth* being perhaps the most remarkable example of this.

The reader may like to see the titles of the books for which the James Tait Black prize was awarded during my term as judge:

1936:	V. Sackville West	*A Flame in the Sunlight*
	Winifred Holtby	*South Riding*
1937:	Lord Eustace Percy	*John Knox*
	Neil M. Gunn	*Highland River*
1938:	E. K. Chambers	*S. T. Coleridge*
	C. S. Forester	*A Ship of the Line—Flying Colours*
1939:	David C. Douglas	*English Scholars*
	Aldous Huxley	*After Many a Summer*
1940:	Hilda F. M. Prescott	*Spanish Tudor*
	Charles Morgan	*The Voyage*
1941:	John Gore	*King George V*
	Joyce Cary	*A House of Children*
1942:	Lord Ponsonby	*Henry Ponsonby*
	Arthur Waley	*'Monkey' by Wu Ch'êng-ên*
1943:	G. G. Coulton	*Fourscore Years*
	Mary Lavin	*Tales From Bective Bridge*
1944:	C. V. Wedgwood	*William the Silent*
	Forrest Read	*Young Tom*
1945:	D. S. MacColl	*Wilson Steer*
	L. A. G. Strong	*Travellers*

T. S. Eliot wrote neither novels nor biography, but I was naturally anxious to lure him to the university, so that my students and other members of the Edinburgh public might have an opportunity of hearing him lecture. Having gained the consent of the Dean, I wrote to him inviting him to give us one or two lectures on Shakespeare. He most willingly agreed, sending me a typescript of the lectures. He stayed with me in Balerno for one night, the second being spent at the hospitable house of my friends the Maitlands in Heriot Row. I told him that we lived in the country and suggested he might like to have a stroll on the Pentland Hills before lunch, since there would be plenty of time to see something of the university on the following morning. My wife was rather nervous of the advent of this great man, but he put her at once at her ease, for when she asked him on his arrival whether there was anything she could do for him, he replied, 'If you have a copy of yesterday's *Times* I should be very grateful, as I never managed to finish the crossword puzzle,' remarking that he always did the crossword puzzle during the lunch hour in a restaurant near his office in order to keep admirers at bay. That he and my wife got on well together may be judged from the fact that he gave her a typescript copy of one of his poems on cats when he left.

When Eliot came down to breakfast he was all ready for the walk, clad in a perfectly new and very magnificent pair of plus fours. We didn't get very far over the hills since a mist came down, but as we walked he explained to me that he was trying to compose a kind of dramatic verse which could be used for any purpose whatever, such as 'Pass the whisky'. I didn't know it at the time, but a little later on I realized that he was then at work on *The Family Reunion*, the second of his plays. As it happened, not long afterwards I was able to see in London an early production of this under the author's own supervision; and when to my amazement three figures representing the Eumenides appeared on the backcloth, I must confess that I laughed. Others must have laughed also, for the Furies disappeared, I gather, at later performances. In any case, I felt the play was a failure, and didn't disguise my opinion from my friend.

It must have been several years later that a member of my staff rang up one morning to tell me that the College of Art was putting on *The Family Reunion* that evening and he had tickets if I wished to go. I said, 'Oh no, I don't want to see that thing. But wait a bit,' I added, 'I'll see if my wife would like to go.' She said she would; and so off we went. The producer was that brilliant young artist, John Maxwell, too soon cut off, and the production was brilliant too, far better than I had seen in London under T.S.E.'s own direction. It gripped me from the beginning, and at the end I said to myself, 'I don't know whether the son of the Family had murdered his wife or not, but—urr-rrgh—I know *I* had!' And that, I believe, was what the author intended spectators to feel.

Also among our friends of those early days were Lord and Lady Normand. He was then Lord Justice General, that is to say, head of the Scottish Law, and as an old Oxford friend of R. W. Chapman and George Gordon (later President of Magdalen) always showed a keen interest in university affairs. And when in due course, as a Lord of Appeal he had to reside in London, he became a member of the Council of University College.

'What do you do in the House of Lords?' I once asked Normand. 'Do? Oh, we try to knock a little sense into them.' And he gave an instance of a recent case in which the English law lords were seeking for a precedent which led them right back to the reign of Edward III. 'Like a lot of dogs,' he said, 'smelling up an almost interminable avenue!'

Normand's interest in university life was shown in his taking the chair for me at one of a series of public lectures in about 1938 to raise money on behalf of academic refugees. These lectures, considerably rewritten, eventually formed the basis of a book, *Shakespeare's Happy Comedies*, published in 1962 by Faber and Faber.

I also got to know two of Normand's successors, first Lord Cooper, who was intensely interested in Scottish history. He was followed, after his death, by Lord Clyde, under whom, as Chairman of the Executive Committee of the National Library, I acted as a trustee.

It is to Normand that I owe one of my best and closest friends, the Rev. David Stalker, now one of my neighbours at Balerno. While in London it was not uncommon for me to find among my students a total ignorance of the Bible; but I must confess that I was taken aback to find the same sort of thing among many of the Scottish students—an ignorance so prevalent that I was frequently held up by it in my dealing with the masterpieces of English literature. What was to be made, to take an extreme example, of Dryden's *Absalom and Achitophel* unless one knows

133

the story of the troubles in the house of King David? I talked about this matter with my colleagues and found much sympathy among some of them. The upshot was that a motion was brought up to the Senatus for the appointment of a lecturer in Biblical History; attendance being of course voluntary and (equally of course) the lecturer a member of the Church of Scotland. But we were wise enough not to bring forward this proposition without having a suitable name to suggest, and this was provided by Lord Normand. He put forward the Rev. David Stalker, the Minister of Aberdour, a man for whose scholarship he had considerable admiration. The motion was carried by the Senatus with two dissentients: Professor Gordon Childe, the world-famous archaeologist and a pronounced atheist, and Professor Whittaker, the equally world-famous mathematician and an ardent Roman Catholic.

My memories of Normand are also associated with those of his friend Stair Gillon, whose character and bearing, it has always seemed to me, must have resembled those of some Edinburgh lawyers of the late eighteenth century.

Stair, who had a very loud voice and a somewhat abrupt manner, never moved about without a book in his pocket, generally in some foreign language; it might be modern Greek or Spanish, though he loved German most. When the war came and petrol was severely rationed, he had to give up driving the eight miles from Balerno into Edinburgh and took to the bus. And the story goes that one day, when Stair was sitting in the bus at the terminus waiting for it to start, with a volume of Goethe open on his knee, a village woman came and sat next to him and, peering at the pages before her, remarked, 'I'ld be ashamed of meself reading *Gairman* in a bus.' Whereat he started up, and crying in a loud voice, 'I never speak to strange women in buses', moved to another seat.

But of all the lawyers, it was Randall Philip whom I knew best —he and his wife and family. He was a man of *embonpoint*, and when we walked along Princes Street together arm in arm, as we not infrequently did, the view of our figures from behind must have amused the passers-by. And though he was as capable of seriousness as any man—was he not the only lay member of one of the committees formed to discuss the reunion of the Anglican and Presbyterian churches?—he was also gifted with an almost Puckish love of fun. One of the great moments of his career was when, as Procurator of the Church of Scotland, he was responsible for the reception of the Queen at the National Service of Thanksgiving and Dedication at St. Giles on 24th June 1953. In connection with this he received a knighthood; and it was reported (by him) that having laid the sword across his shoulders, the Queen said, 'Arise, Sir Cumference!'.

He was a Sheriff, which roughly corresponds with the English Judge in Circuit; and his jurisdiction embraced Renfrew and Argyll. Oban was its headquarters though he, like all Sheriffs, who were advocates, lived in Edinburgh and was only called upon to try criminal cases at Oban, the ordinary course of the law being looked after by a legal official known as the Sheriff Substitute. More than once has Randall driven me over for company to Oban, and I have one vivid recollection of a spring day of sun and showers, when as we threaded our way by lochs, salt and freshwater, we often seemed to be driving through rainbows. But perhaps our greatest prank together was a visit to the Festival of Britain in London in 1951, spending a day seeing all the sideshows and sitting by a parapet overlooking the Thames, each armed with a large tankard of beer—which was not good for his figure—and then going to the theatre to see the Oliviers playing Shakespeare; after which I took him up to the dressing-room of Vivien Leigh whom I knew personally, remarking as I entered, 'May I introduce you to the Procurator of the Church of Scotland?' This was an honour she had dreamed not of, and she almost fell to the floor with delight.

I cannot remember when I first got to know Randall and his family. But what planted our friendship with roots very deep in our hearts was the death of his son Gordon. He was fifteen and playing at football at the Academy, when he fell to the ground and one of the players accidentally kicked him on the head. His father wrote, for private circulation, a delightful little account of him, to which many of his friends, old and young, contributed; and what I recorded then is true now, some twenty-five years later. '. . . His picture hangs in my study, and I look at him every morning before I begin my work. He smiles so gaily and encouragingly that I can't help feeling that I may be able to do something yet, if only to repay *part* of what I owe to his having been my friend.'

Joining the staff of the university in 1936, I was fortunate enough to overlap Sir Donald Tovey by a year or two; he at once showed himself very friendly and I became a regular attender at the concerts given by the Reid Orchestra. And I have a clear recollection of a small luncheon party which he gave—in my honour, I believe—at his house in Regent Terrace, during which as the sweets were brought in he sat down at the piano and sang comic songs. This was in the family, so to speak, since his brother was a music-hall composer, and wrote the famous song, 'When Father laid the carpet on the stairs'.

It was to Tovey, I believe, that I owed my most delightful and rewarding friendship with the Maitlands, Rosalind Maitland being a favourite pupil of his with whom he would play piano duets. The Maitlands lived in a large house in Heriot Row with a drawing-room full of Gauguins, Matisses and others, together with statues by other great artists. (All these were presented by Alexander Maitland to the Scottish National Gallery after the death of his wife.)

The room at Heriot Row was large enough to seat seventy persons, and the Maitlands made it a kind of salon, inviting their friends from time to time to spend the evening listening to some famous singer or other musician, for example Jelly d'Aranyi or Kathleen Ferrier, whom they had invited to their house as guests for the occasion. The hour on our cards of invitation would be 9 p.m., the name of the artiste being printed in the corner. And after the guests had enjoyed an hour or an hour and a half's ravishing music, they repaired to a stand-up supper downstairs. Those were the days—or rather the nights—never to be forgotten, especially when Kathleen Ferrier filled the room with her divine contralto.

The name of Kathleen Ferrier leads me to speak of neighbours of mine at Balerno, one of them, Julian Allan, being a sculptor, and as a Roman Catholic usually engaged in work for some church of that denomination. But she greatly admired Kathleen Ferrier, and after the latter's death, with the aid of photographs and her own memory she produced a head which all who saw it pronounced a very striking likeness indeed. I in particular was so delighted with it that I persuaded the Maitlands to come to see it. They did so; on their advice Sir John Barbirolli also came. He at once declared that there must be a copy of it in the Free Trade Hall in Manchester. Edinburgh followed Manchester, and another copy is to be seen in the Usher Hall.

That the sculptor had a remarkable gift of portraiture was proved in my own case, as she made a head of me which both my friends and family regard as a striking likeness; so a 'Dover head' is to be found both in the Arts Faculty Room at Edinburgh University, and in the Parlour of my own college, Gonville and Caius, Cambridge.

These delightful musical evenings at the Maitlands' house, like other pleasures of Edinburgh society, came to an end with the war. But music has always been one of the main interests, almost a passion, of my life, and Edinburgh supplied a permanent means of satisfying it. And yet I cannot read a note of music. I found a real help, however, in that strange invention which was available to the amateur for a few years before the gramophone and wireless rendered it commercially out of date. I refer to the pianola. I purchased one when I set up house at Purley in 1918, and by means of it I familiarized myself with the crude outlines of some of the masterpieces. After grinding one out I would go to the concert hall and come to realize some of its splendours. When I came to Edinburgh I expanded and deepened what had already been built on this slender basis by the help of weekly concerts given during the winter months by the Professor of Music, in the Music Classroom of the university with the Reid Orchestra. In addition to all this, of course, the long-playing records can now give me even whole operas in my room at home.

It was not long before Tovey retired and was succeeded by Sidney Newman who became a close friend—as indeed did all those members of the university staff interested in music. Perhaps, however, the most intimate of all was Dr. E. H. Cameron (commonly known to us as Bob), who was by profession an oculist. He shortly after retired and has since been able to devote his time almost entirely to playing Bach on any available organ that he can find.

For some years he acted as unpaid organist at Roslin Chapel, a little church built some centuries ago by a Portuguese architect and actually a private chapel belonging to the St. Clair family. And it was my practice to go over by bus on Sunday afternoon to the service at Roslin and to remain on listening to my friend sitting up in the organ loft above me while he played Bach until the church got so cold we had to stop and resort to a tea-room for a warm cup of tea.

In point of fact, I first got to know Bob Cameron as an oculist when he examined my eyes. He had retired before the time for the necessary operation arrived, but he had trained the oculist who operated upon me, and indeed many of the other oculists in Edinburgh. He is therefore somewhat of a father-figure in the medical fraternity and has in previous years given many lectures to the medical students of the university, often choosing for his text, as he told me, Milton's description of his blindness at the beginning of Book III of *Paradise Lost*.

This leads me to record the debt I owe to another great doctor, the late Sir James Learmonth, but for whom I must have fallen by the way long before this book, or indeed my edition of Shakespeare, could be completed. Another patient of his was King George VI; his wife, now Queen Mother, being an ardent patriot, insisted that her husband be operated on by a Scottish surgeon, who should bring Scottish nurses with him to Buckingham Palace.

Learmonth kept me under observation for some time before proceeding to business. And in the end he performed two operations at an interval of a year or so. As a friend and colleague he refused to entertain any question of fee, so the least I could do was to dedicate *The Fortunes of Falstaff*, published shortly after,

To
his friend and colleague
JAMES RÖGNVALD LEARMONTH
an ever-grateful patient
dedicates this autopsy of a
'trunk of humours'

The following story about him may be found in a footnote in
the official *Life* of George VI, and was obviously supplied by the
Queen Mother herself:

Some weeks after the operation Learmonth returned to the
Palace just to give the King a look-over and see that all was going
well. This accomplished, the King, getting out of bed, said,
'Mr. Learmonth, will you kindly give me my dressing-gown?'
And when Learmonth returned to give it to the King, the latter
produced a sword from under the bed, saying, 'You've been
knifing me; I'm going to knife you. Kneel down, please.'
Whereupon he knelt down, was clapped over the shoulders, and
got up Sir James.

I retired from the Chair in 1946 and, believing that retirement
should be absolute, I took great care to keep away from the
English Department at the University (though as Emeritus I
continued to make use of the university and especially the
university library). By what I have always regarded as a piece of
very good fortune, in the same year I became immersed in the
working of another great institution in the city, the National
Library of Scotland. My invitation came from the first librarian,
Dr. Meikle, whom I had previously known in London as
Librarian of the Institute of Historical Research. The National
Librarian for most of my trusteeship was, however, Dr. William
Beattie, the most modest of men, who is nevertheless considered
by all who know his work to be one of the ablest librarians in the
country.

The Advocates' Library, attached to the Law Courts, was in
existence since 1682; early this century, however, it was
expanded, with a new constitution, to form the National Library

of Scotland. Though the foundations for its new buildings had been laid before the Second World War, in 1946 the erection consisted of merely a structure of girders on George IV Bridge.

I became a trustee of the Library in 1946; shortly after, upon Randall Philip's falling ill, I took his place as Convener of the Standing Committee, while in 1951 I was asked to become Vice-Chairman; thus, though the trustees in my day were committed to the pre-war architectural design of the building, I was intimately concerned with all the internal arrangements, including details such as the lay-out and seating of the reading-room, the colour and texture of the curtains, the lighting, the engraved designs in the great staircase windows—all this, of course, as an assistant to the Chairman, Lord Crawford and Balcarres, one of the most charming persons I have ever known, who became a close friend. And that the furnishings seem so satisfactory—and I think I may add, so beautiful—is largely due to his exquisite taste, combined of course with his devotion to the care of books; his own library at Balcarres is remarkable for its wealth both in quality and quantity.

I am proud to say that during my trusteeship I took a leading part in securing for the Library the finest collection of printed dramatic literature in the country, apart from that in the British Museum. And the story of its discovery and purchase is as follows:

Early on in the war (before I was a trustee), I was having lunch in the New Club in Princes Street when a solicitor of my acquaintance came up to me, and said, 'You're interested in old books, aren't you?'

'I am,' I replied.

'Well, come round to my office. I've got some to show you.'

To my amazement, when I went there I found on a table rows and rows of Shakespearian quartos—most of them late seventeenth-century editions. 'Good heavens,' I exclaimed, 'have you got policemen guarding this building? Some agent from Texas would dearly love to run off with the whole lot.' The solicitor then told me that they had come from Falkland Palace, the Hereditary Keeper of which is a Major Crichton-Stuart who belonged to a junior branch of the Bute family. And he, fearing that the palace might be bombed, was negotiating with the National Librarian to have them housed with his rare books in a chosen hide-out, the place of which would be revealed to no one but him and the Chairman of the Trustees.

The existence of early quartos at Falkland Palace was known, and had been recorded by Polland and Bartlett in *A Census of Shakespeare Quartos* (1916), but evidently not inspected by them, since no particulars are given, as in the case of quartos in other libraries. When the war was over, the Librarian received another request from Major Crichton-Stuart, asking whether the Library might not be willing to buy these quartos; he himself, not being a literary man, and feeling that they should be available to the public in general, would be glad to use their price for the development of his own property. At the same time he said that his library contained other books which might interest the National Library, if we would care to go and see them. One memorable day, then, Dr. Beattie and I went off to Falkland Palace. I had not previously met Major Crichton-Stuart and his wife but had heard of them from my friend Archie John Wavell, the son of Lord Wavell, upon whose staff Crichton-Stuart had been at Cairo; and the two had actually been married at Cairo, with Lady Wavell acting as the hostess after the ceremony. After lunch we were taken to the library, where, to our astonishment, we found row upon row of printed plays, mostly in single volumes, though sometimes three or four bound up together, stretching from Lyly's *Sappho and Phao* (1584) down to the end of the eighteenth century.

We went back to our fellow trustees and declared that whatever happened these books must never be allowed to leave Scotland, and our colleagues agreed. Major Crichton-Stuart showed the utmost generosity in his negotiations with us; he would tell no one but ourselves about the books and would agree to any price at which a reputable second-hand bookseller from London valued them. An emissary from the famous firm of Quaritch was engaged and worked for more than two days in listing and pricing the books; and when the valuation was complete it amounted to forty-one thousand pounds. This was just after the Second World War, when the whole country felt impoverished, and it seemed idle to look to the Treasury for any financial help whatever. Various rich merchants in Glasgow were sounded and turned a stone-deaf ear. Yet in the end the money was secured in this interesting fashion.

We decided that first we must get the thing started, so we began with ourselves—in other words, the body known as the Friends of the National Libraries. This consisted of scholars who were led to subscribe their guineas per annum to help libraries like the British Museum, the National Library of Wales and of course the National Library of Scotland to meet the unexpected appearance in the book market of items which could hardly be appropriate purchases under the libraries' annual Treasury grant. This association was able to put down five hundred pounds, practically all they had at their disposal just then. Such a beginning was a proof that British scholars felt that the cause for which we were appealing was one of first-class importance.

The next stage lay with the Pilgrim Trust. Here our Chairman, being a member of the Trust, was able to play a brilliant hand. Reminding his fellow trustees that they usually spent their money on restoring churches and other buildings of various kinds, he asked them, why not spend it on books for a change? And he returned to us triumphantly with a promise of twenty thousand pounds. Then we might perhaps with more assurance approach the Treasury itself, the Chancellor of the Exchequer (be it noted) at the time being a Scotsman—or at least half a Scotsman—Mr. R. A. Butler. Since the Chancellor could, with the story of the scholars and the Pilgrims behind him, face any awkward questions in the House of Commons, he gave us the rest. It's a wonderful story, and a fine example of how necessary it is for individual endeavour to lead the way to State action. So the Bute Collection, as it is now called, became Scotland's for ever.

How did the collection come to exist? It was an American, Professor Alan McKillop, who discovered the clue which led to an explanation of its origin. He was an historian interested in the career of Lady Mary Wortley Montagu and, turning over some of the volumes of the plays in the Bute Collection at the Library, he noticed that there were indications in the margin and elsewhere of little notes which were clearly made by the great lady herself who was known to be a passionate reader of plays. The results of the investigation that followed were set forth by Miss Linton, a member of the staff of the National Library, and were published in *The Times Literary Supplement* for 21st December 1956.

'It may be remembered that Lady Mary was in the habit of marking her books with "M" or "Ma", and also of adding to the beginning and end of the text her comment on the work, always terse, often only one well chosen adjective—"badd" is the favourite, with variations of "meane", "undelightful", "incomparable nonsense", and "extreamely silly", though a few plays earn the approbation of "good" or "exceedingly pretty" . . . Further examination has shown how close is the connexion between Lady Mary and the Bute Collection: not, of course, surprising since Lady Mary's daughter was the mother of the first Marquess of Bute, the chief architect of the Collection. The excellence of the foundations on which he built is now revealed by the discovery that there are twenty-nine plays with Lady Mary's sign-manual and forty-nine with her comments.'

This Marquess of Bute is chiefly remembered in history for having helped to lose us the American colonies; but he may seem to have made honourable amends by preserving this wonderful collection of books which have come down to us in this way.

The news that the Bute Collection had been acquired was first announced publicly by Her Majesty Queen Elizabeth in her speech at the opening of the new building of the National Library on 4th July 1956; and on this occasion, after she and the Duke of Edinburgh had made a tour of the building, I was entrusted with the task of showing Her Majesty a few of the more interesting volumes.

The acquisition of the Bute Collection was followed by an almost miraculous parallel some years later in the acquisition of a scarcely less valuable collection of dramatic material by the University Library of Edinburgh. In Sotheby's catalogue the librarians of both the National Library and of the University

Library noticed that a large collection of books, originally bequeathed by the late J. O. Halliwell-Phillipps to the Public Library in Penzance (of all places) was to be sold. The collection contained Shakespeariana of various kinds. The two librarians agreed that the university should send a representative to bid for it at the sale, with authority to go up to a sum of, I believe, twenty-five thousand pounds; and in the upshot he secured the whole for twenty-two thousand pounds. But before proceeding to the bidding, the librarian had, of course, to obtain authority from the University Court. Such a large sum could not be found within the limits of the regular grants received from the University Grants Committee. But as it happened the university had some years previously received a bequest from a private source which more than covered the upward limit for the bidding. And even so, what persuaded the Court to draw so largely on this nest-egg, for which they were not accountable to the State, was the fact that a body consisting of scholars interested in the Library and calling itself the Friends of the University Library (a title invented by Mr. Fifoot, the University Librarian, in imitation of the Friends of the National Libraries), was able to claim an interest in the Halliwell-Phillipps Collection by offering to contribute several hundred pounds. This gesture had the same effect upon the Court as the similar gesture by the Friends of the National Library had had upon the Pilgrim Trust— the effect, in a word, of conversion. Nothing less, in fact, would have persuaded the Court.

In the days when Shakespeare was reaping his greatest triumphs in London, with Falstaff on the one hand and *Hamlet* on the other, in Edinburgh the drama and the acting profession were struggling for their very existence against the General Assembly. And now Edinburgh has become the home of two of the finest collections of dramatic material, especially that bearing on Shakespeare himself, in the British Isles. And though the war ruined most of the plans for the study of Shakespeare which I had proposed in my Inaugural Lecture it was some consolation to know that I had been able to play a part in the acquisition for Scotland of this great body of Shakespeariana.

7

Balerno

To pass now to Balerno, which has been my home for the last thirty years. Since I could not disengage myself from King's College, London, until the beginning of 1936, I was correspondingly late in starting to look for a house in Edinburgh. We commenced house-hunting in Morningside in the early summer, and the many vacant houses we inspected horrified my wife, for she had been brought up in a country vicarage near Cambridge and our bungalow in Purley had been set in an expansive woodland garden on a hill. Here, however, there were small back gardens, area steps, long flights of stairs and so on. At last she turned to me wearily with, 'Isn't there a village near Edinburgh?' 'Well,' I said, 'I did find a house in a village eight miles away, with the impossible name of Balerno; and though the house has a fairly large garden with trees in it, I don't like its style and I believe it is built of very bad brick.' We went out to see it next day, and I have lived in Three Beeches, patched up and extended, ever since; while, looking back now, I can see that the move to Balerno was one of the best things I ever did in my life.

It is an ugly village, as many Scottish villages are, lying just across the Water of Leith, and communicating with Edinburgh, when I first knew it, by a village road branching off the main route to Lanark along which our house lay. Many of the villagers' houses were most insanitary; and indeed the slums of Balerno were worse than some of the slums of London of that date. Yet how genial—merry, indeed—were the dwellers in those slum houses; and how kindhearted and ready to help in any emergency! In fact, I soon found the myth south of the Border that the Scots are dour and mean was as far as possible from the truth. Both among the villagers and my Scottish friends in Edinburgh I found much hilarity and almost overwhelming generosity.

But Balerno was surrounded by larger houses, such as the one we were to live in, inhabited partly by businessmen and others who went in to Edinburgh by car or train every day, leaving their wives and families behind; it also contained a number of still larger houses, some of them built by rich Leith merchants.

The village had a school, a grocer's shop, an inn, a public house, a nearby smithy and three churches—a Presbyterian church, a Roman Catholic church, and a little Episcopalian church which we attended. This last claimed to be the oldest church in Balerno, being older in fact than the much larger Episcopalian church now in Colinton. Mrs. Jock Anderson, the good body from the village who first 'did' for us, when my wife remarked, 'I see, Mrs. Anderson, there are three churches in Balerno', tossed her Presbyterian head in the air and exclaimed, 'There's more Ca-a-a-a-atholics in Balerno than ye'ld like to think.' The same good lady might have come out of Shakespeare's plays, had he introduced the inhabitants of Balerno into *Macbeth*. For her humour had a sulphurous whiff that is truly Scottish. Speaking of a man she particularly disliked, she once remarked, 'I met him on the street and I gave him a *sinking* look.' And again, 'If I saw him in hell fire, I wouldn't spit on him!'

Very different was the speech of the delightful wife of the blacksmith, an elder of the local kirk, in a neighbouring village. When I called one day early in the year, just before taking flight for South Africa, and asked her to get her husband to fetch my mowing machine to put it in order for my return, remarking, 'We shall get back early in May when the grass is growing; for we are flying home—unless we crash', she looked at me and exclaimed, 'Ye'll no crash; and if ye do, ye're sure of yer wings.' The compliment, I felt, was to my wife, whom she adored, and not to the husband. But I felt myself uncomfortable about the shoulders for a day or two.

The smithy I speak of was at Currie where there is a charming little Presbyterian church standing back from the road which I (though what the Scots call a 'Pisky') often attended. For the minister, Dr. Stewart, was a very remarkable old man, full of humour and stories (neither of which he kept out of the pulpit), from whose sermons I learned a great deal about Scotland. When I went there I sat above him in a gallery, and further along at the same level sat Sir George Adam Smith (recently Vice-Chancellor of Aberdeen University), his wife Lilian and many of the rest of his family, including some of his grandchildren. His only son to survive the wars, Alick Buchanan Smith, since become Lord Balerno, had also come from Aberdeen to live not far from his parents. They had arrived a couple of years before we did and became great friends of ours. Sir George's most famous book, *The Geography of the Holy Land*, was actually used by Allenby when he conquered Palestine, there being no other book on the subject so topographically precise, its author having tramped all over the country for his material. And I possess a walking-stick cut from a thornbush on these tramps, given me by his widow when he died.

Lady Adam Smith survived her husband by many years, but she continued to drive her own car until her son told her she was becoming a danger to the public. When, therefore, she went to the Maitlands' musical evenings in Heriot Row I would take her there in my car. One night, returning about 11.30 p.m., I suppose, I drove her home and put her down at her front door; as I turned, the car stopped. I looked at the register; not a drop of petrol in the tank. And I had been driving a very old lady up Slateford Hill at close on midnight. I left the car and walked home, of course. And when she got up in the morning, she found to her amazement an empty car standing at the front door, and no Professor Dover Wilson. Fled was that vision; did she wake or dream? The Adam Smith family suffered as many losses by war or otherwise as any I have known, yet no family is more cheerful and even full of fun. And none of them bore bereavement more courageously than Lady Adam Smith herself, two of whose sons had fallen in the First World War. And on one occasion during the Second World War, when she was grieving for a beloved daughter whose husband had died, I sent her, thinking it might help her, a copy of my British Academy obituary of Alfred Pollard, who had so bravely endured the loss of two sons in 1914 and 1915. The offprint contained a passage touching upon his interest in Matthew Arnold's poetry. She replied with a long letter stating that while she was very fond of much of Arnold, it was Wordsworth above all which was nearest her heart. And the letter concluded by giving an example of what he meant to her. 'When I go to the village,' she wrote, 'with my basket to get my rations and no kind friend picks me up on the way home, I find time to say over to myself the "Ode on Intimations of Immortality". I come to "Sing, happy birds" when I reach my own gate, and to "Thoughts that lie too deep for tears" at my front door.' And then the letter broke off, '—don't think me mad; only an old woman with a basket.'

The year 1950 saw the centenary of Wordsworth's death, celebrated by a great gathering at Grasmere. There were many tributes, some of them long essays read aloud to us. Not expecting to be called upon, I had come with nothing. But Helen Darbishire, who had organized the whole conference, catching sight of me at the back of the room, called me on to the platform. And when there I repeated, from memory, the letter I have just quoted; and many of my audience afterwards assured me that it was one of the truly Wordsworthian touches of the conference —'Only an old woman with a basket'.

Towards the end of her days, Lady Adam Smith had to take to bed; but when she wanted to chat she would send me a message. On the last occasion, I remember arriving to find a notice pinned to her front door, 'Professor Dover Wilson. No one at home; walk upstairs, second door on the right.' And there I found her, sitting up in bed with a little list of things she wanted to talk about, while I too had brought a list on my part. And so we went on for about an hour, until I could see she looked a bit tired. It was my farewell; for ten days later the family did me the great honour of allowing me to hold one of the cords that lowered her into the grave.

When war broke out in 1939, Balerno, of course, had to have its Home Guard; and my experiences as a humble member thereof deserve a paragraph or two. Like Home Guards elsewhere, we had no rifles to start with, nor do I remember that any of Lord Croft's famous pikes found their way to us. But we soon got our organization going. From the beginning one of our duties was that soon after midnight small parties of us would march off up the road towards the hills, and at about three in the morning change guard at a hut just above Marchbank Hotel on the edge of the moor with a squad already assembled returning from above Bavelaw Castle. What the squad was supposed to do when it got up on the hill was never very clear, except I believe that if we noticed anything that might be a German descended or descending from the skies, we were to ring up the police from the castle. In point of fact, before the end of the war an unhappy young German lad crashed on Black Hill close to where we kept guard, and bits of his body were distributed over the hillside. Nevertheless, neither Edinburgh nor Balerno was really troubled by any bombing. But these night watches gave those who took part in them a tremendous sense of importance and responsibility. And many of the gamekeepers and gardeners and mill-hands who filled our ranks were clearly anxious that the Jerries should come, so as to finish the job off quickly.

When the rifles arrived, shooting practice of course was the order of the day, one of the several quarries on the moor not far from my house being chosen as the most suitable shooting-gallery. And the rifles needed a headquarters where they could be stored, cleaned, etc. An old, partially-disused village club was taken over for the purpose; and I made it my business to render it more comfortable and hospitable for the guardsmen when off duty by collecting funds for its furnishing and maintenance. I marked down as a victim the owner of one of the larger houses in Balerno, called Ravelrig, only a few doors from where I live; and ringing him up I told him that the Home Guard was defending him and his house, that I wanted a fiver from him to add to their comfort and asked when I could call. 'If you come in,' he said, 'at about a quarter past seven, you'll be certain to find me, as I shall just be sitting down to dinner.' I did so; and there he was, in full evening dress, tails and white waistcoat and everything, dining by himself alone in the house. Ravelrig is now a Dr. Barnardo's Home.

I also managed to do a little recruiting. The manager of the local paper mill was a neighbour of mine, and I persuaded him not only to join but to get a number of the mill-hands to join too. Unhappily for me, I fell sick after about a year from the beginning of the war, and my local doctor, persuading himself that it was due to my getting thoroughly chilled as I listened to the long lectures from our captain in the school playground, instructed me to find an indoor job. His diagnosis was quite incorrect, as I discovered later on when I had to undergo a major operation; but I secured my indoor job as corporal to the quartermaster who was, when in civil life, the village postmaster. The job consisted of sweeping out the headquarters on Sunday mornings, clearing out the grate and lighting the fire in the main room, and getting the beer ready for the men when they returned from their route march at midday. These were the corporal's duties; but the quartermaster who supervised condescended to share a bottle of beer with him when the task was over.

So much for Sunday mornings. On Wednesday evenings I became a tailor's assistant; for then the young recruits who had just come of age arrived to be fitted for their uniforms. Finally there was the business of keeping the rifles clean. All this I found very pleasant, for my quartermaster was a matey fellow, and I have always been a handy man. But if, as sometimes happened, a brass hat appeared to inspect us, the quartermaster would assume a stern aspect and the corporal had to stir his stumps under a rain of brisk commands, 'Look sharp, Professor; come along!'

I had a rich reward for 'serving my country' at this time. For it brought me into touch with nearly all the men in the village. And as long as I had sufficient sight to recognize people as I walked about the roads or rode in the bus, many were the greetings I exchanged. But the greatest reward came to me only lately. One of the men I became most familiar with was Harry Rankine, whose work in life, of recent years at any rate, had been mowing the grass at the bowling green—a very important task, as bowling is a great sport with the men of Balerno. (Not long ago they won the Scottish Cup and bore it in triumph home from Glasgow, filling it I don't know how many times with whisky before the club went to bed.)

For many years my gardener had been an old man called John Love, originally a farm labourer, who had become a great friend of mine; though not an expert he did all I wanted very well indeed. But as it happened, in the spring of 1964, just before starting out to celebrate Shakespeare's four-hundredth birthday at Stratford, I found him digging in the garden in a manner which was obviously causing him pain. 'What's wrong, Mr. Love?' I said.

'Ah'm gawn lame.'

'What,' I said. 'Going lame! Have you seen the doctor?'

'Doctor!' he said scornfully.

'Don't you ever see the doctor?'

'Na-a-a-a.'

'Well, what do you do then,' I asked, 'for sickness?' To which he replied, 'Whusky for men; and twar [tar] for sheep.' But, alas, what was wrong was a slight stroke; and he had to submit to the doctor and leave my service. There was sorrow on both sides; but disaster threatened for the garden, with the potatoes and all the seeds still to be put in. I knew all the roadmen in the district, and as I walked round cajoled one after the other; but, friendly as they were, no one was prepared to leave the lucrative service of the Midlothian County Council.

And then, just as I was in despair, Harry Rankine came round. He was sixty-five, and had earned his release from mowing the bowling green. 'D'ye want a gardener, Professor?' he said to me. 'Harry!' I exclaimed, almost throwing my arms round his neck; 'will you be *my* gardener?' 'I'ld love to be yer gardener.' And so he is: one of the friendliest and most serviceable kind. Had I not done well to serve my country in the war?

I must not omit to mention that one of the best shots with the ·22 rifle was not a member of our Home Guard but a private member receiving instruction in shooting from a guardsman of Currie—so expert a markswoman that she is said to have hit the bull's-eye every time. I refer to my own wife who made up her mind that if the Jerries came anywhere near her home they should pay for it dearly—the more so that she had her little daughter, Carol, to protect.

Balerno

I am not continuing the Dover Road beyond my eightieth year. Of the friends and neighbours, all of whom, especially in the immediate neighbourhood of Three Beeches, who have been most kind and ever ready to sympathize in times both of family happiness and affliction, I will say no more here. But I cannot close what I have to say about my home without an affectionate bow to Mrs. Lambert who lives with her husband and her father, Mr. Melrose, in Balerno village. For twelve years she has come up from the village to serve me and my wife for three or four half-days a week, and on many other occasions also, not only on washing days but for much cooking at mealtimes, and always with the utmost cheerfulness and loyalty of service. She knows the house better than any of its inmates, so that if I can't find anything I have only to ring her up and ask where it is. Moreover, never have I seen her downcast or depressed at any mishap. And when I asked her how long she had been with me, it was like her to reply, 'Twelve years of happy memories!'

8

How I came to edit Shakespeare

When the Cambridge University Press offered me the joint editorship of the *New Cambridge Shakespeare* in June 1919, it took me quite by surprise; yet, looking back, it is not difficult to see what led up to it. The first step was the elaborate essay on John Lyly which was awarded the University Harness Prize for 1904 and appeared as a small book in 1905. A study of Lyly, one of the more important of Shakespeare's predecessors, involved as well a study of the great dramatist himself, especially in the comedies. I had also to consider Lyly as a novelist, his place in the history of Elizabethan fiction, and the character and significance of the style of *Euphues*. But Lyly was a pamphleteer too, and he played an obscure part in the Marprelate controversy as a writer of anti-Martinist tracts.

In the Preface to my little book I acknowledged my deep indebtedness to A. W. Ward, the Master of Peterhouse. (I still retain memories of calls upon him at the Lodge and watching him standing, as was his custom, to write letters at a large desk inclined at an angle from the wall.) It is evident that one result of my Lyly was a request from the *Cambridge History of English Literature*, edited by Ward and Waller, that I should contribute two articles to that serial history—one on Martin Marprelate (Vol. III, 1909) and the other, 'The Puritan Attack upon the Stage' (Vol. VI, 1910). The first of these led directly to my acquaintance with the scholar, Alfred Pollard, and indirectly later on to my edition of Shakespeare's plays.

The Martin Marprelate tracts, as their name suggests, were an attempt to attack Episcopacy by ridiculing the bishops and so discredit the Elizabethan settlement of Church discipline. Their authorship has never been decided—though I attempted to fasten it upon Sir Roger Williams in articles in *The Library* (edited by

Pollard) in 1911. But apart from that mystery and the ecclesiastical controversy they took part in, the tracts give rise to a number of bibliographical problems connected with their publication, since they were printed in a secret press which moved about the country and which the Archbishop's pursuivants did their best to track down. The printers were forced to resort to different types, partly because cases of type are not easy to carry on horseback. It was not long before I was up to the eyes in a most devious piece of detective work, attempting to identify types and to discover if possible where they came from (some, for example, certainly came from the Low Countries). In short, I was indulging in amateur bibliography, a game I had first learned to play years earlier in the Cambridge University Library under the direction of Charles Sayle, who taught me the difference between a folio and a quarto, the meaning of printers' signatures[1] and various other elementary facts necessary to bibliographical studies.

I was able to identify one of the Marprelate printers from his peculiar method of signatures; he was a man called Waldegrave who saved his skin from the Archbishop by flying to Scotland, where he afterwards became Printer to King James VI. Pollard took an interest in my work from the beginning, made me join the Bibliographical Society in 1906, and in October 1907 published the first of my articles on the Marprelate tracts in *The Library*. Meanwhile, as a sidelight on Waldegrave, I began preparing a detailed study of a Dutch printer called Schilders, on whom I later (in 1911) read a paper before the Society, which was printed with an elaborate list of books which I attributed to Schilders's press. All this involved research work at the British Museum and many meetings afterwards with Pollard at an ABC near by, where he generally had lunch and where I might also meet other friends—McKerrow, who worked at the publisher's office of Sidgwick and Jackson close to the Museum, and occasionally W. W. Greg, when he happened to be up in town. Most of this took place during the summers of 1907 and 1908;

---

[1] i.e. the letters or figures which are printed at the foot of the first page of each sheet so as to facilitate the sheets being stitched or bound in the correct order.

the University of Helsingfors, at which I was by this time *Lektor*, being closed in the summer months. And it meant, of course, much talk about bibliography.

I must turn now, however, to speak of the other studies in Elizabethan Puritanism that I had been pursuing at the Museum side by side with my work on Marprelate, and only slightly and indirectly concerned with bibliography. These were studies for the writing of the article already referred to, on the Puritan attack upon the stage. This formed a sort of sequel to the essay on Lyly, and gave rise to notes or articles on Lodge, Lyly and Munday as pamphleteers, printed in *The Modern Language Review* by the English Editor, G. C. Moore Smith of Sheffield, who was also often present at our summer luncheon parties. And these articles led to a close study of that masterpiece of editing, McKerrow's *Works of Thomas Nashe* in five volumes (1905–1910). It led too to my earliest contribution to Shakespearian scholarship, the book of Elizabethan prose, one of the *Cambridge Anthologies of English Literature* prepared for the students at Goldsmiths' College. It was arranged as a kind of background to Shakespeare and later entitled *Life in Shakespeare's England*. I managed to find most of the material required in volumes I could borrow from that admirable institution essential to scholarship, the London Library; I got my wife to copy out the passages, which I then arranged to illustrate the various aspects of Elizabethan life which might themselves throw light upon the different stages of Shakespeare's career. I then posted the whole thing off to A. R. Waller, then Secretary of the Cambridge University Press, asking whether he thought the Syndics would like to publish it.

He sent me a rather off-hand letter back and said he would give me fifty pounds for it. I was delighted, having never earned fifty pounds as an author before; and I went dancing into the kitchen, Waller's letter in hand, crying, 'Look! We've got fifty pounds for our book!'

'Fifty pounds,' my wife said, 'isn't there a royalty?'

'Don't be absurd,' I replied. 'I don't get fifty pounds offered me every day.' To which she retorted, 'You go back and tell that man you'll take forty pounds down and ten per cent after the sale of five thousand copies.' I obeyed. Waller accepted the offer pityingly. 'Poor young fellow,' he seemed almost to say, 'if you want to throw ten pounds into the sea, I won't stop you.' He thought differently when a second edition was called for in a couple of years. It was then reprinted half a dozen times before I went to Scotland in 1936, and it joined the Pelicans in 1944. It became in fact one of my most popular books.

The first edition was dated 1911, and next year I had left London to be an H.M.I. in Leeds. I was almost cut off from the British Museum. The material I had been collecting, bibliographical and otherwise, for a book I was projecting on the Marprelate tracts was laid in a drawer, never to be looked at again (though still there). And the dream I had cherished of devoting the rest of my life to writing a first-class history of Puritanism in England, from 1588 to the Hampton Court Conference, was put aside. The First World War, when it came, brought more immediate and more terrible issues to occupy the mind. I had two brothers at the Front. Pollard lost both his sons; a whole generation of young Englishmen was being trodden into the mud of Flanders.

As the war dragged on, I had nothing, as an unhappy official in a 'reserved occupation', but routine duties to think about, and could do little to keep at bay the growing anxiety for family and friends; when suddenly—after a fashion that William James might have recorded in his *Varieties of Religious Experience*—I was converted. Converted—to Shakespeare! That may seem a strong way of putting it; but it will not, I think, seem absurd if, after asking readers who know it already to forgive the repetition, I draw upon an account I gave of the experience in an epistle to W. W. Greg, in which I dedicated *What Happens in Hamlet* to him, published about twenty years later.

The passage begins by describing a railway journey late on a Saturday evening some time in November 1917. Tired out after six days' knocking about Yorkshire, I began to open an accumulated post and found among it a copy of *The Modern Language Review* for October, containing a long article by Greg entitled 'Hamlet's Hallucination'. In this, turning aside for a spell from bibliography, he launched out into an essay on dramatic criticism. Arguing from the fact that the action of the players' dumbshow is repeated in the Gonzago play that immediately follows, Greg maintained that the King did not recognize his own crime, and that therefore the story told by the Ghost was a mere figment of Hamlet's imagination.

Such was his fundamental point, which I later attempted to meet by arguing in my turn that the King either did not see the dumbshow or was not watching it when it appeared. This contention I supported by a series of perhaps over-subtle assumptions.

I must have read the article half a dozen times before reaching the station I was bound for; and when I passed a pillar-box on the platform I stuffed in a postcard to the editor of *The Modern Language Review* bearing these words, 'Greg's article devilish ingenious but damnably wrong; will you accept a rejoinder?'

Though I was very far from realizing it at the time, in reading Greg's article and deciding that I could or would prove it entirely wrong, I had really embarked on being an editor of Shakespeare. My mind was going back to when a dozen years or so before I had made a close study of *Hamlet* as a stage play, when in 1912 I had undertaken the production of the play with a company of young students at Goldsmiths' College. It was only at this point that I began to draw upon my previous experience of *Hamlet* as an example of dramatic art, then (as the psychologists would say) below the threshold of consciousness. I am even doubtful whether I had ever perceived its full significance before, as I try now to recall how it all happened. Such a production was an ideal way of studying *Hamlet*. That the performances were so remarkably successful was because every line had been wrestled with to establish the meaning Shakespeare intended and every dramatic situation reconstructed in imagination as if in action on an Elizabethan stage. In a word, I had set myself to discover what happens or should happen in *Hamlet* in the theatre. I had not then thought out at Goldsmiths' the dramatic principles involved. But they soon took shape once I began translating my memories of the production into writing.

Greg attempted a reply in *The Modern Language Review* to my 'rejoinder' to his article. But long before that my ideas had out-run the limits of the original dispute. Moreover, I soon discovered that to reply to Greg was only the beginning of things. His article raised problems which had never before been faced by critics of *Hamlet*, and these in turn led on to other problems of which he seemed unconscious.

An important issue here, one that struck at the heart of Greg's theory, was the question of Elizabethan spiritualism, the current beliefs about ghosts or spirits that walk by night, a knowledge of which forms one of the main keys to the understanding of *Hamlet*. This, Greg ought to have realized since it had been well brought out by F. W. Moorman[1] in an important article on 'Shakespeare's Ghosts' in *The Modern Language Review* (Vol. I, 1906), upon which I drew in a paper on the subject read before the Shakespeare Association shortly after Greg's article. And ten years later I followed this up by getting the Shakespeare Association to publish an edition of Lavater's *Of Ghostes and Spirites walking by nyght* (1572), with an introduction by me and an appendix by Miss May Yardley, a student of mine, entitled 'The Catholic Position in Ghost Controversy of the 16th Century, with Special Reference to Pierre Le Loyer's *IIII Livres des Spectres* (1586)'.

Side by side, however, with the dramatic studies just referred to, I turned my bibliographical knowledge to an investigation of the text of the play; for it soon became obvious that the textual criticism of *Hamlet* was as unsatisfactory as the aesthetic, and that until the textual foundations were properly laid, there could be no security for dramatic interpretation. Here too I had been favoured by fortune. For just before Greg's article, 'Hamlet's Hallucination', set my feet on the road to Elsinore, epoch-making books by A. W. Pollard, Edward Maunde Thompson and Percy Simpson on the bibliography, handwriting and punctuation of Shakespearian texts had appeared; while Greg himself began at once to check and supplement those bibliographical findings by

[1] F. W. Moorman, father of the present Bishop of Ripon, was Professor of English Language at Leeds University; I found him there in 1912 and became a close friend of him and his family.

criticism and studies of his own. Thus I found new instruments of the utmost value to my hand when I began work on the text of Shakespeare.

As a disciple of Pollard's, and sharing his beliefs that many of the 'good' quarto and folio texts were printed direct from Shakespeare's manuscripts, I hoped to discover something about the way Shakespeare wrote and spelled by studying the aberrations of the compositors who had set up those manuscripts in type. Accordingly I made lists from the 'good' quartos[1] of the obvious misprints (i.e. misprints which have been corrected in all modern editions), and of the 'abnormal' spellings. I began with the 'good' quartos, because they were the texts Pollard suggested in *Shakespeare's Folios and Quartos* (1909) as likely to be closer to the dramatist's drafts.

By 'abnormal' spellings, I meant spellings that I thought a reputable compositor of the time would not have wittingly introduced into the text itself. Many compositors' spellings which now seem to us archaic were of course then quite normal. Yet even those spellings were on the whole far more modern than those of the average author with whose manuscripts they had to cope. And far more consistent, too, since manuscript spellings at that time differed not only from author to author but often from page to page, even from line to line in the same author. In short, it was a blessed age when every gentleman spelled as he liked. Yet this wide variety of usage by authors gave the printers one of their chief problems, for to set up a manuscript in type, letter by letter, would have been not only tedious but costly, since time was money and speed (then as now) an important element in compositorial skill. Speed meant the compositor carrying a number of words at a time in his head as he turned from the 'copy' to set up the type in his 'stick'. And the head-carrying process almost inevitably meant translating

---

[1] As then understood, these were: *Titus Andronicus* (1594), *Richard II* (1597), *Richard III* (1597), *Love's Labour's Lost* (1598), 1 *Henry IV* (1598), *Romeo and Juliet* (1599), *The Merchant of Venice* (1600), *Much Ado About Nothing* (1600), 2 *Henry IV* (1600), *A Midsummer Night's Dream* (1600), *Hamlet* (1604–5), *Lear* (1608), *Troilus and Cressida* (1609), and *Othello* (1622).

the spellings of the copy into his own spelling or the spelling he had learnt from his master when a 'prentice.

Why then is it that abnormal spellings frequently crop up in the quartos, so that my list when completed numbered many hundreds of examples? The answer is that they came, a large proportion of them, from the manuscript. They are words which caught and arrested the compositor's eye. An unskilful compositor (i.e. one not yet able to carry more than one or two words at a time in his head) will, of course, keep his eye on his 'copy' and so introduce a number of his author's spellings into print. Even an accomplished craftsman will at times let copy-spellings through—when he is tired, when the light is bad (as it often was in Elizabethan printing-houses) or when a difficult or unusual word confronts him which has to be spelt out. In this connection, it is important to notice that the commoner the word, the less likely was it to be given an abnormal copy-spelling in print, since (other things being equal) common words are the easiest for a compositor's eye to pick up. Such is the theory of the business, which I believe I was the first to work out; and Greg confirmed it by reproducing one of the few specimens of sixteenth-century printer's copy side by side with what the printer made of it in print—namely the manuscript of part of Sir John Harington's translation of Ariosto's *Orlando Furioso*.[1]

I got busy with my lists towards the end of 1917 and they were ready early in 1918, so that I could put them to use, which I did first of all, naturally, on the text of *Hamlet*; and I drafted an article on 'Spellings and Misprints in the Second Quarto of *Hamlet*'. After submission to Greg, and a few alterations, it was published in *Essays and Studies by Members of the English Association*, edited by E. K. Chambers, 1924. Meanwhile, however, I had found an unexpected application for these lists; by a coincidence which seemed almost providential, it was at this point, in September 1916, that Sir Edward Maunde Thompson discovered in *The Booke of Sir Thomas More* in the British Museum three pages of manuscript in what he was convinced were Shakespeare's own

---

[1] *The Library* (4th ser.) IV, 102–18. September 1923.

handwriting and spelling. He published his findings in his book, *Shakespeare's Handwriting*.

I cannot, to my annoyance, remember at this date when it was that I first began to study *Shakespeare's Handwriting*. Perhaps not at once, as I was an exceedingly busy government official in 1916 and 1917, the middle of the First World War. But it was some time before 1918; and there followed almost immediately a series of letters between Maunde Thompson and myself which was for me in the nature of a 'correspondence course' with the greatest English palaeographer as instructor and the 'secretary hand' as the subject of instruction. For Maunde Thompson, by his study of the six extant signatures, had demonstrated that Shakespeare wrote the then rather old-fashioned 'secretary' hand. The older man took an ardent believer to his heart, made me write my letters to him in 'secretary', which he diligently corrected and wrote letters (beginning 'Dear Shakespeare') in reply, also in 'secretary'. Thus he gave me a working acquaintance with the hand that 'went together' with the mind which I was to spend my leisure hours for the rest of my life trying to follow through the plays—little as I dreamed of such a sequel at that time. It was a gift beyond price, for which I can never express gratitude enough. And he was a wonderful and formidable old man, irascible and impatient of contradiction or criticism but intensely human and full of fun; and if the fun was a little heavy at times, he wore

> 'all his weight
> Of learning lightly like a flower.'

Happily I was privileged to repay the debt in a small measure and while he was still alive.

For with my lists of 'good' quarto spellings and misprints I felt, already in 1918, that I had evidence in my hand which might corroborate or conflict with Maunde Thompson's claims for the Three Pages. Pollard now marshalled a team in support of it, and published a little book, *Shakespeare's Hand in the Play of Sir Thomas More* (1923), with articles by himself, Greg (now a supporter), Maunde Thompson (an elaboration of his previous argument) and a remarkable contribution by R. W. Chambers

with the title 'The Expression of Ideas—particularly Political Ideas—in the Three Pages and in Shakespeare' which was almost enough by itself to convert the doubters. To this book I contributed a chapter, 'Bibliographical Links between the Three Pages and the Good Quartos'. For no sooner did I hold Maunde Thompson's book in my hands than I turned to his transcript of the Three Pages to see how far their spellings tallied with those I culled from the quartos. To my delight, they fitted in like pieces of a jig-saw puzzle. Modern or normal spellings of the Three Pages were not contradicted by abnormal spellings in the quartos; spellings of the Three Pages which are common in sixteenth-century manuscripts but rare in print could all be paralleled in the quartos either directly or by implication through misprints; and finally all the abnormal or old-fashioned spellings in the Three Pages, some of them very old-fashioned or unusual, had also their parallels in the quartos.

One of these, the very odd spelling 'scilens' for 'silence', made quite a little stir among scholars who had in vain searched for a parallel to it in printed books of the period. 'Silence', being quite a common word, had by then acquired its modern spelling in all the London printing houses. Yet it is spelt 'scilens' on the second of the Three Pages (its only occurrence in them) and after the same peculiar fashion eighteen times, either in full or abridged, in the first Quarto of 2 *Henry IV*. The simple reason is that, in that play, 'Scilens' is the name of a character, though a compositor tends to normalize spelling, a wise one leaves names alone; and hair-raising as the notion may be, it looks as if 'scilens' was Shakespeare's spelling, or at least one of his spellings.

And the evidence of spelling was borne out by that of misprints. My list of these consisted of a large and heterogeneous assortment, many of which may, of course, be due to other causes than compositorial misreading. Yet the prevalence of specific types of misprint, in a dozen or more quarto texts produced by some seven or eight printing-houses over a period of some fifteen years, can be safely attributed to the one common factor behind them all (sometimes at more than one remove)—the pen of William Shakespeare. These common types fall into five classes

according to their apparent derivation from a confusion between certain letters in the 'secretary' handwriting.

For example, in that hand the letters *e* and *d* have the same formation and differ in size only. In a second type of misprint, *a* is sometimes confused with *u* or with *or*, there being two forms of the letter *a*, one the modern form (in which case, as Shakespeare sometimes wrote it, the final downstroke was detached so as to resemble *or*), the other often resembling a modern *u* introduced by a flourish above the line. The third type of misprint is one that may occur in the handwriting of any period—namely when minim letters (i.e. short-stroke letters such as *m*, *n*, *u*, *i*, *c*, and even badly-formed *w*, and one type of the 'secretary' *r* which is not unlike a *w*), are written in combination and the writer neglects to count his strokes. Classes four and five comprise *e* and *o*, and also *f* and initial or medial *s*.

Now an examination of the Three Pages showed that the hand which wrote them was prone to just the sort of pen-slips as would naturally give rise to these five common misprints. The two hands, I felt sure, were the same. But how was I to convince others, unfamiliar with 'secretary' script? Or how could I prove that a compositor faced with the Three Pages would have stumbled in the same way and as frequently as his brethren who set up the quartos? I could not prove it; but I was able to point to a rather persuasive and not unamusing piece of circumstantial evidence in its favour. Once again Greg came to my aid, though without meaning to this time. He and Maunde Thompson had recently and independently transcribed the Three Pages. And in these transcripts their readings of three words differed, while in that of a fourth Greg's reading, as he later admitted, was wrong. It so happened that these four readings illustrated four out of the five classes of misprint just described. That is to say, modern palaeographers with magnifying glasses had fallen into four of the five traps which most commonly led to the undoing of the compositors of the quartos. I could not have hoped for better evidence. Incidentally, in my opinion it provides an answer to Greg's criticism, put forward in his review of my edition of *The Tempest* (*Modern Language Review*, April 1922), that while

resemblances between letters or groups of letters in the 'secretary' hand may justify an emendation, one cannot argue that such
resemblances need be reciprocal—a criticism which, following
him, is often advanced by other critics—inasmuch as Greg's and
Maunde Thompson's readings had themselves been examples of
such reciprocal resemblances.

But I must apologize for spending this much time over these
spellings and misprints. My excuse is their relevance to the main
theme, namely a modern editor's attitude towards the text of
Shakespeare. For in dealing with any given passage, what he
needs above all things is some knowledge of how Shakespeare is
likely to have, or might have spelt or written the words, and
some knowledge of how those words are likely to have been or
might have been misread and/or misprinted. And in point of
fact, the lists of spellings and misprints referred to have proved
a constant help with individual cruxes during forty years of
editing.

We shall probably never be able to prove that Shakespeare
wrote the Three Pages in *Sir Thomas More*. But a case which, in
the words of Greg, rests on 'the convergence of a number of
independent lines of argument—palaeographical, orthographic,
linguistic, stylistic, psychological—and not on any one alone',
can never be disproved and has won acceptance from an ever-
widening circle of scholars. Indeed, two editors have actually
included it in *The Complete Works*. We may say, then, that it has
now been canonized. Moreover the primary value, for editors,
of Maunde Thompson's work is not so much his claim that
Shakespeare wrote the Three Pages as his demonstration, originally in the first volume of *Shakespeare's England* (pp. 299–309),
that Shakespeare wrote the 'secretary' hand, with a number of
small peculiarities individual to himself.

My work on the 'good' quartos just mentioned was based on
Pollard's *Shakespeare Folios and Quartos* in which he claimed that
the 'good' quartos were probably for the most part printed from
Shakespeare's drafts and were to be distinguished from those
'stolne and surreptitious copies' which the editors of the First
Folio spoke of in their introductory Letter to the Readers. The

latter which Pollard identified with the four 'bad' quartos, *Romeo and Juliet* (1597), *Henry V* (1600), *The Merry Wives of Windsor* (1602), and *Hamlet* (1603).

In 1918, applying my bibliographical knowledge to the bad quarto of *Hamlet*, I was led with Pollard's approval to an incorrect hypothesis—as to the relation between it and the good quarto. At this period two theories of bad quartos had been advanced. One, that they were corrupt versions of earlier drafts by Shakespeare—a theory advocated by Furnivall (see his Introduction to *Hamlet*, 1604). Pollard knew Furnivall, who had been responsible for the production of the Griggs-Praetorius facsimiles of the quartos. The other theory was that the bad quartos were merely versions of the good texts imperfectly memorized and reported by actors who had played in them. The technical term 'reported texts' was subsequently applied to these bad quartos. This theory, which to the best of my belief I was not aware of when I worked with Pollard on the bad quarto of *Hamlet* for *The Library*—nor, I think, did he know of it—had been put forward by Halliwell-Phillipps who was then lying under certain suspicions as a collector of books. And my attention was not drawn to it until 1945.[1]

Unfortunately Pollard and I were following Furnivall's theory, which was a false trail, and we applied it first to the bad quarto of *Hamlet* in two articles entitled 'The Copy for *Hamlet* 1603' and 'The *Hamlet* Transcript 1593', published in separate numbers of *The Library* for 1918. This theory had originally strong support in my eyes in the fact (which was the chief point in the earlier of the two articles just mentioned) that certain passages of dialogue in the first act of *Hamlet* seemed identical in spelling and even in punctuation in both the 1603 and 1604 texts. This seemed to imply that the 1604 *Hamlet* was, at any rate in part, a revision of the 1603 text. It was some years later that I was first made aware in an article by Miss Greta Hjort that these coincidences could be explained in quite another fashion—namely that the compositor or compositors of the good quarto actually

[1] In F. P. Wilson's article, 'Shakespeare and the New Bibliography', in *Studies in Retrospect*, the 1945 volume of the Bibliographical Society.

made use of some pages of the bad quarto as copy, printers being under standing temptation to turn to any piece of printed copy they thought suitable in preference to an author's manuscript, often in difficult handwriting.

About the same time as these articles on the bad quarto of *Hamlet* in *The Library*, Pollard and I submitted a joint paper at a meeting of the Bibliographical Society on 16th December 1918, in the course of which we quoted the following passage from the beginning of Act 5 of *A Midsummer Night's Dream* (from the quarto of 1600).

Hip.   Tis strange, My theseus, that these louers speak of.
The.   More straunge then true. I neuer may beleeue
        These antique fables, nor these Fairy toyes.
        Louers, and mad men haue such seething braines,
        Such shaping phantasies, that apprehend / more,
        Then coole reason euer comprehends. / The lunatick
        The louer, and the Poet / are of imagination all compact. /
        One sees more deuils, then vast hell can holde:
        That is the mad man. The louer, all as frantick,
        Sees Helens beauty in a brow of AEgypt.
        The Poets eye, in a fine frenzy, rolling, / doth glance
        From heauen to earth, from earth to heauen. / And as
        Imagination bodies forth / the formes of things
        Vnknowne: the Poets penne / turnes them to shapes,
        And giues to ayery nothing, / a locall habitation,
        And a name. / Such trickes hath strong imagination,
        That if it would but apprehend some ioy,
        It comprehends some bringer of that ioy.
        Or in the night, imagining some feare,
        How easie is a bush suppos'd a Beare?

I have printed these twenty lines with diagonals showing the ends of the lines of verse, and in two types: the italicized lines consisting of verse in which the lining has gone wrong, while the lines in roman type are in regular verse.

This illustration afforded a conspicuous example of Shakespeare apparently revising a playhouse manuscript (his own or possibly that of an earlier dramatist). The scene, at Theseus's court, opens with eighty lines of irregularly divided verse—an irregularity which was clearly not due to the incompetence of the compositor. For why (in the extract quoted above, for example) should he go wrong in the verse-lining of the two passages which I have printed in italics, while in those which I have printed in roman type the verse is regularly divided? As this verse runs straight on in sense and metre, it seems obvious that the irregularly divided passages were additions, probably in the margin, which afforded insufficient room for verse to be properly arranged. The compositor, left without any clue, attempted to insert them into the text. Moreover, these additions are clearly Shakespeare's since they supply much of the poetry and some of the fun to the original scene. It was a discovery of prime importance; and I well remember the moment when I stumbled upon what Pollard called 'this nugget'; for we were sitting side by side on the sand at Hunstanton when I passed my copy of the Furnivall facsimile across for him to share in the find. The inference we drew has never been seriously questioned, though even such irregularities in the good quarto must be considered on their merits when they occur. It certainly does not apply to irregularities of lineation in the folio texts, most of which we know were due to Jaggard's compositors.

Shortly after this Pollard and I contributed a series of articles to *The Times Literary Supplement* during 1919 under the general title of 'The Stolne and Surreptitious Texts', attempting to explain the origin of all Shakespeare's bad quartos as springing from early drafts. These articles created a considerable stir among Shakespearian critics, and they prompted Greg to undertake a far more exhaustive enquiry into the nature of non-Shakespearian bad quartos in his *Two Elizabethan Stage Abridgements: The Battle of Alcazar and Orlando Furioso* (1929). This he published as a special volume of the Malone Society reprints, dedicated to Pollard and myself, followed by a quotation from *Chu Chin Chow*, 'Work can only be done one way'.

And as a matter of fact, in his edition of the bad quarto of *The Merry Wives of Windsor* 1602, he had made a contribution to the problem by demonstrating that this pirated text owed a good deal if not everything to the actor who played 'Mine Host' in Shakespeare's final version. Greg's *Alcazar* volume led us to suspect that there was something unsound in our theory. But it was not until Peter Alexander's *Shakespeare's Henry VI and Richard III* was published in 1929, with a long introduction by Pollard, that he himself adopted the idea that bad quartos were reported texts.

Our previous explanation of the bad quartos was as I say a false trail, and Pollard's change of mind left me stranded. Later, in my volumes of the New Shakespeare, I made use (unwisely, as I see now) of Furnivall's theory in those descriptions of the text which we came to call the 'Notes on the Copy'. Nor did I lightly recant; and I still believe that there may be older versions by Shakespeare himself behind some of the folio and quarto texts.

For example, it is, I think, certain now that the folio *Twelfth Night* is a revised text, since the 'Lady of the Strachy' jest concerns 'a reference to actual persons and events subsequent to 1616'.

As for the bad quarto of *Hamlet* 1603, by the time I came to give my Sandars Lectures at Cambridge in 1932 (published in 1934 as *The Manuscript of Shakespeare's 'Hamlet'*)[1] I had already come round to the theory that it was a reported text. I could lay aside detailed consideration of the theory for some later stage, though I was already prepared to use it as a 'control in our investigation of the other versions'. And when I came to Edinburgh and found in my class a brilliant student, G. I. Duthie, who showed a special interest in textual studies, I handed over the question of bad quartos to him; and in 1941 he published a volume in the Shakespeare Problems series entitled *The Bad Quarto of Hamlet* of which the introduction deals in general terms with the other bad quartos.

To return to the question of the 'Notes on the Copy' in the New Shakespeare, these were necessary in a new and confessedly provisional edition, and were intended for the 'judicious' readers —namely Pollard, Greg, McKerrow and any who were following

[1] Vol. I, p. 20.

the adventure with intelligent understanding of the issues involved. Their primary purpose was to explain the nature of the manuscript (or possibly printed text) which the printers used; and where two or three texts were involved, to explain the relationship which I believed existed between them. There was also—at any rate at the beginning—an attempted conjectural textual history of the play before it reached its final form in quarto and/or folio. This last topic was gradually dropped; and as the general character of the quartos and the Folio came to be accepted by scholars as a whole, the 'Notes on the Copy' became less and less important.

My excursions in these elaborate Notes had been harmless enough, since they very seldom affected the choice of the text or the editing of it—though they gave birth to endless discussion among reviewers and lecturers in university English departments; indeed, they seem to form the principal subject of a recent popular book on Shakespeare by an eminent professor. Had I had time, I ought to have produced new editions of my earlier volumes, leaving them out or rewriting them; but a serial editor always pressing forward to the next play is allowed no time. And I had on each occasion to content myself with a dated postscript when a reprint of a volume was called for. It is perhaps fair to myself to add that it was Greg who had originally been responsible for these excursions, for he had always held, and later laid it down in his famous British Academy lecture delivered in 1928 on 'The Principles of Emendation in Shakespeare',[1] that 'no emendation can or ought to be considered *in vacuo*, but that criticism must always proceed in relation to what we know, or what we surmise, respecting the history of the text'. For the rest, as his review of my first volume, *The Tempest*, showed, he was himself at that stage unaware of the main direction which the road he later did so much to construct would take.

But my readers will be asking, how did the edition come into being and when did it begin? To answer these questions it is time to turn back to 1918. In that year I was publishing emendations of *Hamlet* in *The Times Literary Supplement*—the famous (to some

[1] *Aspects of Shakespeare*, 1933, p. 133.

critics, notorious) instance being Hamlet's 'sullied flesh' in the first line of the opening soliloquy, an emendation which appeared on 16th May and was followed in 1919 by others, as also by the articles on the 'Stolne and Surreptitious Texts' by Pollard and myself. It was clearly these publications which lay at the back of a letter dated 7th June 1919 from A. R. Waller, Secretary to the Syndics of the Cambridge University Press, offering me the textual editorship of the edition. I write with the letter before me, and I quote from the opening paragraph, which shows what part in the edition he and his Chairman, my old friend Adolphus Ward, Master of Peterhouse, were asking me to play:

Dear Dover Wilson,

I have had you and your Shakespeare studies on my mind ever since you told me of those railway journeys with a quarto in each pocket! Now the Syndics have undertaken the publication of a handy, inexpensive Shakespeare in forty volumes, in a format designed by Bruce Rogers. They propose a critical introduction, some few textual and bibliographical notes, possibly a very brief glossary. They have decided to offer the joint editorship to Sir Arthur Quiller-Couch and you; it being understood that in those cases where you did not wish to edit the plays yourselves, you would be responsible for the selection of other editors and for their work being in accordance with your general plan. And they would like you and Sir Arthur to outline the scope and nature of this plan during the Long Vacation. Sir Arthur has consented; will you? I need hardly add that you *must*; and that I very much hope the proposal will be to your liking.

The letter was subscribed 'Ever yours', and its proposal made as attractive as possible with a smell of cheese about it for the young mouse in its next sentence: 'I still have hopes that you will some day come back to Cambridge to work.'

It also gave me an address at Whitby to write to, Waller being just about to go away for a short holiday there; Q was enjoying the vacation at Fowey meanwhile, and was as usual impervious to correspondence. On the other hand, as I was then still at

Leeds, I could run over to lunch with Waller, where I met for the first time Harold Child, who was, I found, to be responsible for the Stage Histories and who in consequence later became a great friend of mine.

Thus it was not until October, when presumably Q was back at Cambridge, that Waller managed to extract his signature to the agreement about the edition. And when I received this for my signature, I observed that Q had made a slight alteration. One of the conditions stipulated by the Syndics was that the editors should deliver 'copy' for the Press at the rate of seven plays per annum, a figure which Q, as he told me later, considered 'rather much'; and so he altered the seven to six in red ink. In a word, it was assumed by all concerned in the enterprise that the forty volumes could and would be produced within a period of, say, ten years at the very outside. Alfred Pollard himself, whom I consulted in the negotiations throughout, thought the period possible, even desirable; for his comment was, 'I don't think you will ever produce a standard text of Shakespeare. I hope you won't, as it would mean giving up too much of your life to it. But you ought to be able to produce a provisional text which will be better than anything existing.' How wise that was, every word of it. He didn't want me to become 'Byzantine' (an epithet that I once heard him apply to Greg) and would have grieved had he foreseen how much of my life came to be given up to production of what I have never claimed to be more than a 'provisional' text. For, as he showed me by his example, and as I have always thought myself, there are greater causes to live for than writing notes and making emendations on the text of even Shakespeare—for instance that of public education, in the service of which I was looking forward at that time to a lifelong career, having just completed my memorandum, *Humanism in the Continuation School*.

Most significant of the attitudes of the bibliographical school to the New Shakespeare was an elaborate review of the first volume contributed by Greg to *The Modern Language Review* for April 1922, and covering no less than seventeen pages. This notice was on the whole favourable, indeed most helpful, to the textual editor's share in the enterprise. But what Greg was critical of was the general plan of the volume. He complained of the absence of line numeration on the page, of the tiresomeness of a stage history being interposed between the notes and the glossary which belong closely together, and above all of the textual editor's being confessedly so short of space as to be unable to develop his argument properly—and that in a volume in which some forty-five pages were devoted to literary introduction. These criticisms were in fact recommendations, and all of them were later followed in the edition. The Stage Histories, for example, ultimately found their place next to the Introduction and continued to be written by Harold Child until his death in November 1945.

In his review of 1922, Greg was careful to be polite to Q, but clearly was of opinion that he had been allowed too large a scope. He never mentioned Waller, though obviously regarding him as mainly responsible for the defects he condemned. He could never conceal his contempt for Waller's scholarship. There was therefore no love lost between them; and my belief is, not only that Greg was hitting at Waller in his review of the New Shakespeare Volume I, but that Waller had decided to offer the joint editorship to me partly in order to show the world that the University Press could produce a bibliographer on its own account without turning to Greg or McKerrow.

Greg's opinion of Waller was nevertheless a very partial one. Waller's arrival at the Cambridge University Press opened the first chapter in the present brilliant phase of its history; while he himself was always a good friend to me, even though he tended to overestimate my bibliographical attainments. Furthermore, in 1922 he was succeeded as Secretary to the Syndics by S. C. Roberts (afterwards Sir Sydney) who as Assistant Secretary had fathered the New Shakespeare from the beginning, even to the extent of designing the brown buckram covers for the little volumes.

But to return to Waller's letter of June 1919. The invitation was quite unexpected, and I was duly flattered. Nor did I allow myself to trouble much about the stipulations. As for the six volumes per annum of Shakespeare, I actually felt that now the memorandum on continuation schools was finished, I could find time for these as a parergon from my official duties. Was not Chambers doing the same kind of thing, while acting as Second Secretary in the office at Whitehall? As a matter of fact, however, in the ten years suggested in the agreement I was only able to produce thirteen volumes.

Who first started the idea of the New Shakespeare? Legend (though I believe Waller told it me as a fact when I saw him at Whitby) related that Q, having garnered his lectures into published volumes, among them *Shakespeare's Workmanship* (1918), had the idea of an edition which would give him an opportunity of writing a series of introductions on the individual plays that could be used as lectures at the university. And if my surmise is correct, it looks as if the idea of the edition was Q's. If so, Waller must have been responsible for the word 'bibliographical' in the letter to me, and it was he, perhaps in agreement with his chairman, Adolphus Ward, who had suggested my name as joint editor. In a word, it looks as if the invitation to me was an afterthought, on Waller's part, which Q had not reckoned with; and this in turn would account for the ill-balanced contents of the first volume of which Greg complained in his review. It should be observed that by June 1919 I had published little as a bibliographer, or indeed on Shakespeare, with the exception of the scrapbook called *Life in Shakespeare's England* already referred to. To Pollard and Greg, on the other hand, and to McKerrow also, in view of my work on Marprelate and Schilders for the Bibliographical Society, I had for some years been known as being interested in bibliography. And when the invitation came, after consulting Pollard I accepted it with some self-confidence.

At that date Pollard was sixty, McKerrow forty-seven, Greg forty-four and I thirty-eight; but though Pollard was my spiritual father, Greg was very much a grown-up bibliographical son of his, who had given him invaluable help in the composition of his epoch-making *Shakespeare Folios and Quartos*; so that I have little doubt that when Waller offered me the editorship, they agreed that it could do no harm to encourage this youngster who was trying to learn a little bibliography to produce an amateur text within the next ten years—by which time both expected that McKerrow, as good a bibliographer as either of them, would have been ready with a far more scholarly edition of the plays for the Oxford University Press. But, to the irreparable loss of English learning, McKerrow died an early death in 1940, when only a fragment of his great Shakespeare had been completed—alas, still a fragment. On the other hand, I went struggling on with my 'pioneer' text for forty, not the stipulated ten years. The grounds of my self-confidence—however misplaced—may be found boldly stated in the opening paragraphs of the Textual Introduction to the whole edition.

Hitherto my study of Shakespeare had been almost entirely confined to the quartos; and of them I had naturally to select the 'good' ones. Where only a folio text exists, the Folio had to be the inevitable choice. But here I ran into trouble at the outset, for as soon as I began editing the plays, committed as I was to their order in the First Folio, I was confronted by five folio texts for which no quarto existed (except a bad one for *The Merry Wives*). And my work had left me quite unprepared for dealing with anything but a good quarto. It was not until eight years later, indeed, that I attempted to recover my ground. The chance came from a request from the publishers, Faber and Faber (then Faber and Gwyer), that I should prepare facsimiles of folio texts with textual introductions.

The request was made in a personal letter from Richard de la Mare, son of the poet, who recalled the fact that when he was a schoolboy at the Whitgift I had talked to the sixth form, at the headmaster's suggestion, about the text of Shakespeare, illustrating the handwriting of Shakespeare on the blackboard. The talk had made a deep impression, and he wrote now as a director of Faber and Gwyer, wondering whether they could not supply facsimiles of individual folio texts for classroom use. Since only about half the plays of Shakespeare had appeared in quarto form, we agreed that we should start by publishing individual plays from the Folio which had not appeared in quarto. So we set to work and he published some ten of these texts. But they did

not sell well, and it seemed necessary to drop the scheme. The
truth was, however, as my friend Peter Alexander, Professor of
English at Glasgow, pointed out to me, that we had started off
on the wrong foot. We should have begun by publishing individual folio texts of which quarto versions existed. These would
probably have secured a steady sale, since teachers would have
been able to lay the two versions side by side for the purpose of
textual study in class, and in the end the public would be ready
to buy the rest of the folio texts.

Richard de la Mare did me a greater honour than publishing
the facsimiles when he asked me to contribute to a volume to be
presented to Walter de la Mare on his seventy-fifth birthday on
25th April 1948. The essay I sent in was entitled 'Variations on
the Theme of *A Midsummer Night's Dream*'; and I was later to
enlarge it in my chapter on *A Midsummer Night's Dream* in
Shakespeare's Happy Comedies, published in 1962 by Faber and
Faber.

The Tempest, however, which stood first in the folio, seemed
straightforward enough and gave me at the time a false sense of
security; its stage directions were more elaborate and in some
instances more beautiful than any to be found anywhere else
in the First Folio—a fact which has suggested to many that
Shakespeare might have begun to prepare an edition of his plays
on his own account and never got farther than the first one. But
what was one to do with the succeeding texts, namely *Two
Gentlemen*, *The Merry Wives* and *Measure for Measure*, which are
practically devoid of stage directions? They set a problem for
which no really plausible solution was to be suggested for many
years to come. Nevertheless, I had committed myself to offer
some explanation in a Note on the Copy; and I did this by
supposing that the text had been made up by stringing together
players' parts—a theory which was being put forward at the
same time by R. Crompton Rhodes, a journalist friend of Barry
Jackson's in Birmingham. This theory was discredited in 1930
by E. K. Chambers in his *William Shakespeare*; and F. P. Wilson's
retrospect in 1945 gives a survey of the various theories advanced
up to that date to explain it. Following R. C. Bald's edition

(1929) of Middleton's *Game at Chesse*, Wilson himself a little later showed that such bare texts were probably due to a member of the company being responsible for preparing copy for Jaggard's 1619 edition of the First Folio. On the other hand I sailed into calmer waters with the next five texts which were based on the 'good' quartos, and all seemed well; but I had come to see that I was launched on a perilous voyage indeed.

A word must now be said on the questions of act and scene divisions and of stage directions. Seeing that there are no act or scene divisions in the 'good' quartos, Pollard and I originally assumed that Shakespeare did not think in acts as he wrote his plays. But Greg pointed out in his review of 1922 that there were certainly such divisions in the prompt books of Shakespeare's plays used in the theatre. And act divisions, not always at appropriate points, are to be found in most folio texts. For the purposes of reference (e.g. to Bartlett's *Concordance* or Schmidt's *Lexicon*), it was necessary in my edition to introduce both these divisions and line-enumeration. This I did as unobtrusively as possible in the earlier published plays at the top of each page, but later came to realize that it was in fact more helpful to the reader to introduce line-numeration into the margins as well, as Greg had advised in his review of *The Tempest*.

As to stage directions, seeing that the original texts (with the exception of *The Tempest*) often contained no stage directions or directions occurring haphazardly, and that the traditional stage directions in all modern texts were largely the invention of Rowe and later editors, I saw no harm in filling them out to some extent. This, however, produced a storm of indignation from some critics, in particular from William Poel, that brilliant but erratic genius who wished to return to Elizabethan conditions by ridding the modern theatre of all scenery on the stage. He, however, quite misunderstood; I had no intention of trying to bring back the scenery he abhorred onto the stage but was writing for readers, not for producers or performances—though in my stage directions I always kept an Elizabethan stage performance in mind. The directions were perhaps a little too elaborate in the early plays, and I simplified them to some extent as I went on. But I still believe that the average reader is helped when he is made aware of the kind of background Shakespeare had in mind, when it is possible to discover that. And I have even been thanked by some prominent actors for it.

Quiller-Couch and I had signed on for ten years, at the end of which we had produced, as I have said, thirteen, not forty, volumes; and I concluded the decade by writing an article which appeared in *The Modern Language Review* in October 1930, entitled 'Thirteen Volumes of Shakespeare: A Retrospect', in which I attempted to sum up the hazards and achievements of our voyage of discovery.

The article was also in the nature of a farewell to 'Q', as he resigned after the completion of the comedies, since he was persuaded that he was going blind. I don't think he ever really understood the 'New Bibliography', but he was a most delightful companion, and I visited him at Fowey three or four times, if I remember rightly, mainly to discuss stage directions. *The Tempest*, with its opening scene at sea, was very much to the mind of the President of the Yacht Club. And I can remember another occasion on which I found a large square basket with a lid in his room when I arrived, into which he proceeded to pack himself, by way of showing how Falstaff might have managed it at a crucial moment.

Of the visit to Fowey which resulted in Q's 'making it up with Lytton Strachey' I have spoken elsewhere. And when Q retired and neither Strachey nor Walter de la Mare could be secured to write the introduction in his place, I had to shoulder that burden myself, beginning with *Hamlet* which I dedicated to Q, 'as a slight acknowledgement of encouragement and tolerance extended over twelve years of unclouded friendship'.

The departure of Q and the publication of *Hamlet* opened a new chapter in more senses than one; for the appearance in 1930 of Edmund Chambers's *William Shakespeare* and in 1931 of Greg's *Dramatic Documents from the Elizabethan Playhouses* placed for the first time in an editor's hands nearly all the essential material, whether in documentary or theoretical form, needful for his task. And it was necessary for me to rethink a good many of the theories I had formed and expounded in previous Notes on the Copy—though I must emphasize again that it did not involve the text of the plays. But I now departed from the folio order and began this new chapter with *Hamlet* because I had been working at it on and off, as time allowed, since 1917; I felt that the moment had come to gather it all up and publish, as it were, a model edition, as I conceived it, which would be not only the culmination of what the New Shakespeare had hitherto stood for, but a foundation for improvements in the future. During this period I experienced what amounted to a series of strokes of good fortune. In the first place, in about 1928 I quite unexpectedly received a visit from the German millionaire, Count Harry Kessler, whose ruling passion was his private printing press at Weimar. Among books he had published had been a German version of *Hamlet* by Hauptmann, illustrated by a series of woodcuts by Gordon Craig. This Kessler was now anxious to follow up, using the same woodcuts, in an English edition; and enquiring who was the appropriate editor of such an edition, he was given my name.

The upshot was the appearance in 1930 of the finest edition of *Hamlet*, I dare to say, in the world. I used the second quarto text (punctuation and all), the only departure I allowed myself being the correction of what I considered obvious verbal misprints. The type was specially designed by Edward Johnston, and the pages by Kessler himself. Into them he fitted the marvellous woodcuts by Gordon Craig, each a piece of dramatic criticism of a high order. And the foot of the page was occupied by a border piece consisting, on the left-hand side, of the *Saxo Grammaticus*—the Latin source which Shakespeare used—and, on the right-hand side, an English translation of it by Oliver Elton. And when the *Saxo* was finished, the Belleforest text, also consulted by Shakespeare, with a contemporary translation, followed for the remainder of the volume. For the rest, the title page was designed by Gill; Kessler was content with nothing but the best.

The volume is beautifully bound in red calf, while a little pocket inside the cover of the book, at the back, contains a booklet of textual notes, jottings for later expansion. Lastly, the colophon gives the names of all those concerned in the making of the book, including the names of the compositors. Seven copies were printed on vellum, fifteen on imperial Japanese paper, and three hundred on hand-made paper, plus one specially printed for me.

The book was published in 1930; but at that date the depression had hit America, and Kessler could hardly have sold the copies he expected to sell to millionaires over there. And not long afterwards Hitler and his Nazi troopers began their career in Europe, which led to the expulsion from Germany of Harry Kessler, who was known as a friend of the Liberal politicians. His press was ruined and he himself died in poverty in Paris.

How many copies were actually sold I do not know, but it cannot be regarded as a text easily available to students. It was not until I was appointed Sandars Reader at Cambridge in 1932 that I began the production of my trilogy of books on *Hamlet*, the first of which was *The Manuscript of Shakespeare's 'Hamlet'*, itself an elaboration and expansion of the Sandars Lectures which had been in their turn a development of the jottings in the Kessler volume.

In the second place, a later stroke of good fortune was the grant of the Leverhulme Fellowship which gave me a year's vacation (for the session 1933–34). During that time I continued to work on my three *Hamlet* books: *The Manuscript of Shakespeare's 'Hamlet'* (published 1934); an edition of the play (published 1936) and *What Happens in 'Hamlet'* (published 1935). This last contained in different chapters much material published earlier, some being actually a revision of replies to Greg printed in the *Athenaeum* issued in 1918.

The first of the trilogy extended over two volumes in the Shakespeare Problems series and was in fact a 'Note on the Copy' *in extenso*. It forms the basis of the other two books, but is of course not popular reading. During the years of the publication of these three books there was a good deal of talk about *Hamlet*, of which I heard an echo one day. I was sitting waiting for lunch in the Athenaeum, reading *The Times* on one of those three-fold armchairs in which the sitters face different ways, when two men unknown to me came in and occupied the other two seats. One said to the other, 'Have you read this fellow Dover Wilson's book about *Hamlet*?' 'Which one?' asked the other; 'Do you mean *The Manuscript of Shakespeare's 'Hamlet'*?' 'Good Lord, no!' was the reply; 'I'd rather read Bradshaw!' Clearly it was the 'shocker' of the series, *What Happens in 'Hamlet'*, which he had found interesting.

The third stroke of good fortune was my appointment to the Chair of Rhetoric and English Literature at Edinburgh in 1935. And to crown all, I was appointed a Companion of Honour in 1938.

In the Day of Judgment that awaits all editors long after their death, I suppose that the feature of my text which is likely to remain permanent is a selection of some emendations it offered. I began emending in *The Tempest*, the first volume of all; and the readers of Greg's review on this volume (*Modern Language Review*, 1922) can see some of the emendations of which Greg registered either absolute or qualified approval. They will note that all are based on the assumption that the copy used by the printer was in the 'secretary' hand which Shakespeare employed —as I have already explained.

When I was editing *The Tempest*, however, I was still very much under the influence of the 'revisionist' theories. *The Tempest* was a Court play, without a doubt; and had therefore to be shorter than the plays written for the public. Had it not also been shortened? Was it not originally a full-length play, dealing with the events that led to the treacherous expulsion of Prospero and his baby daughter from Milan—events which Prospero has to relate, in the play as we have it, in an inordinately long speech which stands as the second scene?

Such a thesis raised the hackles of the sceptical Edmund Chambers, and he administered a good drubbing to me in a British Academy lecture (1925) entitled 'The Integrity of *The Tempest*'. And when his *William Shakespeare* appeared in 1930, quite a large proportion of the first volume was devoted to the Shakespearian theories of a former inspector in his department of the Board. And if there was anything unfair in his criticism, it was simply that he, unlike Greg, gave no allowance to the fact that my fancies as developed in successive Notes on the Copy were admittedly merely provisional. In this connection I am proud to quote Greg's Presidential Address to the Bibliographical Society in 1959,

'Whether his [J.D.W.'s] conclusions stand or not—and I am sure he himself would be the last to claim finality for them—he has at least introduced a new spirit and a new outlook into the secular task of editing Shakespeare, and it will never be the same again. And whether we agree with his arguments or whether we do not; to follow him in his attack on age-old problems or down new vistas of unsuspected possibilities is always an exhilaration and a delight.'

But Chambers came to realize, I think, some years after the publication of his book at any rate, that he had been a little hard on the young man. For he wrote me a special article confirming my dating of *Hamlet*.

Edmund Chambers was a very great man; but his most readable book on Shakespeare was an early one, entitled *Shakespeare: a Survey*, written before his full-blooded humanity had frozen into the monolithic Second Secretary of the Board of Education. But what marvels he accomplished! On the one hand, seven volumes on the history of the English stage, including that masterpiece, the reproduction of all the documents connected with the life of the greatest dramatist. And on the other hand, he had been one of the chief architects of the state system of education in England.

Of the other giants in whose shadow I grew up, Pollard is dealt with at length in another chapter. Though I never knew McKerrow intimately, I don't think anybody else ever did either, except Greg and his own wife. He was a shy man, very diffident, and one of those persons who always seem to have bad luck; so that when I met him in town, as I often did, my wife would say to me when I got home, 'What's happened to poor McKerrow today?' Perhaps he tended to regard as bad luck what other men would welcome; certainly I well remember the gloom with which he announced to me that his wife had just presented him with twins. And perhaps it was because he felt that good luck pursued me that he astonished me one day when he called upon me at King's College with Mrs. McKerrow and asked me to be named in his will as guardian to his boys. I wasn't able for various reasons to consent; but I have always thought of the offer as a very great honour. His bad luck still pursues him for, except the prolegomena to his great Oxford Shakespeare already planned, according to Greg, in 1910, what he accomplished towards the edition itself lies like fragmentary Ozymandias in the sands of time.

As for Greg, about whom I have already spoken a good deal, I need say no more than what I said about him after his death in 1959,[1]

'The edition [New Shakespeare] has inevitably been the main target for his criticism since the beginning and he has dealt me many a hard knock in print, though never an unjust one. And his private letters and comments continued though they grew more infrequent of recent years; because, I like to hope, he found I was beginning to learn a little wisdom. I have a large stack of his correspondence. I only wish I had kept it all. Let me, however, proudly conclude this unworthy appreciation by quoting from his reply to a letter wishing him on his eightieth birthday "as many happy returns as he desired to have":

    ' "It has been a good thing knowing one another and sparring together all these years. If you have learned something from me, I have certainly received constant stimulus from you."

'And he added this P.S.:

    ' "We have had no end of a time celebrating. I find eighty a very good age to be."

'I think he had "no end of a time" all his life. Certainly he gave it to me.'

I do not propose to write later chapters in the history of the New Shakespeare edition. But this account must be rounded off by an almost romantic tale of what happened to it and its editor at the conclusion of the Second World War. As war went on, I came to realize more and more that I was committed to a hopeless task. By early in 1944 I found I had been able to produce one

[1] *The Library*, (5th ser.), XIV no. 3, September 1959.

play only in the last eight years. And with the influx of students in large numbers directly the war was over, my work as professor would inevitably increase and entirely preclude any private studies of my own. The alternatives were inescapable; I must resign either from my Chair or from the editorship of the New Shakespeare. At this moment a series of events took place which were in the end to lift most of the burden off my back.

A few days before going to Caius on 19th April 1944 for one of my annual visits, I received a letter dated 31st March from Lord Leverhulme, the son and heir of the original founder of the Leverhulme Fellowships. In it he said that, at the suggestion of Sir Hector Hetherington (by now Vice-Chancellor of Glasgow University and Chairman of the Leverhulme Trust), he had just been reading a book called *What Happens in 'Hamlet'* and was ashamed he had not read it before etc. etc., more especially as it was one of the first-fruits of his father's foundation. I sent a polite reply and by the same post a letter to Sir Hector Hethering-ton, whom I knew well, telling him of Lord Leverhulme's letter and adding jocularly that it almost made me wonder whether the Trustees could be induced to do something by way of pensions to professors anxious to retire prematurely. To which came the instant reply that he couldn't answer for that, but that I might have a second year's Fellowship whenever I asked for it.

While at Cambridge I went round to the Syndics of the Cambridge Press and told my story to my friend S. C. Roberts, the Secretary, merely as gossip, remarking that I was almost prepared to resign my professorship and to live lean on royalties (which at that date hardly amounted to a livelihood) if only I could get on with the New Shakespeare.

The next step took the form of arrangements between Hetherington and Edinburgh University, the university meeting him halfway, as it were, by granting me a sabbatical term from September 1944 as preparatory to a Leverhulme year of absence in 1945.

Readers will find in the chapter on Edinburgh that I am some-times critical of Sir Thomas Holland as principal of the university, but he was always kind to me, and never kinder or more generous than he showed himself on this occasion—or more sympathetic, since the news of my son's death on 15th May had just reached him. A substitute had, of course, to be found to carry on my duties during my absence as Leverhulme Fellow. But in effect I had resigned the professorship before I walked out of the Principal's office.

So far so good; I had a professor's salary for nearly two sessions in my pocket. But beyond that no provision had been made, or even appeared in the offing, for a means of livelihood for my wife and myself over and above the royalties from the Cambridge University Press. On 5th June 1944, however, I quite unexpectedly received the following letter from S. C. Roberts,

My dear Dover Wilson,

The Syndics of the Press have recently considered the prospects of the New Shakespeare. They are very anxious that the edition should be completed within a reasonable time and are bound to recognize that at the present rate of progress the prospects of completion are very poor.

At the same time they appreciate the difficulties that stand in your way in relation to a more rapid rate of production, and after considerable discussion of the whole subject, they have reached the conclusion that the real solution must lie in your release from other work.

When we had our confidential talk some weeks ago, you told me that if you could secure some suitable endowment, you would be prepared to resign your Professorship and to devote practically the whole of your time for a period of years to the New Shakespeare. The Syndics now ask me to say that they would themselves be glad to consider the question of providing such an endowment (over and above your normal royalties) for a period of some seven or eight years.

They feel that before going into further detail it would be essential for you and me to meet and discuss the whole question. Could we do this and would London be the best meeting-place?

Yours ever,

S. C. ROBERTS.

In the upshot we met at the Athenaeum on 19th June. But before we met I received the following card: 'John has been killed in action. But let us meet on Monday as usual. We will comfort each other as best we can. Yours, S.C.' The meeting at the Athenaeum originally proposed for the signing of a formal compact turned out to be something much nearer a sacrament of brotherhood.

Briefly considered, the Syndics were prepared to allow me six hundred pounds a year for a period of half a dozen or more years, in addition to what the royalties amounted to per annum. It was a financial sacrifice for me, as I was surrendering the professor's salary six years before the date of statutory retirement. But with increased speed of production on my part, my royalties—plus the six hundred pounds allowed by the Press—never failed to equal the loss on salary, and has long since ceased to be required while the royalties have gone on increasing.

'S.C.', as his friends all called him, remained my publisher until he retired to become Master of Pembroke in 1948. Nor were the ties between us in any way loosened when he left the secretaryship. He was indeed one of the closest and dearest of my friends. At my eightieth birthday party organized by John Butt in Edinburgh, in collaboration with the Cambridge University Press, he proposed the toast of the evening; and again he came up to Edinburgh for the reception held there in the flat of my friends, the Sym sisters, after my return from a second honeymoon in 1963. And many are the games of golf he and I played together.

I have never known him to despair, even when death dealt him a succession of terrible blows—even when his beloved second wife completely lost her memory. And now that in 1966 death has claimed him in turn, it is good to know that the blow fell too swiftly for him to suffer much pain or to endure the wrench of a slow departure.

To sum up, it is difficult to imagine happier relations between an author and a publisher than those which grew up over the production of the New Shakespeare. The first two chairmen of the Cambridge University Press in my time were my friend

How I came to edit Shakespeare

Adolphus Ward and his successor John Cameron, the Master of my own college, who always took a great interest in the undertaking. The next chairman was Stanley Bennett, already a friend of mine, who had been a pupil of Pollard's in early days in a class at King's College in the Strand. And in R. J. L. Kingsford, Roberts's successor, I found a Secretary no less helpful and understanding; while as for Kingsford's successor, the present Secretary, Richard David, friendship was strengthened by a knowledge of Shakespearian criticism greater than that possessed by any of his predecessors.

It is not that I haven't tried my successive publishers sorely at times, many times—for example, in swelling out the plays into fatter and fatter volumes. An incident occurs to my mind of 'S.C.' coming up to call upon me in my room at Balerno, armed with complete copy for the glossary of both Parts of *Henry IV*, which he proceeded to go through 'with a fine comb', asking, 'What do you want this one for?' more than once on every page. I bowed my head to the storm; and whether he knew it or not, I don't know, but I put them all back again after he had gone.

When it was known in the university that I was intending to resign, an unexpected offer of help in my Shakespeare work came to me from C. B. Young, a member of my staff. Shortly after my arrival in Edinburgh as professor, he had arrived there with his wife from India, having just retired from being Vice-Principal of the Baptist College in Delhi. He was an Oxford Greats man and had come to me asking whether I could find him work in connection with the English department; and this I had welcomed. Now, when I myself retired in 1945 in order to carry on my edition of Shakespeare, he offered to give me voluntary help. I accepted this offer most gladly; and when he courageously shouldered the Stage Histories, after Harold Child's death later in the same year, he virtually became a collaborator in the edition. He read through all my notes before they were sent off to the Press, often made most helpful suggestions, sometimes even affecting the text itself. Finally I cannot close this brief reference without adding that both he and his wife became dear friends of my own.

Though I had given up my professorial duties in 1945, I felt that on reaching the age of three score years and ten I should be wise to enlist the editorial help of younger minds; I received this from my old pupil Professor Duthie (who assisted with *Romeo and Juliet* and *King Lear*), from Dr. Alice Walker (who did the same with *Othello* and *Troilus and Cressida*), and finally from Professor J. C. Maxwell who has virtually undertaken the whole charge of *Pericles, Timon of Athens, Cymbeline* and *Henry VIII*.

Collaboration does not always prove the short cut it promises; that over *Romeo and Juliet* had to be carried on across the Atlantic, Professor Duthie being at that time Professor of English at McGill University, Montreal. And when he undertook *Lear*, which I felt was his by right after his epoch-making book on the text of the play (published by Basil Blackwell in 1949), he unhappily broke down in health after he had written the introduction and drafted the textual notes and the glossary. I was obliged to take over the commentary myself. Yet though this meant a delay for me of perhaps a year I cannot regret it, as the work I then did is, I believe, one of the best of all my commentaries on the plays. As to Professor Maxwell, it was characteristic of him that when asked to select what outstanding texts he would be willing to undertake, he chose the most difficult and what would seem the most unrewarding that remained; and he accompanied me to the end of the journey by producing an admirable edition of the *Poems* while I was editing the *Sonnets*.

9

Granville-Barker and his Influence on the Acting and Production of Shakespeare

I first saw Harley Granville-Barker in 1904 on the stage of the Court Theatre—now the Royal Court Theatre—in Sloane Square. During the years 1904 and 1905, while I was a schoolmaster in Croydon, he was acting in and producing the plays of George Bernard Shaw—productions that all young London was going mad over. I can still see him as Marchbanks in *Candida*, slinking miserably along the back of the stage while the Rev. Manor Morell preaches at him; then as the dentist in *You Never Can Tell*, leaning triumphantly over the gassed Crampton; later still as Jack Tanner, made up as the young Shaw with a little red beard, bouncing on to the stage with *The Revolutionist's Handbook* under his arm; and lastly as the mad priest in *John Bull's Other Island*. How he enchanted us! And what a lovely voice he had, given full scope in the priest's incantations. To my mind his was the finest voice I ever heard on or off the stage, and its owner one of the greatest actors.

Most people who write about Harley, now that he can't reply, tell us that he owed everything to Shaw. We who can go back to those years say to ourselves that Shaw owed everything to him, or at any rate that the debt was reciprocal. We had read *Plays Pleasant and Unpleasant* and *Three Plays for Puritans* as undergraduates, volumes in which the plays were fitted out with elaborate stage-directions for the reader because the author couldn't get anybody to risk producing them in the commercial theatre; and we all said, 'Very brilliant, but of course quite unactable; since the characters are points of view, not human beings at all.' It was Harley who taught us how wrong we were, and Shaw knew what he owed to him, clearly thought of him as a kind of son.

The plays were produced in the simplest possible manner—
beautifully dressed, of course, but with a minimum of scenery.
What mattered was that we heard every word; for Granville-
Barker made his company work hard, so that not a single syllable
of Shaw's wit should miss its mark. I went off to Finland in 1906
and soon after my return was working as an H.M.I. in the North
of England, so that I was never able to see his famous productions
of Shakespeare, in particular of *Twelfth Night*, *A Winter's Tale* and
A Midsummer Night's Dream; but it is clear from all accounts that
the staging and acting of these plays followed the same lines as
those he had used at the Court Theatre in 1904–5. And though
I never saw them, let me quote here a letter from Masefield
thanking Harley for his production of *Twelfth Night*, so that my
readers may at least catch something of what Harley's Shakespearian productions were like:

'. . . much the most beautiful thing I have ever seen done on
the stage; the play which has delighted me most, quite perfectly
done. The speaking of the verse was beautiful; Lillah often got
most exquisite effects with a sort of clear uplifting that carried us
away, and I believe that the women scenes were never once
allowed to drop to the dreamy and emotional; they were always
high, clear, and ringing, coming out of a passionate mood. The
men were equally good whenever they were called upon for
poetry . . .

'The comedy was divinely done, and kept on the height of
comedy all through; the letter scene of course much the best;
and I liked the way you made the drinking scene a concert,
another bit of seeing with W.S.'s mind; and your ceremony of
the duel was superb. Feste ended the play divinely; and there was
a fine touch when the blacks came down and shut the golden
gates. W.S. does make one feel cheap . . . If I hadn't got to make
a living I would go to every performance; so would Con. My dear
Harley, you have really done a most astonishing thing; intuition
and sympathy and fine and poetical feeling; and you've given new
souls to all your cast, and broken an ancient tradition. Bless you
and thank you and may you enjoy great and long success.'[1]

[1] Harley Granville-Barker, by C. B. Purdom, 1955, p. 142 f.

Perhaps the most important point that Masefield makes is his references to the speaking of the lines in the verse scenes; most particularly to Lillah's uplift as distinct from dreamy and emotional falling-away at the end, so characteristic of many actors, especially women.

When Harley went over to America late in 1914 he met Helen Huntington, a married woman, and in the end he came to the decision that he must divorce the actress Lillah Macarthy while Helen's husband, an oldish man of great wealth, consented to divorce Helen and endow her. It is a tangled story, but the upshot was that in marrying Helen, Harley was obliged to give up not only Lillah but his connection with the stage: for his new wife was jealous of his theatrical life which would inevitably bring him into contact with Lillah again and also with Bernard Shaw, who had taken Lillah's part in the whole affair. It was a tragedy for the English stage; for though his *Prefaces to Shakespeare* will always remain of the utmost value to producers and actors, they could be no substitute for Harley himself. He had, however, made such an impression on the acting profession before 1916 that the Harley tradition was still carried on by some of the best actors, especially by Sir John Gielgud.

Gielgud had first met Harley in 1928, and some years later succeeded in securing direct instruction from him, first about the production of *Richard II* and a little later about that of *Hamlet*. Gielgud had asked Harley whether he had written a preface on *Richard II* to help him in the production of this play. He had not; but later on in the correspondence, after seeing Gielgud's *Richard II*, on 15th October 1937, Harley sent him his impressions:

'. . . The point is that while W.S. doesn't begin to *write* *Richard* till he comes back from Ireland (till he becomes himself, a *man* and not merely a King), he does keep one guessing and wondering what sort of a man he is up to that point, and what the devil he will do next, and the more we see of his cryptic face the better . . .

'But my chief grouse is about the verse. It is a lyrical play. W.S. has not yet learned to express anything except in speech. There is nothing much, I mean, in between the lines, as there is in *Macbeth* (for an extreme example). Therefore—I am preaching; forgive me—everything the actor does must be done *within the frame* of the verse. Whatever impression of action of thought he can get within this frame without disturbance of *cadence* or *flow*, he may. But there must be nothing, no trick, no check, beyond an honest pause or so at end of a sentence or speech. And I believe you'll seldom find that the cadence and emphasis—the mere right scansion of the verse does not give you the meaning without much of any further effort on the actor's part. The *pace* you may vary all you like. Clarity there must be of course. But here, it is really the breaking of the rhythm which destroys it, for, as I said Shakespeare had written one tune and his words are playing that in the treble (say); if one tries to play another tune with them in the base—naturally we can't understand the thing.

'Variety of pace—tone—colour of speech; yes, as much as possible, but within the *frame*. You must not turn W.S.'s quavers into crochets or semibreves—or semiquavers for that matter. And I think each character ought to have his own speech. I thought during the first half of the play they were imitating *you* and your taste for sadder *sforzandi*; good enough for Richard and clearly indicated for "Down—down I come—" and "No lord of thine, thou haught insulting man—" appropriate to him but quite wrong for Augustus Caesar-Bolingbroke or Mowbray or the "Tenor" gallantry of Aumerle.

'The thing got—I began to swear—more and more hung up as it went on, and you began to play more and more astride the verse instead of in it. The scenic invention of the deposition scene was again admirable. B. on the throne; you wandering about below like a lost creature—admirable (but oh if you'd have let the marvellous and sweet music of that verse just *carry you along with it*). The *tune* of that "bucket and well" bit (again the business admirable) and even more of the "No deeper wrinkles yet . . .". It is like an *andante* of Mozart. Shakespeare has done it for you. Why not let him?'[1]

In June 1939, Gielgud was preparing to produce *Hamlet* at

[1] C. B. Purdom, *op. cit.*, p. 253 f.

Kronborg Castle, Elsinore; already armed with Harley's Preface to *Hamlet* (1937), he wrote asking him for further help. Harley attended a rehearsal at the Lyceum, and afterwards spent a whole day and more going over the play with Gielgud. The result was the birth of what is known in theatrical history as the second Gielgud *Hamlet*, a superlative production which Gielgud still gives us. Clearly it left a permanent impression, not only because other actors and producers were able to learn from Gielgud, but because Harley's advice about production in general and the speaking of Shakespeare's verse in particular was shared by other actors and producers. And of course there were still actors who had played in Barker's company: for example, Leon Quartermaine, the most meticulous of actors, who died in 1967.

Of course there were spirits of another sort, actors who either ignored Harley's subtleties, as they would think them, or deliberately flew in the face of them. On the whole, however, I believe Harley's tradition of verse-speaking has become generally adopted. Certainly our great actors Sir Laurence Olivier and Sir Michael Redgrave follow it. In particular George Rylands had produced a wonderful example of Shakespearian verse-speech in the Marlowe Society records which cover the whole canon and are especially remarkable for their clarity of diction. Not a syllable is missed. In a few parts only (which I suspect he gave professional actresses) does the players' habit of exhibiting their own personalities instead of Shakespeare's characters obscure the sense of Shakespeare.

But let me add something here about my friendship with Harley. I can't remember when I first met him personally. Probably it was at a meeting of the Shakespeare Association held under Professor Israel Gollancz's auspices in King's College. But my letters from him begin in 1928, and I am the proud possessor of a copy of *Prefaces to Shakespeare II* (1930), inscribed 'For J. Dover Wilson, in gratitude for much, from Harley Granville-Barker, Paris, December 1929'. This was an over-generous return for a proof of Faber's Folio facsimile of *Antony and Cleopatra*, which I had sent to save him carting the Oxford Folio about Europe as he worked at his Preface to that play. After that we soon dropped formal titles and the correspondence became fairly frequent, culminating in letters fast and furious over *Hamlet*, to the accompaniment of a rain of picture postcards, one of which by an Italian painter represented a number of figures, apparently Greeks, hailing a prisoner before a judgment seat. The figures Harley had initialled in ink, showing myself as the prisoner, Stoll as the executioner and E. K. Chambers sitting on the judgment seat; the whole supposed to take place at a meeting (entirely imaginary) of the Shakespeare Association.

When I discovered that Harley's *Prefaces III* was to be devoted entirely to *Hamlet*, and he learned that I was in the middle of a publication which he dubbed 'What 'Aitches in 'Aitch', he consented to look at a carbon and to make comments thereupon. He was sorry for it later.

My book is *vieux jeu* nowadays, but since it goes on selling some of my readers may be interested in the following letter which Harley wrote after reading the carbon; and one, as I came to realize, which showed great self-restraint.

Paris. Nov: 7, 1934.

My dear J.D.W. Well, I have been a devil of a time—thinks you!—getting through it. But I needed to go carefully and I've only had spare afternoon hours to give (you said there was no great hurry); my own infant Hamlet taking up the mornings, muling and puking as it lies—still!—on my table.

I have scribbled recklessly and often ribald-ly, as you said I might, on the pages.

What is my perspective view, now that I have just turned—and torn—the last page?

The Ghost business. Immensely valuable. I don't think it can possibly be brought out in all its variety in a modern performance —but neither do you. But much could be done, especially in the first scene by marking the contrast between Horatio and the other two—their conduct. I don't agree with your *interpretation* of Hamlet's conduct in the 'Cellarage' scene. I think you make it too calculated. But the underlying 'facts' as you put them— most convincing.

The ambition theme. I think all this is very sound. But you surprise me by saying it has been so little remarked on. I have always rather taken it for granted—too much so taken it, doubtless.

The 'lobby' entrance. By Jove, I believe you have convinced me. I didn't think you would. I still don't feel quite sure, for I have not been 'at' that part of the play since I read you. If I am convinced it is because the theory only (forgive me) clarifies what was discernible before—behind cryptic (*too* cryptic for W.S.? There is the question) allusions. And I believe I am—if I am—finally convinced by the sustained metaphor (image) and the series of double meanings. But will you take your Bible oath that all these double meanings were obvious to an Elizabethan audience? And don't ride off on your 'judicious', now. I still, I expect, shan't quite follow you all the way. And, if the word is very farm-yardy, isn't it odd that Polonius should speak of 'loosing' Ophelia?

The play scene. I just think you are utterly wrong. I don't believe for one thing that any true theory which could be successfully put to test on the stage, could need all that explanation and argument. But I see it is no use counter-arguing. You delight too much in your bastard brat. I wish you had strangled it at birth. It will not grow up to do you credit; at least, that is my conviction. By the way, clear up that superficial confusion about the First Player. Long tradition has it that this is the gentleman who has grown a beard (see Alleyn's; I give you that point. When *did* he grow his? Nice, if you knew!) recites the Hecuba speech and acts the Player-King but does *not* speak the prologue (which is given for economy to Lucianus but need not and I suppose (anyhow; you apart) should not be).

I think that the identification of the Players with Alleyn's lot may be a sound one. But it does not follow that W.S. would spoil (from my point of view) his play scene by continuing and stressing the matter so far and so heavily as that.

After this I make friends with you again. You give me some fine and most elucidating bits about the *Antic Disposition*, the *Ghost in the Closet Scene*, and the *Return*—especially I feel that last.

I seldom quite agree with you, but the question between us will be one of emphasis mainly. But see—and read if you can—my scribbles.

I'd like, if I may, to keep the MS a day or so longer. I want to go back over one or two points to make sure I've not misunderstood you. You are going to run me in for a lot of footnotes in my own book, confound you (and already I can't keep them down). But I expect you'll be 'out' before I shall; so this will be all right, won't it?

I'll launch my revised MS at your head, if you'll be patient enough to look at it again (or would you rather wait for proof?); but I don't know when. I have been largely re-writing and enlarging, trying to generalize a bit about the fellow's stage-craft; and it is troublesome work.

Once I'm through I don't believe I'll ever read a word of W.S. again. Once *you*'re through—oh, my friend, how you face it, right up to *Henry VIII* and *T. of A.*, I don't know!—I'm sure thereafter you'll burst into tears if anyone so much as mentions his name.

But my blessings on you. And forgive me what will seem to you my stupidities about this book. They bulk far larger than they should, for my admiration much outbulks them. You must take that for granted.

H. G.-B.

The ribald marginalia I shall not trouble to repeat. Let this one suffice, scribbled against the middle section of the chapter about the play scene:

'It is 11.30 p.m. And I am now going to bed!

'Sunday, 8 a.m. I have prayed for you *and* taken a walk at Fontainebleau. I will face this terrible business once more!'
What was so delightful about Harley was that he never took Shakespearian criticism too seriously, and I think you will agree that it is the long-faced fellows who are most likely to misunderstand our poet.

What Happens in 'Hamlet' was published at the end of September 1935 and Harley's book did not appear until the beginning of

1937. It was far too kind to its predecessor; I read it with intense interest, closing the book, however, with some sadness, since it brought to an end what had been for me a great experience. As for Harley himself, the inscription on the fly-leaf of the copy he sent me ran as follows,

'J.D.W. from H. G.-B.

'The rest—please God!—is silence. (Still, there'll always be *Titus Andronicus* to talk about.)

'Dec: 1936, Paris.'

—which seemed to show that he was then in the mood to give up writing prefaces. Fortunately Shakespeare wouldn't let him alone.

Yet though the duel over *Hamlet* was ended, the friendship became closer than ever. We saw one another from time to time, he running over from Paris—where in 1937 he was appointed Director of the British Institute—to meet me for breakfast at the Athenaeum, I having come down by the night train from Edinburgh where I was by this time Professor of English.

And when Barrie's *Boy David* (which I irreverently called 'Girl David' because the title-role was played by Elizabeth Bergner, with a strong German accent) was first launched in Edinburgh, nothing would do but Harley must come over from Paris to see the première.

He had a very deep affection for Barrie who, I suspect, must have befriended him as a young man. At any rate, after Barrie's death in 1937 he came once again all the way from Paris to Edinburgh to deliver the funeral oration in the Old Quad—for Barrie was then Chancellor of the University. Whether that tribute is extant, I don't know. I could wish it were, as it was a friendship's garland that would have pleased Barrie himself as it delighted all who heard it.

I think the war came upon us before I met Harley again after that occasion. He was in Paris, of course, and only just escaped with his American wife an hour or two before the city fell. Across the water he found work as Director of British Information at New York. But he was intensely patriotic and grew very miserable while the Battle of Britain was going on, so that I used to try and cheer him up. In one letter I remember I said, 'Don't *worry*; we're all right. It's true our clothes are wearing out, and I've lost two watches since the war began (one trodden into the mud by the Home Guard in one of the fields near Balerno), so that I now have to borrow a watch from one of my students in case I should lecture too long to them. . . .' The reply came by return. Unfortunately I have lost it, but I remember this sentence very well, 'I wouldn't have your students listen to your pernicious nonsense about Shakespeare one second longer than necessary; I am therefore sending you by the next surface mail—not my second-best bedstead but my second-best watch.' It's a good Geneva chromium wrist-watch which keeps excellent time. The only thing wrong about it is it doesn't like golf, gets out of order if I wear it when I am playing. I don't think Harley played games, so it had never been properly trained. But it's one of my proudest possessions—and dearest, as it keeps me still in touch with him.

Since this chapter began with Shaw, it must end with him. I only met him once, but thereby hangs a tale.

I used to go away with Alfred Pollard for a week or so every summer. On one occasion we decided to take serial tickets at the Malvern Festival—one of Barry Jackson's enterprises, unhappily now a thing of the past. The festival always began with a miracle or morality play, followed by an Elizabethan drama (Shakespeare being left to Stratford), continued with a couple of plays from the eighteenth or nineteenth centuries and ended up with Shaw's latest. *And*—as cunning Barry knew would be the greatest attraction of all—there was Shaw walking about the place in his ridiculous Victorian Norfolk jacket and knee-breeches with, as I noticed one day, a little button at the back of each knee, obviously intended for riding gaiters—though I doubt whether Shaw ever rode a horse in his life.

Well, Pollard and I took our tickets and on the Monday were enjoying our afternoon tea in the garden of a hotel, when we suddenly heard a babble of voices from the verandah. Looking up, we saw it full of people, and in the middle Jackson with G.B.S. Presently these two came down, to our amazement made

straight for us and we presently found ourselves being introduced
to Shaw. He seized a chair, planted himself at our table, and
without more ado or preface of any kind proceeded to tell us
exactly what the Elizabethan theatre was like, inside and out.
It was an amazing performance. But it was all wrong, from
beginning to end, and after a time we realized that it was based
on one visit to Oberammergau a few years earlier. Then, having
got it off his chest, he rose, gave us a kind of royal farewell, and
turned away. I was just going to have a really good laugh with
Pollard, when I found myself confronted by a little lady. 'You
are Professor Dover Wilson, aren't you?' she asked, and then
went on, 'I read one of your books once, and thought George
might like to meet you.' What an afternoon! I had met not only
Shaw, but his stage-manager, Mrs. G.B.S.

Was Shaw capable of affection? I think I can say at any rate
that he had once adored Harley and regarded him as a kind of
son—which was natural, was it not, if he fell under his spell
in Court Theatre days, as the rest of London did. At any rate
when Harley died on the last day of August 1946, Shaw was
moved to send to *The Times Literary Supplement* a photograph he
had taken of Harley with his famous Kodak in 1906, at the height
of the Vedrenne–Barker season. It is an ultra-romantic picture;
Harley sits at a table, chin on hand, gazing out through a window
with a Father Keegan look in his eyes. And with the photograph,
which was reproduced in the *T.L.S.* issue of 7th September, he
sent this letter:

Sir,—The enclosed photograph of Harley Granville-Barker,
taken by me forty years ago at The Old House, Harmer Green,
when our collaboration, now historic, was at its inception, may
interest your readers.

We clicked so well together that I regarded him as my contemporary until one day at rehearsal, when someone remarked
that I was fifty, he said, 'You are the same age as my father'.
After that it seemed impossible that he should die before me.
The shock the news gave me made me realise how I had still
cherished a hope that our old intimate relation might revive.

But

> Marriage and death and division
> Make barren our lives.

and the elderly Professor could have little use for a nonagenarian ex-playwright.

G. BERNARD SHAW

The widow read that in Paris, as he meant her to; for she had robbed him of Harley and, like a true Celt, Shaw never forgot or forgave. With all his genius, he was never quite human; that's why he never understood Shakespeare. But Harley did, and in that respect was the greater man of the two. Yet there is genuine grief behind the letter, isn't there?

10

The Acting of Shakespeare in
Stratford and Elsewhere

My first visit to Stratford, if I remember rightly, was in the autumn of 1914, a few weeks after the First World War broke out. It was reported that the Kaiser was speaking scornfully of Britain's contemptible little army; and Benson was playing *Henry V* to wildly enthusiastic audiences, bringing down the house with the words, 'We few, we happy few, we band of brothers'. And it was not long after this that I visited Stratford as an inspector of adult classes. I was pleased to find that, as in most W.E.A. classes, the members were working-class men; and at the end of the discussion I rose at the back to reveal who I was and show, I hope, that an inspector was a human being. And I remarked at the same time, 'You are studying industrial history; I should be interested to know what you think of the main industry of this place.' At which, after a pause, a large man with a red tie rose and replied, ' 'Spose ye mean Shakespeare?'

'Yes,' I said, that was my idea.

'Oh,' he said, 'we don't think nawt to Shakespeare 'ere. 'E's a middle-class superstition, 'e is.'

Later when I was proposing the toast of the Immortal Memory to the Mayor and distinguished citizens and strangers, I told this story as I thought it might be good for them. Whether the workers still feel that way, I don't know. But one can understand that, watching the kind of public that flocks to their town and having been bored at school, I fear, with parsing and analysing one of the plays, they should gird against the dramatist who gave such intense pleasure to the groundlings of his own day.

In 1914, the performances were given in a cinema, for the old theatre built by Sir Archibald Flower's father with funds he had raised in America, had recently been burnt down. A new theatre, built by Sir Archibald himself, was in use at my next visit. And after I had been elected as a Trustee of the Birthplace in 1931, I returned to Stratford almost every year—being honoured indeed by having to deliver on three occasions the Toast to the Immortal Memory on the Birthday.

One of these times was during the Second World War, in 1945, when I was asked to propose the Immortal Memory in Holy Trinity Church itself, standing close by Shakespeare's tomb at the side of the altar. What follows is the speech, 'The Man of Stratford', which I then delivered.

'I am to say a few words about the man of Stratford who was made a Christian in this glorious church on April 26th three hundred and eighty-one years ago and whose body was buried in a place of honour before the altar on April 25th, fifty-two years later. He who blamed Fortune

That did not better for my life provide

Than public means which public manners breeds,

was of a retiring disposition; and the date of his birth is a private affair between Mistress Mary Shakespeare and himself which has been hid from us like so much else that was private about him. Yet we are happy in this ignorance, for it allows us to celebrate his birthday today, and so to enthrone him in memory side by side with St. George, patron of chivalry and guardian saint of England. Not that a very large number of his countrymen will have Shakespeare and Stratford in memory at this moment. We are a practical people with little time (as we think) even in peace to worry our heads over poetry and plays and such matters. But Shakespeare is Shakespeare; and though not everyone reads him or goes to see him acted we are all proud of him, and realize that an Englishman has been accepted by the world as its greatest writer.

'All this he would have understood, for he was himself very English. His command of language, his imaginative sweep, his knowledge of human nature were amazing, so amazing as to seem well-nigh superhuman to many. That was his genius. But this genius, as if to keep him sane, was it seems balanced by a nature of simple tastes and homely aspirations. Men in that age were not interested in other people's biographies, and the earliest "Life" of him did not appear until ninety-three years after his death. But all the facts that have survived go to show that, while he had his London triumphs and no doubt enjoyed them, what he valued above all things in the world was the quiet life of his home, his family and his friends. We do not know when he first went up to London. All we can say is that he took a Stratford wife in 1582, who bore him children baptized like him here in May 1583 and February 1585, and that nine years later, in 1594, he was already famous in London as a leading poet, dramatist and player, though his greatest successes were still to come. The theatres were often closed for most of the summer, so that he may well have paid many visits to Stratford during those nine years. Certainly he kept home constantly in mind; for he began putting by the money his plays and poems brought him, partly it seems to pay off his old father's debts, and partly to buy New Place, the pleasantest house in Stratford. This he made his own in May 1597, but found it in some need of repair—repairs that engaged his attention that summer and next, if one may judge from the long and slightly irrelevant passage about building in 2 *Henry IV*, which was also engaging his attention at the same time. I cannot believe that he bought and rebuilt New Place if he didn't intend to live there, or that he was not, from henceforth if not earlier, to be found at Stratford, a quiet place for writing, as often as he could slip away from his London affairs. And then, after another dozen years or so, while he was still under fifty, he retired. He turned his back upon London, upon his grand friends at Court, upon his fellow-actors and the theatre he had helped to make the best in England. He even gave up, it seems, all thought of writing more plays—and just came home!

'To millions of British and American soldiers, longing at this moment to do the same, it will seem natural enough. But others of us, who think much of what he called "the bubble reputation", find it very hard to understand. Many even refuse to believe it, and declare that the plays must have been written by someone else, some lord at Court—it's always a lord. These are the snobs who think the son of a shop-keeper and provincial mayor, who preferred his little country town to London, not fine enough for fine poetry, or hold it absurd that anyone should count living his own life more interesting than running after success "faster and faster till he sink into his grave". This was not the opinion of another if minor poet, his first biographer, Nicholas Rowe, who wrote, "The latter part of his life was spent, as all men of good sense will wish theirs may be, in ease, retirement, and the conversation of his friends." And if we want to see something of Shakespeare's mood, as his heart turned back to find its centre out, we have only to read *The Tempest*, the play in which he said good-bye to London, King James and his art.

> We are such stuff
> As dreams are made on, and our little life
> Is rounded with a sleep—

that is the text of it. Would a man who thought of life like this be one to worry over-much about fame or a career? And if it came to a choice between Stratford and London, could a *poet* hesitate, even if he had not ties of affection, no Hermione or Perdita, to draw him home? For Stratford, still one of the loveliest of places, must in the days before industrialism ruined the world have been far more lovely, standing with the forest behind it, the Avon before it, and across the river the open fields and meadows.

'The pull of Stratford is naturally most evident in the last plays, when the promise of release was near. But it may be felt in them from the beginning. It is in 2 *Henry VI*, one of the earliest, that I find the most explicit statement of what I take to have been William Shakespeare's worldly ambition. A country gentleman soliloquizes, as he paces his garden:

> Lord, who would live turmoiléd in the court,
> And may enjoy such quiet walks as these?
> This small inheritance my father left me
> Contenteth me, and worth a monarchy.
> I seek not to wax great by others' wanting,
> Or gather wealth, I care not with what envy:
> Sufficeth that I have maintains my state
> And sends the poor well pleaséd from my gate.

The Acting of Shakespeare

'I believe too that this simple passionate homeliness is the true secret of Shakespeare's unchallenged sway over our imaginations. His poetic genius was the gift of Heaven; but what made him a *dramatic* poet was his intense interest in life, the ordinary life of ordinary men and women—for what else *is* life? Because we feel that he understands and loves ordinary people better than anyone else who has ever written, he has been crowned as the greatest of all dramatists, with an empire that spreads to wider and wider circles of humanity in each succeeding generation. And today the man of Stratford, who was made a Christian in this great church three hundred and eighty-one years ago, stands as one of the few unifying forces in a warring world; for he speaks to all nations and all creeds, and from his understanding and compassion they may learn a little to understand and have compassion upon each other.'

Another lecture, which I gave on a special occasion though not in Stratford, stands out also in my memory. This was at the headquarters of the Royal Society, known as the Royal Institution, in Albemarle Street. Sir William Bragg, at the time when my trilogy of books on *Hamlet* was being much discussed, invited me to give one of the special evening lectures there. These were formal occasions; the invited audience, all guests of the Royal Institution and their wives, attended in evening dress after dinner. The lecturer himself, also in evening dress, dined with the president and spent the night as his guest after the lecture. Furthermore, the lecturer was expected to discourse for exactly sixty minutes, neither more nor less, and to lecture without notes.

I was so full of my subject at the time that I felt no nervousness as I stood up. But ten minutes before the end of the appointed hour I suddenly 'dried', as the actors say. There was a horrid pause. I grew very hot under the collar. And then—Heaven knows how, and still less what I said—I went on again, and the audience didn't appear to have noticed anything wrong.

But I must return to Stratford. At almost every visit I saw something of Sir Archibald and Lady Flower, staying more than once in their house. Every now and then there are stupid people who maintain that the Birthplace Trust and the theatre should be run from a committee in London—become indeed a branch of the National Theatre. But fortunately the Flower family still rules at Stratford; and after my friendship with two members of it, serving under their admirable chairmanship on the Birthplace Trust, and watching the varying progress (not always in the upward direction) of the theatre, my motto for Stratford has consistently been *Floreant Flores*.

The quality—one might almost say the genius—of the family may be well illustrated in the following incident, which took place not long after I first came to know Sir Archibald Flower. A famous American professor and Shakespearian scholar, G. L. Kittredge, was lecturing at University College, London, shortly after the conclusion of the First World War, and was being entertained to a farewell lunch by the Pilgrims at which the President, no less a person than the old Duke of Connaught, took the Chair, with the Earl of Derby supporting him on his right. The toast of the day was proposed by Ernest de Selincourt, a delightful man, a great scholar and I am proud to say a great friend of my own—but, alas, not a good after-dinner speaker, for his speech went on and on about Professor Kittredge and William Shakespeare, and William Shakespeare and Professor Kittredge, until I could see from the back of the room where I sat that the old Duke was quite visibly trying desperately to keep awake. At last it ceased, but it had to be seconded.

Happily, however, the seconder was Sir Archibald Flower, the brewer of Stratford-on-Avon. He realized the situation completely. 'Something Professor de Selincourt said,' he began, 'reminded me of those wonderful lines, so familiar to you all, in which Shakespeare describes the horse.' At that word *horse* the Duke woke up with a start, and as Sir Archibald recited the passage from *Venus and Adonis*, describing the horse courting the mare, one could almost hear the Duke saying, 'There's something in this bloody man, Shakespeare, after all!' And though he of course was not expected to speak, the great Earl of Derby— great geometrically and in every other respect—rose to convey the Duke's good wishes to Professor Kittredge on his homeward journey. 'And may I say,' he concluded, 'how apt were the lines Sir Archibald has just quoted, because you see, the Duke and I are on our way to Newmarket. And,' he went on, taking out a large watch, 'as we have a train to catch, perhaps the company would excuse us.' I feel sure that Kittredge enjoyed the incident as much as any of us did.

Sir Archibald Flower was succeeded in 1946 by his son Fordham—later Sir Fordham Flower whom I came to know as well as I had known his father. Indeed he did me the honour of taking me into his confidence from the outset of his 'reign'. He had served with great distinction in the campaign at Walcheren in the war and had been decorated by the Queen of Holland. He had then returned home, as he told me, to find his old father becoming senile, so that he was compelled to take over at more or less the same time the brewery, the chairmanship of the theatre, and the chairmanship of the Birthplace Trust. As he said to me, 'I had grown up in the brewery, and we had a first-rate director of the Birthplace Trust in Mr. Levi Fox, but I knew damn all about the theatre! So I sat in the wings for a year and then got started, making up my mind that the director should be a young actor who had served in the war.'

As I write these words, Stratford is mourning the sudden death of Sir Fordham—is indeed as yet too dazed to appreciate to the full the greatness of its loss. One has only to mention the building of the magnificent Birthplace centre for which he and the director succeeded in raising a sum of money which seemed impossible when the project was first broached to the other trustees; the opening and development, as a convenient resort for visitors, of Hall's Croft, supposedly the house of Shakespeare's son-in-law; and thirdly Fordham Flower's conception of his duty as chairman of the theatre being not that of, in any sense, a theatrical director but one whose function was to encourage and support his director and company, and if necessary to defend them.

It is natural to pass from visits to Stratford to my friendships and acquaintance with actors I have met there and elsewhere. In the previous chapter I referred to a visit to Sir Barry Jackson's

Malvern Festival. To that great gentleman, director and patron of the Birmingham Repertory Theatre, the English stage owes much; and I personally learned something new about *Hamlet* from his experimental *Hamlet* in modern dress first produced at Birmingham and then at the Aldwych Theatre. He would also let me know of any interesting productions that he was putting on at Birmingham; and I believe I saw several eminent actors there for the first time. Certainly I saw an eminent producer when still unknown. On one occasion Sir Barry wrote to me, 'I have discovered a young genius who is producing *King John* for me at the Rep. His name is Peter Brook. You must come and see it; I'll put you up at New Street Hotel.' Such invitations were not to be neglected; so I presently found myself sitting between a young man who, I was given to understand, had never acted in his life, and Sir Barry, watching *King John*. In due course the Bastard came on with his well-known soliloquy on Commodity —a word which no modern audience is likely to understand but which was rendered explicable by a spurious line added by Brook as follows,

'Commodity which men do call advantage.'

Thereupon both Jackson and Brook looked at me quickly. I 'neither winced nor cried aloud', and so was acquitted of pedantry.

In this extreme instance a little doctoring of the text may be permitted; but I am afraid that when the same producer took such liberties with Shakespeare that he felt himself permitted to miss out whole scenes (as he did in a production of *Romeo and Juliet* which I saw later at Stratford) in order to make room for a tableau à la Watteau, he was indulging in a superfluity of naughtiness.

An actor I met before I saw him at Stratford was Michael Redgrave. Living at Purley during my professorship at King's College but still retaining links with the Whitgift, I received one Saturday morning a telephone call from a master at that school telling me that he was going to a performance of *King Lear* at Cranleigh School in Surrey, given by the boys, and asking if I would care to go with him in his car. Always keen to see amateur performances of Shakespeare, I agreed, and found all the parts taken by the boys—except that of the King, which was wonderfully performed by a modern languages master called Redgrave. When introduced to him afterwards, I ventured to compliment him by saying I thought he ought to be on the professional stage. He smiled, saying, 'Next term, Sir, I shall be joining the Liverpool Rep.'

Another famous actor whom I was often to see at Stratford I first met in London. My friend, C. B. Young, who after the death of Harold Child wrote the Stage Histories for the *New Cambridge Shakespeare* plays, was anxious to discover the date of a performance of some play in which Laurence Olivier had acted and wrote to ask him for it, telling him what he wanted it for. Olivier replied sending the date and saying, 'Please tell Professor Dover Wilson when he is next in London I shall be delighted to see him.' C. B. Young sent on his letter to me a day or two before I was going up to town for a few nights at the Athenaeum. So after breakfast one morning I strolled round to the New Theatre, where Olivier was then acting. At the stage door I put my head in at the office, introduced myself and said, 'When can I see Mr. Olivier?'—he hadn't been knighted at this time. 'Why, he's just behind you, Sir,' the stage manager said. 'Professor Dover Wilson to see you, Sir.' At this Olivier started back, exclaiming, 'Oh, Professor Dover Wilson, what a lot of trouble you give us!' This, I think, was one of the greatest compliments I had ever had paid to me.

After some talk he suggested that I should see his *Henry V* film, which was then taking London by storm—that very afternoon if I would—and arranged that I should have tickets at the Marble Arch cinema if I called after lunch. It really was the best Shakespeare film I ever saw, and Olivier the best Henry V, especially in the courtship scene which so rarely comes over. Olivier and his producer had taken very great pains with the production, even using some of the old French Books of Hours for scenic purposes.

At a later stage, when the Oliviers were playing Shaw's *Caesar and Cleopatra* one night and Shakespeare's *Antony and Cleopatra* the next, my wife and I saw both performances; and after the

9. John Dover Wilson
in Durban, 1949

10. Alfred Pollard

11. John Butt

12. Field Marshal Wavell

second one were invited to supper by Lady Olivier (Vivien Leigh) at their little 'cottage' in Chelsea, we being accompanied by our friend Archie John Wavell. As I drove off from the theatre after the play with Olivier, he said to me, 'I've got to do this Antony next week in New York, and I can't see what you fellows find in him, I can make neither head nor tail of it. What's wrong?' To which I retorted, 'Good lord, I found nothing wrong to-night.' But when I got back home, thinking it over I said to myself I might perhaps make a suggestion or two. And as a matter of fact I had received one from an unexpected quarter; for I had recently been down to the school run by my sisters in Bexhill, the Winceby House School for Girls. When I got there my younger sister, who was taking the Shakespeare class, said to me, 'Do you know, John, what the set book is this year? *Antony and Cleopatra*! Isn't it awful?'

'Yes,' I answered, 'it is a bit.'

'Well then, you must talk to the girls about it,' she replied. So five young damsels were brought in, and when my sister had left the room, I said, 'Now she's gone we can talk. What sort of man was this Antony, do you think?' At which one girl shot up her hand and cried 'Terrific!' This was an excellent start, and we got well away.

Here was the suggestion I was seeking. Olivier's problem, as he saw it, was to reconcile Antony's nobility with his constant exhibition of weakness of character. How much of Antony's nobility should he show, and how? So I wrote to him somewhat as follows,

'Antony's nobility? I think it's more important to make him "terrific"; that's what the man was whom Cleopatra saw in her vision of him after his death and that, I believe, is what Shakespeare wished us to think of him. Everything Philo says about him before his entry bears this out—a terrific man, the triple pillar of the world and looking like it, a plated Mars. And it's only a terrific spirit that could love as "Let Rome in Tiber melt", etc., tells us he did. I don't think you can possibly overdo this, especially as the audience gets its first impression of him. And I do think that other things in the production as I (twice) saw it

militate against it. The lion's skin, for instance, which you got
out of my notes, was a mistake. The Elizabethans knew he was
descended from Hercules and wore the lion's skin by right; but
to a modern audience it just looks "cissy". No: enter as a
"plated Mars" (just back from a little field practice if you like)
and *dominate* the stage, with Cleopatra to boot.'

And I also stipulated that he should engage a new Enobarbus
as his 'feed', in New York.

He didn't answer this impertinence, of course; I never expected it. But a year later I received a letter from Felix Barker
who was writing a life of the Oliviers and asked whether he
might quote this letter of mine which Olivier had sent him. I was,
of course, elated; and when the book appeared, I wrote to my
sister saying, 'Please tell the "terrific" girl to look at page 302
of Felix Barker's book on the Oliviers and she will see how she
helped Laurence Olivier act Antony in New York.'

In 1948 I edited *Titus Andronicus*, in the introduction to which
I declared that the play was probably by Greene and/or Peel,
revised (with his tongue in his cheek) and much inflated by
Shakespeare. I was now to experience a production by Peter
Brook with Laurence Olivier and Vivien Leigh as Titus and
Lavinia, which revealed it by a miracle of transformation as high
tragedy. Brook had given us every variety of blood in the back-
cloths; and the two chief actors were at their very best. Titus's
first sight of his daughter Lavinia after the sons of Tamora had
done with her—Lavinia with her tongue cut out had little to say,
looking at her loveliest, a figure of infinite pathos; and Titus her
father bending towards her with a look full of compassion—
seemed to give us a human Pietà. A picture appeared in *The Times*
and I begged for a copy which now hangs in my library, signed
'with loving admiration' by them both.

The play was a great success at Stratford; and after Stratford
the company triumphed with it through the European capitals.
It was a new Shakespeare of which the German professors had
not dreamed. But the triumph was an old story; Ben Jonson's
jibe in his *Bartholomew Fair* (1614) shows that *Titus* was still
holding the stage for admiring audiences twenty-five to thirty

years after it was first produced. It was a bad play but excellent box-office.

It was not only at Stratford and in London that I saw Olivier; when he played in Edinburgh he almost always managed to spare the time to come up to our home at Balerno for a quick lunch. It was on one such occasion that he asked me what I thought of his *Hamlet* film—an awkward question!—which I attempted to parry by telling him that the most important character in the film Shakespeare never thought of. 'What do you mean?' he said. 'The staircase at Elsinore,' I replied; 'I didn't count the number of times you ran up and down it. Like Burbage, you will have your acrobatic tricks.' We lunched together at another date just before I saw him acting in *The Entertainer*, when his mind, still running on the filming of Shakespeare, was full of a project of doing so with *Macbeth*. In this I did all I could to encourage him, for it seemed to me a splendid subject; but, alas, it came to nothing, as he found that the atmosphere of Scotland was never clear enough for the purpose.

At our first meeting he told me I had given him a lot of trouble; on the other side he might be ready to turn to me for help in an emergency. For instance, returning from Stratford in 1964 I found a telegram from him which ran something as follows, 'Be a dear and tell me the names of the actors that appear in the Quarto in place of the characters they were to perform. Wanted for Royal Academy address. Larry.'

I managed to find the passage in the Quarto and wired 'Quarto *Much Ado* 1600 demonstrably printed from the author's MS. At Act 4 Scene 2 instead of Constables Dogberry and Verges names of comic actors in Shakespeare's company Kempe and Cowley appear.' Next evening my wife and I listened to Olivier pouring scorn on the doubters and quoting the Dogberry and Verges entry as proof that the plays were written by Shakespeare himself. He, of course, quoted me as his authority for the evidence he gave.

The three Parts of *Henry VI* are a group of plays which like *Titus* I had argued were Greene, Peel and perhaps Nashe re-written by Shakespeare. But when they were put on as a group in London, by the Royal Shakespeare Company, my experience of them on the stage shook my previous resolution. I witnessed them, I remember, with my friend Richard David of the Cambridge University Press; and he reminded me recently how I exclaimed every now and then,

'There! *That's* the Master! Isn't it? Isn't it?'

I am sometimes critical, as my readers will have observed; but my debt to the actors and producers cannot be over-estimated. And so often they reveal the true character of the play which has completely baffled the editor. An outstanding example of this is *Love's Labour's Lost* which cost me two years and more of wrestling with the text and attempting to understand its quips and quiddities. And then I went with my friend, Alfred Pollard, to a production by Tyrone Guthrie; and what had been flat-footed plodding on my part took wings. Or rather, it turned out to be something like Gilbert and Sullivan's *Patience*, or better still Mozart's *Cosi Fan Tutte*—a thing of coloured gossamer on tiptoe, an ever-moving stage pattern.

I cannot omit the one meeting I had with Dame Edith Evans, whom I originally saw when she was enchanting audiences as Millamant in Congreve's *The Way of the World*. I was at Stratford with my friend S. C. Roberts, where she was acting Emilia in *Othello*. When 'S.C.' learned that I had never met her, he said, 'I know her very well. I often see her, as I'm chairman of the Film Institute. Come and meet her in her dressing-room.' So he went in, followed by an expectant Dover. But they greeted each other as old friends and were soon deep in conversation, until at last he remembered I was there. 'Oh,' he said, 'may I introduce Professor Dover Wilson to you?' I took her out-stretched hand into mine and bent over it as if about to kiss it, murmuring, 'I have never met you before, but I have loved you often.' The rest of the conversation was mine. 'S.C.' in his *Adventures with Authors* tells this story, but gives it a somewhat different slant.

I I

Shakespeare sends me Abroad

One of the results of my rising reputation as an authority on Shakespeare, which reached a peak with publication of the three *Hamlet* books in 1934 and onwards, was that during the next decade I was asked to travel abroad and lecture on Shakespeare. Of such visits those I made to Germany, France and South Africa were especially noteworthy.

EUROPE

After *What Happens in 'Hamlet'* was published I received a number of letters about it. One morning at breakfast, I said to my wife as I opened an envelope, 'Good heavens, here's an old woman has written me four half-sheets about the book!' I turned over the letter, to find it signed 'Neville Chamberlain'. I now print it, both because it belongs to the story of this book and because it is an historical document owing to the importance of the writer.

> *Westbourne,*
> *Edgbaston,*
> *Birmingham.*
> *June 7*, 1936.

Dear Dr. Dover Wilson,

I expect you will be rather surprised to get a letter from me as we have not been 'introduced'. But as we are both public characters perhaps we may dispense with formalities.

The fact is I can't help telling you what immense pleasure I have had out of 'What Happens in Hamlet'. I had asked for it as a Christmas present, and when it duly appeared I sat up several nights into the small hours reading it (for it cannot properly be read too hastily). When I had finished it, I did what I don't think I have ever done before with any book; I immediately read it all over again! And that won't be the last time of reading, for there is much meat in it.

Well, you have made plain much that has always puzzled me and you have made the great play even greater and more interesting [than] before. I am sure I am only one of many thousands all over the world who will be deeply grateful to you and who will rejoice in the honour which has just been conferred upon you.

Having now expressed what I wanted to say I feel emboldened to ask a question or two.

I was a little bothered on hearing that the Ghost came from Purgatory for though I confess to a very hazy idea of what happened there I had not associated it with 'sulphurous and tormenting flames'. However the encyclopaedia tells me that according to the orthodox after Thomas Aquinas souls in Purgatory *were* tormented with fire, and as you do not allude to the passage above or to the 'fasting in fires' I presume you are not conscious of any difficulty.

The 'tables' speech or rather the passage about the tables has always bothered me, since it seems odd that a man, all by himself, should write down for his own satisfaction what he could always go on saying to himself. Bradley of course felt the difficulty and tried to account for it. I should like much to know what your view is.

Your ingenious and convincing emendation of a dram of eale etc. is very happy. But to my ear a dram of *ill* would sound better than *evil*. 'Bear those ills we have' is a good precedent.

One last question and I have done. In Act IV Scene III Hamlet calls Claudius 'dear Mother' and on correction gives his sardonic explanation. I am sure you have thought over this passage and can tell me what exactly is in Hamlet's mind in affecting to make a mistake. I am satisfied that it signifies something but I can't make up my mind what.

I read the Mousetrap chapter first. Splendid!

Yours sincerely,

NEVILLE CHAMBERLAIN

The letter gave me much pleasure for it was clear that apart from his high office (at that time he was Chancellor of the Exchequer) Neville Chamberlain was a genuine critic, knew his *Hamlet* thoroughly, and raised relevant questions. These I had already dealt with in notes to my edition of *Hamlet*, which he had not yet seen. So I sent him a copy, saying that it would be a great privilege to be allowed to write his name in it. The result was an invitation for my wife and myself to dine at No. 11 Downing Street. As we were to talk about *Hamlet* there were just the four of us, and on our way to the dining-room with Mrs. Chamberlain on my arm, she said to me, 'My husband is so fond of your books that I give him one every Christmas,' at which Neville cut in from behind, 'Only once, dear.' A small thing, but evidence of the passionate honesty of a brave man, which I am proud to be able to record.

I have one or two other letters from Neville Chamberlain arising out of correspondence in *The Times Literary Supplement*, but after he became Prime Minister and had to deal with Hitler, we found ourselves writing about another subject altogether. By this time I was also in correspondence with Professor Wolfgang Keller, who was the secretary of the Deutsche Shakespeare Gesellschaft in Weimar and a scholar for whose Shakespeare translations I have considerable respect. Having heard that I knew Chamberlain, in one of his letters Keller asked me to sound him to see whether he would consent to be Honorary President of the society, the last Englishman to fulfil that function having been Edward VII. And Keller added in the same letter that he was sure his fellow-Shakespearians would greatly welcome such consent from one who had saved the world from war. This letter, it may be noted, was written towards the end of 1938.

Chamberlain replied that before answering he must make enquiries; and having waited a fortnight or so I received a note from him telling me that on discovering that the society had been compelled to expel all Jews from membership, he found it impossible to act as President. But, he went on, he did not, of course, want this given as a reason for declining and perhaps I would tell Professor Keller that he had numerous offers of this kind in his official position and found it so difficult to select between the various societies in this country and foreign countries that he had to make it a rule not to accept honorary presidencies unless in very special circumstances.

There was, however, another matter that Keller and I discussed, and which involved me more closely. On 23rd April 1939, the Deutsche Shakespeare Gesellschaft was to celebrate its seventy-fifth birthday; and Keller was to a large extent, I gather, responsible for organizing the celebrations. In the earlier correspondence of 1938 he had arranged that I should give one of two guest lectures at Weimar where the meeting was to be held, the other lecturer being Professor Arturo Farinelli of Turin, who would represent the Rome–Berlin Axis. Letters from Keller also informed me that the celebration was to be a two-day affair—lectures on the first afternoon and an official welcome on the second, accompanied by greetings to be conveyed by myself from learned societies in Britain. These last, it may be noted, included messages from the British Academy which W. W. Greg sent me, with his blessing, and from the Trustees of the Birthplace at Stratford-on-Avon, sent me with a similar blessing by Sir Archibald Flower.

Meanwhile, however, a second occasion for this visit to Germany turned up unexpectedly in the form of a letter from Sir William Bragg who knew me for family reasons. He asked me in the name of the Royal Society to go to Berlin as a guest of the Kaiser Wilhelm Gesellschaft, the German scientific academy corresponding with the Royal Society. It is not commonly realized that an appeasement campaign was being actively pursued on the German side at the same time as it was on the English side—though whether Hitler did not regard it as a useful screen for other designs may be doubted. In any case, the Royal Society and the Kaiser Wilhelm Gesellschaft had been exchanging lecturers, who were of course scientists. But as Bragg's letter informed me, Telschow, the secretary of that Gesellschaft, was suggesting that they might have a literary lecturer as a change, and it was agreed that I should be asked to go, together with William Bragg, the son of Sir William. I was very willing and found Telschow anxious to meet my convenience. Thus it was not long before it was arranged that the week I was to spend in Berlin as the guest of his society should immediately precede my visit to Weimar for the other Gesellschaft. And in the end a third string was added to the bow; for a connection of Professor Bruford (at that time Professor of German in Edinburgh) was a Professor of Education in Jena; and so I was to call in at Jena for a weekend before going on to Berlin.

I set out on my visit to Germany on Good Friday, stopping a night at Caius before going on by boat to the Hook. But while I was in Cambridge, the world suddenly heard that Mussolini had pounced on Albania. 'You mustn't go. War is just about to break out,' said my friends at college. It did seem a facer; but I determined to get in touch with the Foreign Office before turning tail, so I rang up Stephen Gaselee who was then Foreign Office Librarian. His reply was, 'Go, of course; if anything happens when you're in Berlin, we'll send you home in the Embassy bag.' It now occurs to me that Gaselee naturally shared the optimistic illusion since seen to be common to Foreign Office generally at this period; for when I reached Berlin after my weekend at Jena and called at the Embassy, I was taken out to lunch there by a number of happy young men. They all said to me—as I well remember—'What is all this fuss in England about? This is the most peaceful capital in Europe.' How they could justify this ebullience seems difficult to understand now; but when I read Ambassador Henderson's report on the whole sorry business after war had broken out, I could see that he at any rate had been 'had'. Nor can I avoid the opinion that Henderson himself was, at least in part, responsible for Chamberlain's refusal to believe that Hitler would go to the lengths he did.

So I started on my journey to Jena, a cross-country one with two changes, if I recollect rightly, en route. And when I got into a fresh carriage, travelling third class so as to hear what people were talking about, I found those I met at once aware from the cut of my clothes that I was English and very much aware too that a dreadful war was hanging over them. 'You don't want to fight us, do you? We don't want to fight you,' was their pitiable cry. And the most popular man in Germany was not Adolf Hitler but a little black-coated gentleman carrying an umbrella, upon whose meetings with the Führer all their hopes hung.

On reaching Jena, I was most kindly received by Mrs. Petersen and the Professor, who was very anxious for me to see him conducting a class. Unfortunately the demonstration school was not open on Sunday, but he collected together a class of boys and girls about fourteen years of age, and took as his subject the Prodigal Son—which he read from Luther's Bible and then expounded for the rest of the hour. When Petersen was good enough to ask me, at the end of the lesson, what I had thought about it all, I said that I had found it most interesting, but that in our country we did like the pupils to do something during the lesson hour. The 'Diktat' method was then presumably prevalent in German class teaching; but I understand that since the war the pendulum has swung the other way, as pendulums are apt to do in our own schools.

When my weekend there was over, I travelled to Berlin. Having paid my respects to the Ambassador, I then went on to Harnack House, which was the residential club of the Kaiser Wilhelm Gesellschaft. There I was introduced by Telschow to two charming young Nazis, man and woman, who told me that they were to be my guides for the week; a little flat was set at my disposal and the sum of two hundred and thirty marks was given me to spend as I liked, provided I took none of it out of Germany when I left. I was to be entertained, I was told, by a special performance of *Hamlet* at the State Theatre with Gründ-gens in the title role. The play was produced on a revolving stage with a little piece of the *ruins* of Elsinore showing in each scene; and the performance seemed to me terribly *démodé*. I could imagine Harley Granville-Barker snorting at an early moment, and walking out. I felt much happier at *Die Bürger von Calais* on another evening: the Germans in my experience never fail at the opera.

But the peak of the week was to be Hitler's fiftieth birthday on 20th April, which was to be celebrated with a military parade, the first military parade in Germany since 1918. The Führer sat in a little canopied pavilion just wide enough for Goering on one side and the head of the army on the other—Goering holding out his Field Marshal's baton well before his ample frontage, so that the people might see it. And to either side of the pavilion were lower platforms on one of which was exhibited the immense von Neurath in uniform, standing guard over (one might almost say, leading to the sacrifice) little President Hacha in a frock-coat, the puppet head of the newly-formed 'Slovak State'.

Hitler's seat in the pavilion was a simple chair of red plush and gold, like a vice-chancellor's chair—*sancta simplicitas* was the note of the frame as a whole. And when each new regiment marched past him he rose and 'Heil Hitler'-ed—I don't know how many times he 'heiled' himself in the four hours that I sat in the diplomatic stand opposite, feeling hungrier and hungrier, for the lunch hour fell in the middle of the parade: and I hadn't even a stick of chocolate with me. The stand was not over-full, but was there for the boys to learn their lesson from the master on the platform. And when it was all over the master got down from the pavilion, stepped lightly into his chariot with his special banner flying, turned to all of us with a scornful fling of the arm—as much as to say, 'So much for you, you bastards!'—and disappeared.

It occurred to me about a couple of years later that if I had had a Mills bomb in my pocket and known how to throw it, I might have saved the world in a way more effective than Chamberlain ever thought of, for the pavilion was within an easy lobbing distance from where I sat.

A contrast to this was my visit to the house of Professor Alois Brandl, who was then over ninety years of age. He received me in his study—where I can still see him seated on a sofa—and delighted to tell me about a translation of *Hamlet* he was then working out. But what sticks in my mind is the sudden interruption when he broke short and turning round pointed to the picture on the wall behind him. 'But have you seen my picture of the Führer? He is a man! God sent us a man!' That was the tragic moment to me of my visit to Berlin.

I also visited, as in duty bound, the Kaiser Wilhelm Institute at Dahlem, in the biological section of which I was shown a department that gave me the creeps. It was devoted to the study of identical twins. I saw identical twins of baboon and other types of monkey, of other animals also, I think—even of insects, if I remember rightly. Most repulsive of all was a cage through the bars of which I could see two pairs of human identical twins—human specimens, and labelled as such on the door. What was it all about? The Führer believed that his scientists ought to be able to produce not only identical twins but triplets and quadruplets as well, and so on. And in the end the slaves could be produced in the laboratories. Had he not been reading Aldous Huxley's *Brave New World* in which he foresaw a slave race being thus produced?

But I mustn't detail all the events of a very crowded week and will omit dinners and other forms of festivity. One item must however be mentioned, the ostensible purpose for which I was in Berlin, namely my lecture in the Harnack House on Shakespeare, the subject I chose being *Twelfth Night*. Either immediately before or immediately after my visit to Berlin, I spent a night with Professor Deutschbein, the Professor of English, at Marburg, where I delivered another lecture.

Marburg, as everyone who knows it will agree, is a delightful little university town, and my host and hostess were the kindest of people. In the morning I took a walk with Frau Deutschbein on her shopping expedition, carrying her basket for her. Presently we came, halfway up a street full of houses, to a site on which the building had obviously been destroyed. 'What's this?' I said to Frau Deutschbein. She raised her finger to her lips. 'It is *Synagog, Synagog*. We did not wish it. It is that Goebbels. He came down from Berlin and ordered it.' Goebbels, I found, was one of the best-hated of all Hitler's lieutenants. But the Deutschbeins were by no means disloyal to the Führer; and at lunchtime I was told that the great man himself was to make a speech which could be heard over the wireless. We sat and listened, the servants being called in. It was a solemn half-hour, as if at family prayers; only I had the feeling that on this occasion it was God Himself who was speaking in the raucous voice that came over the loud-speaker.

Shakespeare sends me Abroad

The seventy-fifth birthday of the Deutsche Shakespeare Gesell-schaft was, as I said, to be celebrated at Weimar. The meeting assembled consisted of about five hundred 'Anglisten' (English specialists) from all over Germany, mostly school-teachers, two mornings being devoted to sightseeing (Goethe's house and so on) and informal talk, and two afternoons to lectures and speeches. I only discovered later that one of the notorious Nazi concentration camps was within four miles of where we were enjoying ourselves—but I'm pretty sure that very few among those present were any more aware of this than I was.

Two lectures were to be delivered between four and six o'clock on the first afternoon, the first by Professor Farinelli, to whom one hour was assigned, the second being left to me. The Italian professor spoke in very rapid, very fluent German—too rapid for me to follow much. But, despite his rapidity, he occu-pied one hour and twenty minutes out of the two assigned—perhaps presuming on the privileges due to the Axis. My lecture, entitled 'Kingship in Shakespeare, especially as revealed in *Richard the Second*', was therefore a little cramped; but I managed to get in most of what I wanted to say, and at the end the mem-bers of the audience surged forward to shake my hand and to tell me that they had understood my English so much better than Professor Farinelli's German.

An incident worth recording occurred that afternoon. The curator of a great art gallery asked whether he might have a word in private. So he came up to my bedroom, took the receiver off the telephone, and then exploded, 'I hate him! I hate him!' This was not the only occasion on which I seemed to be talking to a soul in prison. And I couldn't help feeling, as I moved about, that I bore the air of a free man whom people looked upon with envy.

The second afternoon was devoted to speeches of welcome from the officials in their brown uniforms. There was the Gauleiter of Thüringen, the Burgomaster of Weimar (a very fat man) and a third, slimmer person, whose name I never caught, but who was obviously an ardent disciple of the prophet of the Aryan race, for he harangued us for ten minutes on Shakespeare as 'the spearhead of Nordic culture in Europe'. Next on the list my name appeared, to convey greetings from the learned societies in England already referred to. And when I had completed my brief mission, feeling more than a little indignant about what the last speaker had said, I went on to ask whether I might take advantage of the honorary membership which the society had just conferred upon me, to say a few words in reply. We in England were very proud that Germany had adopted our national poet, I said; after all, the only thing we could claim was that he happened to be *born* in our country—at which my hearers laughed. But we did like to think that he belonged not only to England, not only to Germany, but to the whole world. 'You must remember,' I said, 'that his noblest soldier was a black man with thick lips and fuzzy hair, and that his most fascinating woman was a gypsy queen of Egypt who took Professor Farinelli's Rome prisoner, in the person of Antony.' And then I suddenly remembered where I was and sat down in rather a hurry, lest I should begin to talk about Shylock—saying to Keller as I took my seat next to him, 'I hope I haven't dropped a brick.' 'Oh no,' he replied. 'The officials do not understand English.'

So I was allowed to leave Hitler's Germany quietly, without having to be sent home in the Embassy bag! Within four and a half months we were at war and before 1940 was out Neville Chamberlain was dead. He had honoured me with his friendship, and though our meetings were few—not more than three, I think—and our conversations confined to Shakespeare, from these and such correspondence as I had with him I received an impression of a man honest-to-God, hating insincerity and sycophancy, who, when faced with a problem connected with matters he thought important, was inclined to suspect traditional or official opinion.

Let me then conclude by quoting Churchill's tribute in the House of Commons, when news came of Chamberlain's death, to one who, in utter sincerity, staked his whole reputation on the chance of saving humanity from disaster.

'The only guide to a man is his conscience; the only shield to his memory is the rectitude and sincerity of his actions. It is very imprudent to walk through life without this shield, because we are so often shocked by the failure of our hopes and the upsetting of our calculations; but with this shield, however the fates may play, we march always in the ranks of honour.'

The tablet in the parish church at Heckfield, Hampshire, reads,

Neville Chamberlain
Prime Minister of Great Britain
1937 — 1940
'Write me as one that loves his fellow men'

Shakespeare took me again to Europe—this time soon after the end of the war that had been imminent during my earlier visit. Some of the French publishers celebrated the Liberation by staging an exhibition of books published by the university presses of Britain. The Cambridge University Press accepted the invitation with enthusiasm and even went so far as to exhibit an author as part of the show they put forward—to wit, myself. This side of the exhibition took the form of a lecture on Shakespeare at the Sorbonne in Paris. Duff Cooper was then our ambassador; the lecture was preceded by a cocktail party at the Embassy where I met the divine Diana who afterwards came on with the Ambassador to the lecture. The title I chose was 'Shakespeare and Humanity', and the lecture itself was a development of a reply I had made just before the war to the Nazi speaker at Weimar who had claimed Shakespeare as a spearhead of Nordic culture. I do not believe I ever spoke better in my life. At that moment of history, at that place in Europe, how could a man cease to be inspired?

The evacuation had been so recent that there was still no milk in Paris. In fact they were as short of milk as we were of sugar; so that of an afternoon when one of our hosts took half a dozen members of our party to tea at his house, and, opening the door of the room where the meal was to be served, showed us a table covered with highly sugared cakes, we simply sat down and ate like wolves. Nor was that the end; for when we went off next day by train to Calais, each of us was presented with a carton containing a delicious cake as a present to our respective wives.

In October 1953, I paid a second visit to Germany in my role of Shakespearian scholar. This one lasted two weeks, from 6th to 22nd October, and was confined to the British Zone. It included lectures delivered at various centres, the most memorable being those at Munich, Berlin and Bochum—this last having become the new centre of the Deutsche Shakespeare Gesellschaft.

From my personal point of view, the most interesting hours during the tour were spent in Munich with my friend Professor Wolfgang Clemen, already at that date recognized as the leading Shakespearian scholar in Germany—and indeed known to English scholars before the war for his famous book, *Shakespeare's Bilder* (1936), rewritten and expanded for English readers in 1951 under the title *The Development of Shakespeare's Imagery*, with a preface by myself.

I had first met Professor Clemen at the meeting of the Deutsche Shakespeare Gesellschaft in Weimar in 1939, where the opportunities of talk were few; but during this visit I spent a weekend as his guest at Endorf, a little village some distance south-east of Munich. His home had been built by his father, a professor of fine art, who had introduced the knowledge of Ruskin to Germany; and it was a house full of his treasures. And there I came to know Clemen's family and found his delightful wife busily engaged in translating Gerard Manley Hopkins's poetry into German. She asked my advice about 'windhover', and I wished my bird-loving wife had been there to answer her. I was fortunate in the weather on my visit and went for a walk up on the hill above Endorf—which led to my talking of the Lake District, telling my host how my two elder children, then Oxford students, had made me walk on one occasion twenty-five miles in a snowstorm. It is chance remarks like this that may in Germany suddenly reveal terrible situations. 'You've never walked twenty-five miles,' I said to my friend. He replied, 'I once walked for four days carrying a rifle from Leningrad.'

13. Richard Pares, 1950

14. John Dover Wilson with his
second wife, Elizabeth

While in Munich, I was able to spend a few hours with another old friend, the veteran Shakespearian scholar, Professor Schücking, who had come over from Leipzig to see me. The meeting had been arranged, of course, by Clemen who looked up to him as a master-spirit; and he was indeed a wonderful old man, who had looked on tempests and had not been shaken. He had even refused to 'wear the button'.

I also visited places of interest in Munich, and gave two addresses, one to the Anglo-German Society and university students, and another, the next day, to the Institute for the Training of Interpreters; and there I was received by the principal who, I came to learn afterwards, had been Hitler's own interpreter—a matter, of course, which he never mentioned to me, preferring to tell me that he had princesses among his students.

The next place I may mention was Berlin which I had been eagerly looking forward to. I need not here record the events of my stay; suffice to say that I was most hospitably entertained both by dinners given in my honour and by attendance at operas. But what must be specially noted is the reception given to a lecture I delivered, entitled 'Shakespeare and Humanity'. I began it by telling the crowded hall that I was repeating a lecture I had given in Paris almost immediately after its liberation. And I took as my text, as I told them, the claim I had made at Weimar in 1939 that Shakespeare belongs to all humanity—not to England, and still less to the 'Nordic race'. At this reference to the Nazi gospel of race the whole audience roared with laughter; and the lecture was listened to with more attention and enthusiasm than any lecture I have ever given.

To pass from Berlin to Bochum was like exchanging comedy for tragedy. I stayed in a hotel but my real host was a genial old gentleman who had been a Jewish refugee in Britain; he showed me, as a trophy of his exile, one of the richest assemblies of detective stories and other shockers that I have ever seen on the walls of a private library. Returning to his old home, he had become chairman of the local Culture Committee; and I sat with him in a kind of royal box in the astonishingly perfect little theatre just completed at a cost of six and a half million marks. The play was Shakespeare's *Richard III* (the Schlegel-Tieck translation); and upon asking the theatre manager, another returned exile, why they had chosen this as their opening play, he gave me a look as he said, 'To remind them of recent events'. It had clearly been selected with the approval of my host sitting beside me; for when we came to the words (in German), 'The bloody dog is dead', he rose from his seat and shouted, 'Dat is vat I said ven Hitler met his end!' Nevertheless I couldn't help noticing that the previous chairman of the Culture Committee, sitting behind us in the box, was not amused.

SOUTH AFRICA

Most of my English colleagues, especially since I retired, have paid visits to America, where facilities have generally been afforded them for time to write their own books. My extended journeys have been southward not westward, to the Union of South Africa. This is mainly due to family reasons, of which a word must now be said.

My only son, Godfrey, became, after reading Mods and Greats at Oxford, a social anthropologist—largely owing to the fact that at one of Zimmern's summer schools he had met a South African girl named Monica Hunter who had just been awarded a First Class in that subject at Cambridge; and her Ph.D. thesis 'Reaction to Conquest' was later published with an introduction by Smuts himself. She had not over-much difficulty in persuading even one of Zimmern's favourite pupils to abandon a life of devotion to Greek scholarship. They both joined Malinowski's class in social anthropology at the London School of Economics (which class, incidentally, included Mrs. Paul Robeson and Jomo Kenyatta) and in the end they were married in 1935.

Monica Hunter came of Scots missionary families on both sides, her father being David Hunter, son of a well-to-do Glasgow merchant, who had settled at Lovedale, the centre of the South Africa mission of the Church of Scotland, where he devoted himself to looking after the finances of the Church and especially of the mission hospital. And her mother was a

MacGregor, daughter of a missionary in China. David Hunter was clearly a most remarkable man—it was never my good fortune to meet him except on one brief occasion—and his wife, whom I came to know better, was no less remarkable, combining force of character with saintliness. It may be noted that the name Monica which they gave to their only child who grew up was that of the most famous African saint known to history, the mother of St. Augustine.

After completing the course under Malinowski, Godfrey and Monica selected, as their area for field-work, an African tribe called the Nyakyusa, living on the borders of what were then Tanganyika and Nyasaland. With this tribe they lived for over two years, mastering the language and filling rows and rows of notebooks—in the Nyakyusan language, transcribed in a phonetic script of their own invention—with details of the life, manners, customs and laws of the people with whom they established almost at once terms of great familiarity. There is nothing hidden from the social anthropologist; and what the man didn't discover, the woman did. I once said to Monica, my daughter-in-law, 'You should make a similar study of the mixed tribe that inhabits Balerno.' She lifted up her hands in horror!

From these notes, Monica Wilson has since written and published three important books on the Nyakyusa—books which have now become well known to social anthropologists all over the world. After they had completed these studies (at least temporarily), the future looked very rosy for both of them, for Godfrey was appointed director of the Rhodes-Livingstone Institute in Northern Rhodesia, which was to be a centre of social anthropology for the whole of the South African area. But he never lived to do more than write two books. One, *The Economics of Detribalisation* was issued by the Institute in 1942; the other, *The Analysis of Social Change*, was completed by Monica and published by the Cambridge University Press after his death. Both these books are, I believe, regarded as classics by anthropologists. The sudden outbreak of war not only brought all their work to a stop but led to Godfrey's death in May 1944, leaving Monica a widow with two infant sons.

So much for the family ties that bound us to South Africa. The primary reasons for our first visit, in 1949, were, however, official.

The South African government, of which Smuts until just before our visit had been prime minister, had set up an organization somewhat similar to the British Council, for the purpose of inviting British scholars to give courses of lectures in South Africa. And the two organizations combined to plan a tour which would enable me to lecture on Shakespeare in all the six university colleges in South Africa.

The other reason was even more important. The two separate colleges in Natal, one at Pietermaritzburg and the other at Durban, were to be united as the University of Natal, the inauguration ceremony to take place on 19th March. On this occasion, four persons were to have honorary degrees conferred on them—Lord Eustace Percy, the eminent educationist, then Principal of King's College, Newcastle; Sir Raymond Priestley of Antarctic fame, then Vice-Chancellor of Birmingham University; Dr. Basil Schonland, now Sir Basil, later at Harwell and then the most eminent atomic scientist in South Africa; and myself.

My wife and I left home on 6th March and travelled from London by Skymaster. Our first stop was Tripoli, then Khartoum and Nairobi, after which we eventually landed at Johannesburg. Since the University of Witwatersrand was the first call in my list of universities and colleges for lectures, we stopped in Johannesburg for a day or two. Our host and hostess were Professor Underwood and his wife who overwhelmed us with kindness, showed us all round the town, and on Saturday afternoon took us, to quote my wife's diary, 'to a large race meeting, the great and monthly social event where the women show off their smart clothes. Lunched with a steward who gave us tips for the races'. Our quarters with the Underwoods were most comfortable; but it is worth noting that they kept three large dogs which were let out at night for protective reasons, ready to spring upon any intruder.

The Professor of English at the university, Professor J. Y. T.

Greig, was endlessly kind; and in particular he drove us over to Pretoria through lovely country, for our visit to Roberts' Heights to visit the military graves, retiring at some distance when we got there for us to kneel together by the little cross marked G. B. Wilson and his 'number'. It is a quiet resting-place high up on a flat hilltop with all the winds of heaven blowing about it.

Next day we took the train to Pietermaritzburg and when we arrived there, at 6.20 a.m., found an almost royal reception; not only were our host and hostess, Dr. and Mrs. Akerman, there but also the principal and real founder of the new university-to-be, Principal Malherbe and his wife, together with others—all inhabitants of Pietermaritzburg. (*En passant*, the name Malherbe will remind my readers of the French philosopher; and there are indeed many descendants of French Huguenot families in South Africa, while there were even not a few Scots religious emigrants as well as Genevan Calvinists. I need hardly say that Natal itself, as everyone knows, contains thousands of Indians, Gandhi himself having lived there for twenty years.)

Our host and hostess were very wealthy, and we were sumptuously entertained in their most comfortable home for a day or two—more sumptuously than either Lord Eustace Percy or Sir Raymond Priestley, clearly because each had, unlike me, come with no wife. The Akermans kept a large staff of servants—four indoor and four outdoor—and, instead of what my wife calls 'those awful dogs', a night watchman. Their best maid, an African woman, had been with them for sixteen years. Eleven years before they had had a battle royal over getting her a driving licence. She had passed all tests four times, and at last Dr. Akerman himself had gone with her to the court and secured it for her. Yet for years she had to drive with her licence open on her knee as no policeman would let her pass; and hundreds of people wrote to tell the Akermans that their car had been seen driven by a native woman. But every African society and club in Natal wrote to thank them. Yet African men and both Indian men and women could get licences.

We stayed at Pietermaritzburg long enough for me to deliver one or two lectures to commemorate the college's union with the college at Durban. Our next port of call then was Durban itself. Our host and hostess here were again a doctor and his wife; but how different from either the Underwoods or the Akermans. Dr. George Campbell was the fashionable doctor of Durban, a product of Edinburgh, an international cricketer, a most charming and lovable man. Two of their sons were then known to us as medical students at Edinburgh University, George junior being serious-minded and also passionately fond of music, and his younger brother, Hamish, ebullient and endlessly talkative. They have now followed their father as doctors in Durban.

Both the doctor and his wife were what were then called 'liberals', the doctor himself being much involved in politics and also being chairman of the University Court; his wife, equally liberal, was a close friend of the Smuts family.

I gave several lectures in Durban, one at my special request to the non-European department, which mostly consisted of Indian students. Its head was, I found, an old friend—Mrs. Mabel Palmer, formerly Mabel Atkinson, a prominent Fabian, whom I had met at a Fabian Summer School in Saas-Fé about 1906 and who was delighted to meet me again. The English department was specially greedy for talks not bargained for in the programme —until Principal Malherbe, discovering what was happening, intervened, as in a climate of this kind a good deal of rest is required in the day.

After one of these lectures we heard that Smuts would like to see us, and a conversation followed in which he talked to me about Shakespeare and to my wife about South African birds. The conversation, she notes in her diary, led on to a discussion of the phrase, 'to enjoy yourself', which Smuts interpreted as getting time to be alone, as Christ did when He went up into the mountains, according to the Gospel—though in point of fact there are no mountains in Palestine, as Smuts had himself found, for he had just been there. How necessary it was, he said to her, if one wished to 'enjoy oneself', to get away from crowds (he did not like the word 'escape'), if one wished to enjoy natural things, birds and so on. She said that we loved to be among the simpler village people too, and he agreed.

He then described how recently he had been halfway up Table Mountain, and met some pleasant-looking people with whom he had exchanged a few words. They asked him whether it wasn't true that General Smuts often walked that way. He said that it was so, but did not tell them who he was, not wishing to have his own walk ruined. At which my wife remarked, 'We shall know how to behave if we happen to meet you there, when we come to the Cape.' 'What a man he was,' my wife writes elsewhere, 'one of those rare creatures whose spirit shines through'—Ichabod!

The inauguration ceremonies of the University of Natal had already begun in Pietermaritzburg; but the culmination of the whole affair, including the graduation, took place on 19th March in the City Hall, Durban, at which Smuts was present as Chancellor of the parent university of Cape Town. Before entering the hall, some of the graduands waited in the square without, Eustace Percy and Raymond Priestley each in his robes of office, while I wore my scarlet Cambridge doctor's gown and the black velvet Tudor cap with the gold tassel to shield my head from the burning sun. The broadcloth of the gown lent little protection to the body; and I have never felt so hot in my life as I did while I waited to be ushered in under the protective roof of the Great Hall. However, the illustration facing page 208, which originally appeared in the commemoration number of the University of Natal magazine under the heading 'Three Wise Men', will show that my perspiration had not damped my ardour for talking about Shakespeare.

Before the degrees of LL.D. were conferred, greetings from various universities were conveyed, including of course those represented by Eustace Percy, Raymond Priestley and myself. I had been empowered to carry a personal message from the Vice-Chancellor of Edinburgh University and was able in my speech to use my Cambridge gown so as to make a special bow to Smuts, who was at that time also Chancellor of Cambridge University.

The somewhat elaborate ceremony of inauguration, together with the conferring of honorary degrees, was followed by an address by Smuts and we then doffed gowns for comfort and adjourned to lunch, some nine women and ninety men. My wife records, of the heat in the room, that 'we women were given fans, and needed them!' Smuts had to catch a plane back to the Cape, but before he hurried away he found time for brief speeches of a laudatory character about the honorary graduates of the newly-founded university. He had a good deal to say about Eustace Percy and Raymond Priestley, and could have said more. And then followed words which became blurred in my memory because of the keen pleasure they gave me, so that I must fall back on the diary of my wife who shared the same pleasure to the full.

'And then his voice changed and with deep feeling he said, "And then there is Dover Wilson, Dover Wilson with whom I have spent so many happy evenings".'

We stayed at Durban in the hospitable house of the Campbells for a week or so, and then flew on to the Cape—for me an unforgettable flight, since in those days one flew low, not far over the lagoons all the way along the coast, and then right over the top to find Cape Town lying below.

Our host and hostess in Cape Town were Vice-Chancellor and Mrs. Davie, both charming people, but he of very delicate health. We came in for a talk by Eustace Percy, our first opportunity of hearing him; but he was, I think, off colour during most of his stay in South Africa—certainly not well, nor up to his usual form. Next day I gave one of my lectures. On the 27th March we were fetched by Leo Marquard and his delightful wife, a lecturer in English at Stellenbosch, whom I had met years before at a tea-party given by Pullinger's daughter at St. Hilda's College, Oxford. He was at that time representing the Oxford University Press in South Africa and is himself a distinguished writer, very much opposed to apartheid. We stayed with them at Stellenbosch for a couple of nights. Both were friends of our daughter-in-law, Monica, and proved very welcoming on subsequent visits to Cape Town.

From Stellenbosch, a stronghold of Afrikaaner culture, we returned to Cape Town and were seen off next day on a thirty-two-hour journey to Bloemfontein, another Afrikaans university.

We travelled first class in a comfortable carriage, but a very shaky train, over that appalling central waste in South Africa known as the Karroo—'a vast uneven desert, with hills and even mountains in the distance, of sand, and stones and rocks in parts, covered all over, hills as well, more or less sparsely with Karroo grass. . . . Wherever there is a dried-up watercourse there are a few houses, and very, very far between each place; elsewhere apparently utter desolation'. The Karroo exemplifies the fundamental problem of South Africa—the dried-up watercourses show the land does not lack rain; what it needs is some sort of conservation so that this is not lost through evaporation.

Bloemfontein gave us an unfriendly welcome—or rather no welcome at all. In fact, we were not met at the train and for some time had no idea of where to go. Though the authorities had been informed of our coming, they clearly took a very mild interest in it.

The next stage of our journey took us to Grahamstown, to stay with Monica, who was then a professor at Rhodes University there, and to meet our two grandsons for the first time—Francis, then aged about nine, and Timothy, aged about five.

We could only stay a fortnight or so, the most memorable days of our whole tour. Though we were saddened by the death of Monica's father, it meant that we got to know Mrs. Hunter. For Monica fetched her to Grahamstown where she resided, till her death, in a house that Monica found for her; and so we came to love her gentle spirit as if we were members of her family. Mr. Hunter's death meant that Monica had to be away from home for a day or two and she left the boys in our charge. I watched Francis playing football and visited him at his school, St. Andrew's—which was one of the country's Church of England public schools—and liked what I saw of it very much.

One memorable incident during our stay was a visit I paid with Monica to Fort Hare, near Lovedale, the one college in South Africa for African students, which later became a constituent college of Rhodes University, which was, of course, mainly for white students. The university's principal, Thomas Alty, was specially interested in this outlying college.

Ostensibly, my visit was to give a lecture; but what stands out in my memory now was a dinner I ate at the Matthews' house, sitting next to Professor Matthews, the black Professor of Social Anthropology, who knew his Plato better than I did and with whom Plato himself might have enjoyed converse. He was afterwards imprisoned, as in the same situation Socrates might have been, had he too persisted in speaking the truth.

On our return to Grahamstown from Lovedale, I had of course to give a lecture, choosing one of my stock topics, 'How Shakespeare Wrote his Plays', which involved reproducing passages from the plays in his handwriting on the blackboard. The lecture was in a large hall full of students and others, with my wife, Monica, Francis and friends of the family at the front. Early in the lecture, a point arose upon which, turning to the audience, I remarked, 'But I will return to that matter later on.' When the lecture was over, according to my usual wish, the chairman, Principal Alty, told the audience that I would be very glad to deal with any questions; whereat Francis, quite unconscious of the large audience behind him, leapt up, 'Yes, grand-dad, you didn't go on with that point that you said you would tell us about.' The grandson got louder cheers than his grandfather.

On the 18th March, Francis and the kind Altys saw us off for another extended journey across a corner of the Karroo, our destination being Pretoria via Johannesburg, reaching the former on the morning of the 20th March.

This was the final stopping-place in our long journey. Here we first came to know Dr. Partridge of the English Department and his wife and family who were our hosts in Pretoria; we saw a good deal of them at our next visit to South Africa in 1956, by which time he had become Professor of English at Witwatersrand. To my wife's delight—and almost confusion—he presented us with a copy of a most expensive book about South African birds, other copies of which she had seen and longed to possess. It was from the Partridges that we first came to appreciate how important it is for English professors and lecturers to visit South African universities. As they explained, the institutions are separated by such long distances that members of the English departments, for example, have little chance of getting to know each other; so that our visit came to them like a breath of fresh air. Nothing could be more ill-advised than the notion one sometimes hears expressed in British university circles, that the proper attitude towards apartheid is to boycott South African universities.

One last point to record before we finally reached home. Our Skymaster which we took from Johannesburg on the 23rd April touched down at Khartoum. We were sitting on the steps beside the Nile before night fell with its usual suddenness, talking about Ernest B. Haddon (or 'Pachy', as his friends called him) who was also at that time visiting Africa. We had just said to one another, 'Fancy, if we were to meet Pachy here'—when a deep but very familiar voice from the foot of the steps said, 'He *is* here!' It was indeed my best and oldest friend, whose plane from Uganda had been delayed.

Our second visit to South Africa was in 1956, mainly for the purpose of attending the wedding of our younger daughter, Carol, to a missionary, Eric Jeffrey, in Nyasaland (as Malawi was then called). The wedding was planned to take place at the little church at Hogsback where Godfrey and Monica had been married, though ultimately the couple decided to marry in Mzuzu which was too inaccessible for us.

My wife and I journeyed by boat as far as Durban, and from there by train to East London, where we were met by Monica, and brought up to Hunterstoun, her delightful summer residence at Hogsback. The garden at Hunterstoun was watered by a mountain stream which had been canalized and caught up into pools, while, by means of piping just below ground with taps at various points to which tubing could be attached, it was kept perpetually green—though at the height of summer the country around might be parched and the cattle in bad seasons dying in the valleys beneath.

This was our first visit to Hunterstoun—so called after Monica's father, David Hunter. He had bought a hundred and fifty acres up in the hills, and enclosed a level portion, five miles up by road from the valley, planted it with European trees, with an orchard towards the back. And while Monica was still a girl they came up from Lovedale in the parched valley below during the heat of the summer months to live in a wooden hut there. Such was the wonderful inheritance my daughter-in-law acquired after the death of her parents. Meanwhile she also inherited a sum of money from an uncle, which enabled her to replace the wooden hut with a most fascinating building for herself and her two boys.

My wife and I slept in a bedroom facing north, next to one in which our grandsons slept; and to our great delight they were on holiday during our visit. We were roused in the morning by hearing shrieks outside the window, as the boys ducked each other in a built-up round pool not many yards away; and as they chased each other across the grass, quite naked, it was like a scene from one of the Greek vases.

I paid two other visits to South Africa, on both occasions staying at Hunterstoun. During the first of these, I took in hand the preparation for my edition of the *Sonnets*, sitting under the shade of a deodar tree not far from the entrance to the house.

Let me conclude by quoting my description from the Preface,

'It lies in a level upland glade shut in by dark forests stretching up to jagged mountain tops, but itself containing a luxuriant orchard and stately trees dotted about it here and there, while it fearlessly exposes its grassy slopes to the midsummer heat of the southern hemisphere, being watered and cooled by running streams and deep dark pools that give teeming life to birds and flowers of many kinds and colours, while to crown all extend the sweeping curves of a stately house, dwelling-place of a great lady. Shakespeare, I fancy, had imagined just such a home of peace and delight as his Belmont.'

12

Portraits

Alfred Pollard I came to know many years before the idea of editing Shakespeare even entered my mind. After my return from Finland in 1909, I lived for three years in London while a lecturer at Goldsmiths' College. So I could often call on Pollard in Wimbledon where he lived, and his friendship and character have been one of the chief influences in my life. Indeed, after the death of his two sons in 1914 and 1915, he accepted my offer of substitute sonship.

This is a sketch of the private life of my friend, as far as he revealed it to anyone. Of Pollard the librarian and bibliographer, and of his work upon Chaucer, the Bible and Shakespeare, much has been published elsewhere by others and in part by myself. Later, when I first became engrossed in the text of *Hamlet* and other quartos, we did much Shakespeare work together.

Though Pollard was a scholar, like many of his countrymen who have earned that title he had much more than scholarship in him; in fact, he was a man more than usually many-sided and complete. He might perhaps have contributed nothing at all to learning but for an accident, the bad stammer he caught from an elder brother at the age of three and was never afterwards able to throw off. For mere acquaintances a sore hindrance to intercourse and understanding, once you got to know him it was felt as almost an added grace, since it lent pleasing ripples to the current of his talk, and ever and again an engagingly explosive force to some wise or witty remark. At times he could manage to speak in public, for example as Professor of Bibliography at King's College; while on one memorable occasion he actually delivered the 1923 British Academy lecture on

237

Shakespeare. It was this stammer which made him a librarian, and hence, for a man of his active mind, a bibliographer and scholar.

His pen was as ready, articulate and direct as his tongue was halting; the one a compensatory effect of the other. Certainly as a writer he was an almost incredible combination of facility, good humour and exactitude. He could write, too, under practically any conditions; a good deal of his bibliographical journalism was, I believe, composed in the train between Wimbledon and Waterloo; and when the line became electrified he found the oscillation a distinct stimulus to invention.

But even though—except for the stammer—a born teacher and a great admirer of other born teachers like W. P. Ker and Walter Raleigh, Pollard himself was less academically minded than any other learned man I have known; while his wide-roving curiosity, his intense and passionate interest in every phase of modern life, would very soon have driven him from 'parochial' Oxford had he begun by settling down there. Thus scholarship was not the first or even the second thing in his life, while he was inspired by no ruling ambition, like his friend A. E. Housman, 'to build himself a monument'.

He worked hard at scholarship, with as much zest as any, and with greater skill, knowledge and urbanity than most; but it was always something of a game, which he found himself unable to take quite seriously, while it amused him, at times even saddened him, to watch others offering it their heart's worship. He was, in fact, in the strict sense of the word, an amateur. When I first realized this it came as a shock. I was speaking enthusiastically of a very learned and very elaborate book by Greg on a subject of great interest to us both, when he broke in, 'Yes, b-but rather B-B-Byzantine, don't you think?' Coming from the Honorary Secretary of the Bibliographical Society and our leading authority on fine books, the sentiment took my breath away. Yet it was characteristic, and not in the least caused by a 'superior' attitude. 'A very self-effacing person', as Sir Frederick Kenyon, the Director of the British Museum, described him, and one humbly conscious of his own imperfections and shortcomings, none of them very evident to his friends, he was always surprised that people he considered far more gifted than himself should devote their lives exclusively to erudition. And when someone once called him a scholar of international reputation, he replied, with his inimitable stammer, 'Do you know what *that* means? S-S-S-Six old m-m-m-men in various countries of the world know my work, and d-d-d-don't a-g-g-g-gree with it.'

For most of his life Pollard was associated with King's College, London. King's College School where he spent his schooldays was at that date housed in the underground corridors of the college itself, the same cellars in fact which I refused to accept as fit quarters for the Education Department when I arrived in 1924.

When Pollard left school he went up to Oxford where he formed a remarkable friendship of considerable importance to English literature. Let me quote from an unfinished autobiography which he left behind him and which I shall refer to as the 'Sketch',

'In November 1876 I tried my luck for a Balliol scholarship, with the pleasant reward of beginning a long acquaintance with A. C. Clark, one of the successful candidates. The following Midsummer I got a scholarship at St. John's College, Oxford, thanks to having read the early numbers of the *Nineteenth Century*, in which the setter of the Essay paper seemed also to have been interested. Alfred Housman won the other scholarship at the same election, and to my great profit we were given rooms on the same stair. His friendship was the best thing I got from Oxford.'

Both were fellow scholars in the same year at St. John's, living on the same staircase for three years and during the fourth sharing rooms out of college with another undergraduate, Moses Jackson. At the most critical period of their lives, Pollard and Housman enjoyed a close friendship which must have been an especially tremendous experience for the former; cut off from the world by his stammer, a day-school boy, and early robbed by her illness of a mother's attention, he had probably never before known intimacy with a fellow human being. And the intimacy soon ripened into affection on both sides, which lasted the rest of their lives, though for reasons presently to be explained they drifted apart after 1881. That Pollard admired Housman and regarded him as a great man goes without saying. Yet, while he paid full honour to his friend's powers, he could not help regretting the use he put them to. Of *A Shropshire Lad*, the title of which he was proud to think had been suggested by himself, he often spoke to me, as it was for a time one of my favourite books of poems; but, highly as he placed it for craftsmanship, he could only groan in spirit over the gallows and graveyards which formed its principal themes.

What then did these two young men, so utterly different in temperament and outlook, talk about in those four years? It is an easy guess that poetry and religion provided them with their chief topics. Housman's 'favourite English poet in these early days', Pollard recalled some fifty years later, 'was Matthew Arnold, whose *Empedocles on Etna* he recommended to me'. This recommendation was an important event for Pollard. I find several references to Arnold's poetry in letters we exchanged in 1916. In one he observes, 'I think some of it has entered more deeply into my outlook on life than any other poetry'; and in a later letter still, written in reply to one preferring the claims of Robert Browning, he says,

'Yesterday evening I read *Rabbi Ben Ezra*, *Empedocles on Etna*, and *Saul*, one after the other, and think all three of them very wonderful. I grant you that *Saul*, and *Rabbi Ben Ezra* too, are much bigger than *Empedocles*, and yet I think that personally and in my own life the feeling of strength and certitude I have derived from Arnold has been of more practical help than the hope and consolation I have got from Browning. So there!'

As far as his studies were concerned, Pollard tells us in the 'Sketch',

'I was not expected to achieve more than a second in Classical Mods, but my attention to set books and a little polish conferred on my proses (verses I gave up!) by an excellent coach, C. H. Gibson of Merchant Taylors, I secured a First, to the pleased surprise of my tutors. When "Greats" was drawing near I was perturbed by an invincible habit of falling asleep whenever I tried to read any treatise of philosophy, especially if by T. H. Green, then the leading Oxford philosopher. One day, in the Undergraduates' library at St. John's, I took down a bulky volume by a disciple of Herbert Spencer: John Fiske. To my surprise I kept awake and soon found myself provided with a handful of formulas which could be applied without much difficulty to a considerable variety of topics. Thus at Midsummer 1881 I was placed in an unusually small First Class. When during 1882 I tried in succession for two "prize" fellowships at Queen's and Jesus, the examiners were more exacting. An opinion obtained for me from one of those at Jesus was that I might make a good journalist.'

At the time he wrote this, Pollard had a special reason for reflecting on examinations. A fall from a step-ladder in his garden in 1935, though it did nothing to impair his spirit, virtually put an end to authorship; he only managed, as far as I can discover, two pieces of continuous composition, apart from letter-writing: the 'Sketch' and 'Some Reminiscences of A. E. Housman', contributed to a memorial number of *The Broms-grovian*, the magazine of the poet's old school. And since the reminiscences were chiefly of Oxford days, it was inevitable that they should include some comment upon Housman's amazing failure in Greats, the same Greats in which Pollard had himself scored a First Class.

These contrasting results cast a shadow on Pollard's friendship with Housman. Bewildered and grieved at his friend's failure and ashamed at his own success, 'I got it into my head,' Pollard records, 'that the sight of me reminded Housman of his troubles, and was unwilling to thrust myself on him more than he might welcome.' And so—though he occasionally saw him after they began life in London, Pollard at the British Museum and Housman at the Patent Office, helped him unobtrusively when-ever he saw a chance, got him to contribute three verse translations for a volume of *Odes from the Greek Dramatists* (which I suspect was partly devised in order to draw his friend out); persuaded Kegan Paul to publish *A Shropshire Lad*, and even wrote him a testimonial in support of an application—the intimacy ceased. As Housman lived in rooms with the cheerful and ebullient Jackson, the sacrifice was probably mostly on Pollard's side. But selfless self-effacement and a delicate consideration for the feelings of others were part of his nature. The story, however, has a joyful ending, which shall be given once again in his own words,

'After 1899,[1] when I moved from Kensington to Wimbledon, I saw still less of Housman, though occasionally we corresponded, and there was a jolly interlude when Jackson, who had left the Patent Office for the Headship of a native college in India, was home on leave, and he and Housman dined and slept in my house. When I retired to rest I found an apple-pie bed awaiting me and I think the Professor of Latin was a fellow victim, though I'm not quite sure he wasn't an aggressor. Anyhow, we became very youthful and light-hearted. In 1911 I went up to Cambridge to hear his inaugural lecture in his second Professor-ship and was richly rewarded by the cry of pleasure with which I was greeted when he caught sight of me after it. I think that somehow my presence seemed to him a recognition that he had reached his haven at last.'

But to return to Oxford, which Pollard discovered, despite his 'double first', had no use for him. He returned home and in due course obtained from the Archbishop of Canterbury— through the instrumentality of his godfather, the Vicar of Brompton—a nomination to compete for a place in the British Museum. Whereupon, to continue in his own words,

'I attended at the Secretary's office at the Museum to fill up a form in which I had to state what languages I could offer, and was persuaded by a friend there "just for the sake of appearances" to add to my meagre stock of languages, Latin, Greek, and French, a fourth language—Italian, in which I had read a few cantos of the *Divina Commedia* with the aid of a crib. In November (1882) I was warned that I should be examined in the following January, and that translation from Italian would be one of the subjects. Others were Geography, Arithmetic (including Civil

[1] The correct date is 1897.

Service Tots), and Algebra, in all of which I was pretty rusty—more so in Algebra than I realized, as at half time I had only answered 3½ questions out of 13. Fortunately I pulled myself together and nearly finished the lot, while having made a diligent study of Manzoni's *I Promessi Sposi* in the intervening weeks, I got a higher percentage in translation from Italian than I dare mention. It was my last examination, and my old luck carried me through.'

This tale of the Lucky Examinee's Progress was obviously written by a man of unusual humility who enjoyed a more than ordinary sense of humour; an auspicious endowment for one destined to have much dealing with Chaucer and Shakespeare. And if we add to humility and humour and a quite exceptional mental agility, other qualities which proceed therefrom, such as a self-effacing administrative ability of a high order, a complete lack of pompousness or fuss in dealing with others and a literary style at once 'delightfully informal' and engagingly personal, we have most of the characteristics which were later to bring him honour with the officials of his department and in the world of scholarship.

Pollard was twenty-four when he entered the Museum, and he married four years later. Unhappily I never met their two sons, Geoffrey and Roger, born in 1888 and 1891 respectively; but after their deaths in 1914 and 1915, Mrs. Pollard and their sister, Joyce, welcomed me as son and brother. And so though I only came to know three members of the Pollard family, I knew three of them so intimately and learned from them so much about the sons that I could feel certain that it would have been hard to find any family happier, saner, richer in intellectual and spiritual values, or more conscious of its social responsibilities.

Pollard's own personal loss affected him in a way at once surprising to his friends and yet entirely in keeping with his character. In 1915 he was fifty-six years old and prepared, I was told by his wife, to descend by easy stages into the vale of old age, becoming a little of a valetudinarian (even in beginning to fancy walking was bad for him) and more and more engrossed in his books to the exclusion of other interests. His boys' heroic deaths rejuvenated him; he felt that he must do what in him lay to take their place in the world.

Previously he had sometimes ventured—despite his stammer— to speak in public, although his lectures were generally read for him by a friend. However, after the death of his two sons he was inspired with new courage and energy. Roger fell in October 1915; and in November Pollard was at Cambridge for his Sandars Lectures. They were delivered by Stephen Gaselee; but as an experiment he spoke himself for five minutes at the beginning of the course, and for another eight minutes at the end; 'quite successfully', he wrote to me at the time, and added:

'It may interest you to know that I think I can trust myself to speak without risk of a breakdown on three conditions:

(i) I must be quite sure that what I have to say is reasonably worth saying.

(ii) I must be quite sure of the order of my ideas.

(iii) I must leave the words pretty much to the inspiration of the moment.'

In the same dreadful year, he thought out and wrote out two of his principal contributions to Shakespearian scholarship, *Shakespeare's Fight with the Pirates* (the Sandars Lectures) and *King Richard II: a new Quarto*, published early in 1916. The second, with its elaborate tabulation of the errors and corrections in the four successive Quartos before 1623 and the folio of that date, involved more sheer drudgery than any of his publications before the *Short Title Catalogue* which was also completed at a time of bereavement, at his wife's death. In his last book he built himself a monument of a different kind; and if the results of the first two have been absorbed or superseded by those of later scholars, they will always be remembered for the heroic mood in which they were written.

With the utmost vigour, Pollard threw himself into all sorts of social and religious activities. Of these his membership of the Anglican Fellowship and of the committee of the Central Library for Students were perhaps the most conspicuous examples—the one a small body of active-minded Anglicans of every shade of churchmanship who combined devotional fellowship with the untrammelled discussion of religious problems; the other an offspring of Albert Mansbridge, which was struggling at that time to get onto its legs (though now a national institution well known to all as the National Central Library).

Many individuals as well as societies found gain in his loss. One of them was myself, who was bereaved of my father in the same twelve-month as Pollard was of his sons. It seemed natural that we should adopt each other. He was helped by it, I believe; and I received more grace from that adoption than from any thing, except one, that has happened to me in life. It is, I think, due to his memory to record also that the example of unflinching courage which he set in 1915 proved a great inspiration when a single ordeal of the same kind as his double one came to me a generation later.

At the beginning of 1936, I moved to Edinburgh and became much absorbed in a new life; and though I now had an excuse to go and stay at No. 40 Murray Road whenever I was in London, those occasions could not be very frequent, so that I did not see Pollard more than two or three times in the year. The war came in 1939 to make visits far more difficult both for me and for his daughter, now Mrs. Roberts, while for one reason or another nearly all his friends left the neighbourhood; all in fact, I believe, except Sir Henry Thomas, his successor as Keeper of Printed Books at the British Museum, who stuck out the blitz at Wandsworth Common and continued to visit him right up to the end. 'His last years,' Greg wrote to me, after Pollard's death on 8th March 1944, 'must have been rather miserable and dreary, I'm afraid.' Lonely they certainly were; and one often thought of him sleeping in that little house in Murray Road, while the Nazis bombed South London. Yet though he confessed, in a letter written on 10th August 1942, that he was growing 'tired of excess of solitude', I doubt whether he ever found life dreary, still less miserable—except perhaps during the last ten days, when he suffered pain from his thigh, fractured by a second fall. What he complained of was not solitude but *excess* of solitude. Always, as I have noted, something of a recluse, he was, as he once told me, 'much more contented with his own company than most people'.

But contentment was not merely the fruit of habit, and solitude did not mean to him, as it means to many, vacancy of mind. For he had an inner life to retreat to. About the matters he ranked higher than scholarship he did not often speak. 'No one,' he wrote, 'has any business to talk about the big things of life unless he is really feeling them in his bones.' But he gave much time and thought to them, and their effect upon his character was felt by all with whom he came into contact.

Scholarship, I repeat, was not the first or even the second thing with this scholar. What stood second was what he called 'practical morality', or his duty to his neighbour; what stood first was religion, which was in his eyes 'practical' too, if it was anything at all.

In 1911, Macmillan published a book, *Life, Love and Light: Practical Morality for Men and Women*, whose author was anonymous. Addressed to a generation which still implicitly accepted the utilitarian philosophy, it opened by asking them to reconcile these assumptions with the historical accounts of three deaths— those of Socrates in Athens in 399 B.C., Brythnoth and his loyal companions at the Battle of Malden in A.D. 991, and Father Damien on Leper Island in 1889—which the author had selected as supreme examples of the three ideals of conduct most admired by civilized men and women, namely courage, self-sacrifice and the pursuit of truth. After this, the writer, who was of course Pollard (as he publicly admitted on 19th October 1916 in an article entitled 'The Faith of One Layman' in *The [Anglican] Guardian*) went on to discuss with penetration, sympathy and wisdom, and with complete lucidity and candour, the chief moral problems that confront human beings in modern society as they make their way through life. Roger, the youngest of his three children, came of age the year after the book was published, and as it was dedicated 'To the writer's domestic critics', the year of publication was no doubt a father's choice. But, as he explains in the Preface, 'the idea of the book dates back some thirty years' to when he was reading for Mods.

'It is hoped,' the Preface continues, 'that it is none the worse for having been kept simmering for a good many years, during which the author has had his share of the common joys and sorrows of life.'

Life, Love and Light was the work of a Darwinian, who was always ready to remind himself and others that he entered the world in the same year as *The Origin of Species.*

'A great part of my intellectual life,' Pollard wrote in *The Guardian* article, 'has been spent in trying to harmonize with the doctrines of the Church of England a whole-hearted belief that man has ascended to his present stage of development through a series of lower forms during tens of thousands of years.'

And when he said 'a great part' he meant it, surprising as it may seem to those who have followed his crowded life up to this point. A devoted and devout son of the Church of England, a man for whom a daily service was as necessary as daily bread, he felt nevertheless that some of her doctrines and formularies were out of keeping not only with modern cosmology but even with Christianity itself as understood by the modern conscience. He once told me, for instance, that he could find very few psalms appropriate for use in an office of Christian worship. But he rejoiced in the Athanasian Creed. One form taken by this dis-content was an attempt to find light by studying the religions of others. Accordingly, some time before 1910, he joined The London Society for the Study of Religion, founded in 1902 by von Hügel, Claude Montefiore and others. The society had a restricted membership consisting in fairly equal proportions of Moslems, Jews, Anglicans, Roman Catholics and Free Church-men. Pollard was a regular attender, often wrote papers (I can remember reading a paper for him there). The last paper recorded under his name was one in 1932 on idolatry, but he remained a member down to 1937. It is noticeable that, apart from *Life, Love and Light*, Pollard's intense interest in religion found expression in print only after the death of his sons. Between 1915 and 1925 a number of pamphlets and other publications on religious matters appear among the books and articles on Shakespeare and bibliography in a *Select Bibliography* of his works presented to him in 1938 by Sir Stephen Gaselee at the British Museum. Most of these were written for or in connection with the Anglican Fellowship, of which he became a member in 1916 and a committee member in 1918. From its meetings he derived very great stimulus and encouragement, both in his personal life and in regard to his ideas of prayer-book reform; and they brought him the valued friendship of men like Clutton Brock, Percy Dearmer, and Kenneth Mozley.

But this did not really touch more than the periphery of that inner life which, I believe, occupied his thought more and more after 1915. It is unnecessary to discuss it here, even had I the knowledge to do so. Yet the portrait I have been trying to draw would be incomplete and untrue without some indication of its existence.

After the death of his sons it was our habit to spend part of our holidays together. One wet evening on such a holiday, only a couple of months after the death of Roger, we found ourselves, owing to circumstances beyond our control, at a 'concert party' on a pier. It was a deplorable show, cheap in every way, and full of equivocal jests about the men in the trenches. I was in agony for his sake, the more so that the large audience enjoyed every moment of it; and having no opportunity of a word with him after it was all over, I went to bed thinking how dreadful an experience it must have been for a man who had just lost two sons at the Front. I little knew him.

Next morning I no sooner began to stammer out my shame-faced words of dismay than he cut me short by declaring that he had spent a very pleasant and instructive evening. 'You see,' he went on, 'it set me thinking. The Church will never be right until it can attract big audiences like that, and give them as much pleasure. And, thinking this as I went to sleep, I dreamed; and in my dream I saw the universal Church. It was made up of three distinct Orders. The first, to which the vast majority of people belonged and whose votes determined everything, called itself the Order of the Children of God. Two rules only were required of its members; to have a good time, and never to do anything which might prevent other people having a good time; which last,' he added, 'if you think of it, embraces almost the whole of practical morality. The second, to which only a small minority belonged and which possessed very little power, was the Order of the Disciples of Christ; and they had to live up to the Sermon on the Mount. No hanky-panky! Live up to it!'

I can still hear the fierceness in his voice as he said, 'Live up to it!' He stopped, and I thought for a moment he had forgotten the third order. But presently he went on, almost shyly, in low tones, 'And there was another order with no power at all; for there was no Pope in this Church. They were very few indeed, and no one even knew who they were. People called them the Passionates, and they took upon them all the sins and sorrows of the world.'

I cannot, of course, reproduce his exact words; but what I have written is not far out, for I remember those moments well. And when I thought of him in his last lonely years, lying night after night on Wimbledon Ridge while the Nazis rained their bombs from the sky all about him, I used to wonder whether he had joined the Passionates.

THE HERO AS SCHOLAR
WAVELL

This is the greatest and noblest man that it has been my good fortune not only to encounter but to call a friend.

I first met Wavell just after he had been appointed Viceroy of India in 1943; but coming to know his son I was able to glean many hints about his life on active service in the field. When I met him, behind him lay that most brilliant of all our military campaigns, the defeat of the Italians in North Africa, which came very near to bringing the whole Italian empire crashing to the ground, though they were to be saved by the intervention of the Germans. But even Rommel, we are led to believe from the latest life of Wavell (one by Connell) would have failed to stop him had it not been for the downfall of Greece and the disaster of Crete. And after all this there were campaigns in Burma and Asia, so that those who watched him from Britain could not help feeling that he was a Hercules usurping the function of Atlas.

When I first saw Wavell, he was just about to set out for India.

With my gift of visual memory the scene is before me. I was lunching one Friday in the New Club in Edinburgh with Lord Normand, Lord Justice General of Scotland, sitting against the wall, right round the corner of the dining-room, when Normand said to me, 'Look, there's Wavell.' And there Wavell sat in Field Marshal's uniform against the wall on the opposite side of the room, lunching alone; and Normand exclaimed, 'What an extraordinary people we are. We take our best general and make him into an administrator'—a remark which shows what ordinary thinking people then thought about Wavell; and Normand was far from ordinary. My excitement at getting even a distant view of Wavell was great, so much did I and most other Britishers admire his desert campaign, which had kept our hearts up while the Battle of Britain was raging here. He was, as I said, alone, but when I went out of the Club I saw Lord Rosebery's shooting brake on the other side of Princes Street, and at a guess I thought that Wavell might be staying with the Roseberys who knew him well.

At breakfast next morning my wife went to answer the telephone and coming back said, 'Lady Rosebery has asked us to dine at Dalmeny tonight. I told her I am very sorry I'm engaged. What about you?' 'Oh dear,' I cried, 'you've missed it. I bet you anything we should have met Wavell there.' She could not alter her engagement, but finding I was free went back to the telephone and accepted for me. She was asked to tell me that it was quite an informal dinner, just a black tie, and that a car would call for me at seven o'clock to take me over to Dalmeny from Balerno. Accordingly the bell rang at seven and I was somewhat surprised to find a sergeant standing at the door to fetch me. As we got in I said, 'This isn't Lord Rosebery's car.' 'No, Sir; Field Marshal Wavell's.'

The party at Dalmeny consisted of the Roseberys, Lord Primrose (only a boy then), Wavell and myself; and I dare to think that Wavell had especially asked to meet me, for the talk was mostly about Shakespeare. It was evident that he was following my edition with keen interest. But the talk that evening naturally was also much on the war and particularly upon Stalin's persistent but impossible demands for a second front, a subject upon which Wavell recited with great gusto a highly entertaining ballad which I thought at the time was by A. P. Herbert; but I later discovered among Wavell's papers a copy of the verses, claimed by Alanbrooke as Wavell's own. In any case, it left us in fits of laughter.

Wavell was in a very happy mood that night and was evidently looking forward to the viceroyalty as a relief from multifarious and at times overwhelming problems that the war had laid upon him, much as he regretted losing contact with his troops. Before I went home, or at some meeting soon after, I asked him whether he would care to hear about the edition as it went on, and the consequence was that a correspondence began between us mainly about Shakespeare. What survives is now deposited in the National Library of Scotland and includes eight letters written during his period as viceroy of India and nine after his return. Together with these papers, the Library also preserves a number by his son, including letters written to myself.

The quotations from these letters will illustrate how the friendship which sprang up between the Field Marshal and myself developed. Here is the first of the surviving letters, written from the India Office and dated 3rd October 1943,

Dear Dover Wilson,

So many thanks for *Falstaff*. I always try to take my mind off the day's work by reading something quite unconnected with it before going to bed—usually poetry, as state documents are prose (or meant to be); and *Falstaff* has greatly cheered me lately. I enjoyed the book thoroughly. As a groundling I had not realised that the critics had made such a pother over the relations between Prince and Buffoon (the Prince of Buffoons). I had just enjoyed the plays and accepted the ending as coming quite naturally and logically as Shakespeare meant. I am glad you have put the matter straight, for I think your argument is quite convincing.

Many thanks. I will tell the publishers to send you a copy of my anthology of verse [*Other Men's Flowers*] when it appears. . . .

He referred in the same letter to a quotation from James Elroy Flecker's *Hassan* which became one of my favourite passages and which I often used in my lectures. It runs as follows,

Caliph: Ah, if there should ever arise a nation whose people have forgotten poetry or whose poets have forgotten the people, though they send their ships round Taprobane and their armies across the hill of Hindustan, though their city be greater than Babylon of old, though they mine a league into earth or mount to the stars on wings—what of them?

Hassan: They will be a dark patch upon the world.

There follows a letter from me, dated 10th March 1944, thanking Wavell for *Other Men's Flowers* and his *Life of Allenby*. I read the *Allenby* with the greatest interest, more especially because Wavell had been on his staff and had entered Jerusalem walking by his side. As to *Other Men's Flowers*, after expressing astonishment at his memory, I ventured to say, 'Your choice of poems is all the more interesting because instinctive rather than deliberate. And the prominence of Browning and his disciple, Kipling (for R.K. was a pupil of R.B.'s, you will, I think, agree) is what one might expect, if I may say so, in a man of action.' I reminded him that Shackleton had declared that men of action, men whose lives are lived in hard places, love poetry and beauty. My letter continues, 'What does a little surprise me is the absence of any Wordsworth and of all but one of Milton's poems. I get more out of each every year I live.'

To this he replied on 13th May 1944, from the Viceroy's House, New Delhi,

'I agree with you that Kipling was a disciple of Browning. I think in many of his poems you will find that two of the chief influences are his knowledge of the Bible and of Browning. I am afraid that Wordsworth for some reason or another has never rung a bell with me, though I have read a good deal of him. Even *The Happy Warrior* does not appeal to me. I think he got a bad start with me, in that the first of his poems I was made to read as a child was *We Are Seven*.'

He went on later,

'I have also read a great deal of Tennyson, in fact I think I have read almost everything he wrote; but again he does not somehow appeal to me. A homely comparison that arises in my mind is that Tennyson's poetry is rather like eating an egg without salt, and Wordsworth is like eating one with sugar instead of salt. This is probably unfair to both poets, but it is just how they impress me.

'I have not read Lascelles Abercrombie's *Sale of St. Thomas* which you mention, and should much like to.

'I am very busy and hard worked, and have little time at present for reading. I have never had to work harder; some of it is dull routine work, but some of it is interesting, and I have had the opportunity to see a good deal of India. We have plenty of anxieties and worries out here, but on the whole things are going reasonably well. Very much will depend on whether we get a good monsoon or not. Without it our food situation will be very bad.'

The foregoing will give my readers an idea of the attitude of the two correspondents to each other. I cannot now quote the further letters so fully and will note only the outstanding points made by either side.

A letter of mine, dated 17th June 1944, told him that my edition of the two Parts of *Henry IV* was nearly complete and I was already working upon *Henry V*. And at the same time I told him of the death of my only son in South Africa as a result of the war. He replied on 20th September 1944 most sympathetically about my loss and telling me that his own son, Captain Wavell, who had recently lost a hand in the Burma Campaign and was coming to Edinburgh to be fitted with an artificial one, would like to call on me, being a diligent reader of my Shakespeare work. He asked me for my views on the Bastard in *King John* who was, in his opinion, one of the most attractive characters in Shakespeare and resembled Henry V.

In my next letter (5th November 1944) I wrote,

'Many thanks for . . . sending Captain Wavell to call on us. . . . Both my wife and I, rather son-hungry just now, were delighted and cheered by your boy's visit, which left us feeling that life and living was more worth while, when such spirits as his lived to carry on the world. If, when you write to him, you would tell him how much he helped us and ask him to come again when he is next in these parts, we shall be very grateful.'

Thus began another great friendship, for 'Archie John' became almost like one of the family. My letter continues,

'You are, I think, right about the Bastard and Henry V. The one is in many ways a first sketch of the other; *King John* being written about 1594–5 and *Henry V* in 1599. But one must remember too that both characters were almost certainly played by the same actor, Burbage.'

And I also posted him a copy of my *King John* and told him that I was just about to send off my two Parts of *Henry IV* to the printer. The correspondence at this point naturally turned to the character of Falstaff, and the Field Marshal agreed that nearly all men but very few women admired him. I amused him by quoting Mrs. Elizabeth Inchbald, the early nineteenth-century bluestocking. 'This is a play which all men admire and which most women dislike. Many revolting expressions in the comic parts, with most boisterous courage in the graver scenes, together with Falstaff's unwieldy person, offend every female auditor; and whilst a facetious Prince of Wales is employed taking purses on the highway, a lady would rather see him stealing hearts at a ball.' And on the other hand I told him the story of the morale of the H.Q. of a newly formed army division being restored by getting the officers to take part in a play-reading of *Henry IV*; 'proceedings which began in gloom but ended in hilarious laughter'.

Wavell replied on 21st January 1945, thanking me for *King John*,

'I read your preface with much interest, it threw a great deal of fresh light on the play for me. I took the opportunity of reading the play again, which I had not done for some years. I suppose it is an indifferent play, but I have always had a considerable interest in it since it was one of the first of Shakespeare's plays that I saw on the stage. I think *Julius Caesar* was the first I saw as a schoolboy, done by Tree. He was a very good Mark

Antony, and the production was a very good one. . . . These
two plays, seen while I was still a schoolboy, did bring home
to me that Shakespeare was meant to be acted and was extraordinarily effective on the stage.'

Henry V formed the chief topic of the next correspondence
as, on 25th September 1945, Wavell was thanking me for a
draft preface to the play and wrote saying he would be highly
honoured to have *Henry V* dedicated to him as I had requested.
Further, the discussion among critics as to the real character of
Henry led Wavell to the following reflections:

'. . . no-one knows the real truth about any man, except the
man himself (and that only if he is both intelligent and honest);
and . . . one of Shakespeare's greatest qualities is that he realised
this fact; that he gives the external observations of the man, so
far as he has been able to ascertain them, and gives them with
the most brilliant perception; and leaves it to the reader himself
to judge from his own knowledge of men what the man's
character really was like, inside itself.'

If we read 'actor' for 'reader', as I am sure he would allow,
we have a profound piece of Shakespearian criticism, applicable
to *Hamlet* above all but true of every other character as well.

In a letter (not among those in the National Library) which I
made use of elsewhere, I told Wavell that one item in the play
I found very puzzling was Henry's sudden order to kill the
prisoners in the middle of the battle; and I asked whether he
could help me, noting at the same time that there was a sort of
parallel in the Irish wars of Elizabeth's reign when, in November
1580, Earl Grey, in command of the English forces found it
politic to slaughter five or six hundred Spanish filibusters
captured at Smethick in Ireland; these were prisoners who
could not have been conveyed through a hostile country by a
force little greater in number than themselves without endanger-
ing the whole position of English rule in Ireland—an act which
nobody in the Europe of that day looked upon as anything but a
necessary military precaution. Wavell's reply (in his letter of
25th September 1945) was,

'I have been puzzled not by the ethical considerations—I am

quite prepared to accept that it was pardonable by the standards of the time—but by the tactical considerations. Presumably the prisoners had already been disarmed and were not therefore formidable; and it is the time factor which interests me. With a sudden counter-attack, such as is imagined, the vital consideration would be to get one's troops in position to meet it with the least possible delay. Now to kill the prisoners, if they were at all numerous, must have meant quite a considerable delay in those times of hand weapons, it was not possible to turn a machine gun on them and to kill many in a short time, it would have taken quite a lot of men quite a while to kill off the prisoners, especially if they resisted. From the point of view of a commander, I should have thought it much more advisable not to attempt to kill the prisoners, but to keep them well away from their arms which they had presumably surrendered, and to put a few determined archers in charge of them with orders to shoot any man who moved. The only circumstances in which it would have struck me as advisable from a military point of view to kill the prisoners on such an occasion would be if the prisoners were only a few and were highly placed officers who might break back to the enemy and provide information and leadership. Had this aspect of the problem ever struck you or any other commentator of Shakespeare?'

This set me digging further into the records of the battle itself and I found that Monstrelet, the Burgundian historian who has left us the only impartial account of what happened (*Chronique* 1400–1444) tells us that before the battle it had been raining for days so that the French knights were stuck in the mud up to their girths—sitting birds for the Welsh archers who slaughtered them in their hundreds. Shakespeare knew nothing of Monstrelet, and there is no mud in Holinshed—thank Heaven!

On 12th May 1946, I wrote to Wavell thanking him for sending me his volume of lectures entitled *Speaking Generally*, and continued,

'The historians will bless you for it too. What would they not give for a similar volume by Henry of Monmouth after the Agincourt campaign! By the same token, is there any parallel in disparity of numbers and completeness of victory to the battle of Cyrenaica except that of Agincourt in English history?

'My edition of *Henry V* has long been finished, and should be out towards the end of the year, though *Henry IV* Parts I and II are to appear first. I am now nearing the end with *Macbeth*, which I have taken up as a change from the histories, though it must have been very much of a history for James VI and I, whom Shakespeare obviously had in mind from first to last. There is not only witchcraft, one of his majesty's hobbies; the portrait of Banquo, his (mythical) ancestor, very much touched up after Holinshed; the prophecy about his descendants . . .' (Here I mention other points.)

'Among other matters I am trying to work out, two may interest you. The first, which has very little to do with Shakespeare, is how Macbeth who, as far as history which knows precious little about him can tell, was a more than usually strong and enlightened monarch for his time, came to be the Bad Boy of the Scottish chroniclers. The answer seems to be that the custom of succession changed shortly after his time from the old practice (found in Ireland and Kievan Russia also) of alternate or collateral inheritance to that of primogeniture; that Macbeth had the bad luck to be one of the latest monarchs to stand up for his rights under the old system, Duncan being really the usurper . . .'

I also propounded my theory that *Macbeth* had been a longer play but abridged by Shakespeare himself, possibly for per-formance at Court on the occasion of the visit of the King of Denmark; and I suggested that in the longer play Macbeth was a much nobler figure than the shortened version allows us to imagine. I concluded the letter,

'I don't apologise for writing of affairs so remote from those in which you are now immersed. For I know that distraction must sometimes be welcome . . .

'By the bye I am adding a footnote in my *Henry V* about the tactical aspect of the killing of the prisoners, which you raised in your last letter—without of course referring to you by name.'

To this Wavell replied on 27th June 1945,

'Many thanks for your letter of May the 12th, and for the

copy of your pamphlet about *Henry IV*, in which I was much interested. I shall look forward very much to your *Macbeth*; the points you raise in your letter are very interesting indeed. I knew that Macbeth had been very much maligned by history and was in fact one of the better of the early kings, but I never heard any theory as to how he came to be written down as a villain. I have not read the play for some time, nor have I ever seen it acted (I think it is the only one of the great Shakespeare plays that I have not seen on the stage), but the impression Macbeth has left on my mind is that of a good and gallant soldier, probably with not too much brains, who was dominated by an ambitious wife and had not the strength of will to resist her. But I do not think I should ever put him in the class of a great spirit overthrown by circumstances, like Hamlet or Othello, as the play now stands. You seem to think that parts of the play which have been cut out would show him in a better light. I must try to read the play again, but I have very little time for reading at present, as you may imagine.'

The letter ended with a passage marked 'Confidential' from which I may now be allowed to quote the following sentences,

'The negotiations here have concluded, rather disappointingly . . . I feel gloomy about the prospects of being able to form an effective coalition Government, and not very optimistic that the Constituent Assembly will live long enough to produce a Constitution. We were very near success at one moment . . .'

The last letter from India in my collection, dated 20th September 1946, repeats some of the observations he had made in earlier letters, and seems to show evidence of the great strain under which he was working at this point.

'Thank you so much indeed for the two volumes of the Cambridge Edition of *Henry IV* which arrived a little time ago. I have read your preface with very much interest, I have always liked those two plays; and I deeply regret having missed seeing them in London recently with Richardson as Falstaff and Laurence Olivier as Hotspur and Shallow. It came on just after I left London last time.

'What are you busy with now, have you finished *Henry V*?

It is not a play I care for as well as the two Parts of *Henry IV*, but I think it is a more popular play on the stage. The film of it seems to have been a very great success, but I am afraid I did not care for it very much. I believe that *King John* would make a good film if it was well done.

'I am afraid that my preoccupation with the very tiresome politics of this country gives me very little time for reading, I am in the middle of another attempt to try and get the two parties to come together in a coalition Government, but am not very hopeful of doing so.'

His remark to me, in the letter of 27th June 1946, that his plan of keeping a united India nearly came off, showed that with the patience at his command he could still hope to pull it off. But his forebodings in the last letter were to be justified in a way he had only too well foreseen. He had given warnings of what would happen, but these were disregarded, others preferring to believe Nehru and Gandhi. The new Labour Government under Attlee had come into power in 1945 and was impatient for results; it decided to anticipate Wavell's aim of granting India independence during his viceroyalty by granting it forth-with. For, within six months of the 20th September, Wavell found himself recalled and his place taken by Mountbatten, charged with the task of partition. The operation cost a million lives; for at once India and Pakistan flew at each other's throats—a horrible massacre, the full extent of which was concealed from the general public in England.

It was Archie John who told me of the reception his father got at Downing Street when he went there after his return from India to report to the Prime Minister. He was instructed to call, I believe, about noon. There were only two or three members of the Cabinet present, and after a short conversation Attlee rose, with his watch in his hand, and said, 'Excuse me, Field Marshal, but I have a luncheon engagement.' Clearly Attlee had done with Wavell, so that the interview was a piece of mere courtesy. India was now off the Prime Minister's plate, and his whole attention was concentrated on building the Welfare State in Great Britain.

It is interesting to note that when Allenby had to make a similar report on Palestine after a similarly brusque dismissal, he had been treated by Curzon in much the same way.

Wavell came almost directly from the interview up to Balerno, sending me a wire telling me he would be in Edinburgh on 5th April and would ring me up during the morning in hope of seeing me during the day. My memory of him sitting in my little library after lunch is almost too vivid. He was ever a silent man, and his first words, blurted out, were, 'You know I've been sacked.' I had not realized it until then, and was suddenly faced with a great human tragedy. What could I say, except to suggest that he would now have time to write, and that I knew he had much to tell the world, but the depth and rawness of the wound were evident when he almost shouted, 'Not about India!' 'But you can write about the poetry you loved, and the history of the war.'

After this meeting in April he paid several visits to me at Balerno, while I sometimes met him at the New Club in Edinburgh. Moreover, his letters about Shakespeare and other things continued, in spite of everything. On 12th October 1947, he writes,

'. . . I am most grateful for the amusing article on the Porter in *Macbeth* and now I have just received from the publishers a copy of your Cambridge *Macbeth*, which I am taking to the country tomorrow to re-read . . .'

The article he referred to was an offprint from the Edinburgh Bibliographical Society proceedings suggesting an emendation in the Porter's speech and also throwing out the idea that what had made the grooms sleepy and Lady Macbeth bold was nothing less than whisky.

A letter, dated 6th November 1947, gives me news about Archie John,

'. . . I think he is probably in Delhi at present, he has just wound up his Education School and said he would be going to G.H.Q. to report and find out, what next. I don't know whether he will come home.

'Bernard Fergusson about whom you asked is due home

shortly, I believe. . . . I hope your work prospers and that we may have an opportunity to meet soon. Please remember me to your wife.'

After this I have eight letters from him between October 1948 and October 1949. From one of them I learned that Archie John had refused to take up his vacancy for the Staff College (much to his father's disappointment), clearly preferring to go on with his army education work, which he continued to do.

In a letter written on the way to play golf at St. Andrews where, as I learned later, Archie John with only a left hand was able to hold his own with him, Wavell thanked me for a copy of *Titus Andronicus*, the introduction to which he was then reading with interest. *Titus* was referred to in the next letter also, as Archie John had been reading it; and at the same time I was told that Walter Oakeshott, then headmaster of Winchester, had asked him to go there and teach for a year, if the War Office would allow him leave; but, alas, the War Office refused.

Sometime before our departure for South Africa in 1949, Wavell had recommended me to read Alan Paton's *Cry the Beloved Country*; so I owe my acquaintance with this noble book, as so much else, to Wavell himself.

On 31st May he welcomed us back, hearing of our return from Buchanan-Smith, now Lord Balerno. And most of the last letter in the collection, dated 2nd October 1949, must be quoted, since it again shows the Field Marshal as a Shakespearian critic,

'Very many thanks for *Julius Caesar* which I found on my return . . .

'I also read your article on Ben Jonson and *Julius Caesar*. But I really do not understand why Jonson should have criticised the remark about brute beasts and reason as if it were meant as a serious philosophical observation. It is nothing of the kind, it is part of a speech meant to move a mob, who knew nothing of philosophy and cared little for reason. One might as well treat Mr. Aneurin Bevan's recent observation about Tories and vermin as a reasoned philosophical statement!

'Again, the words put into Caesar's mouth, that he "never did wrong, but with just cause", are of course nonsense taken by themselves, but it is just the sort of remark that a pompous self-satisfied tyrant, such as Shakespeare is making out Julius Caesar to be, might utter without reflection. It is well within the part as portrayed by Shakespeare, in fact I think it might well be treated as rather a masterstroke by the dramatist. Shakespeare was writing for the stage not for analysis in the study, and I am prepared to bet he said something of the kind to Ben Jonson, though he may have added at the end: ''But if you make such a point of it, old boy, I'll tell them to alter it in the prompt-book.''

'When I get back to London, I'll send you a copy of Thornton Wilder's *Ides of March*, which gives quite another view of Caesar, a fanciful one but it may amuse you.

'Archie John will be disappointed at missing you when he comes to Edinburgh for the Highland Brigade meeting, I don't think he arrives till after you have gone.'

Wavell was much interested in university life and had been Chancellor of Aberdeen University since 1945; he would have been willing to become master of a college at Oxford or Cambridge had such a post been offered. A few years after his death I was dining at the High Table at Clare College, Cambridge, and, being a guest of the Fellows, found myself sitting next to Sir Henry Thirkill, the college's delightful Master, who had been Vice-Chancellor when Wavell came home, and had been the means of offering him an honorary degree of the university. 'I think you will like to know,' he said to me, 'that this degree was some help to that great man in trouble, for he said to me there were only two things that lit up the sky for him at that time: the honorary degree of the University of Cambridge, and the dedication to him of *Henry V* in the New Cambridge Shakespeare.'

Being a lover of history, Wavell had been pleased when the Queen appointed him Constable of the Tower in 1948. But he did not long enjoy these various honours that came to him, for he was untimely cut off by early death in 1950.

Archie John succeeded to the title and took his seat in the House of Lords where, I am told, he made not a few good speeches; nor could anyone who knew him doubt that a great future—I think as a statesman—awaited him. His father, as I have already mentioned, was a silent man, and one cannot suppose that he would have been a great Parliamentary orator. But Archie John was also the son of an Irishwoman, and his talk in private life was endless and fascinating. His enthusiasm for Shakespeare equalled his father's, as his charming little essay in the Proceedings of the Royal Society of Literature is enough to prove; and I enjoyed several performances of Shakespeare in London in his company. On one occasion, as I have elsewhere recounted, he came out with us to a midnight supper with Laurence Olivier and Vivien Leigh at their 'cottage' in Chelsea.

In spite of having no right hand he insisted on joining his regiment when they went out to deal with the Mau Mau trouble in Africa, and was shot within a fortnight of his landing. The news reached me over the wireless on Christmas Eve, and I felt I had lost a second son.

My last sight of him was a happy occasion when I took him to an academic garden party which he greatly enjoyed, for though he had not been himself at a university he loved university people. And when I said goodbye to him he was going on to stay with a friend of mine and a still more intimate friend of his father and of himself, Major Crichton-Stuart, Hereditary Keeper of Falkland Palace, of whom I have already spoken in reference to the Bute Collection.

THE SCHOLAR AS HERO
RICHARD PARES AND JOHN BUTT

W. P. Ker, that master of learning, who wrote more than most of his fellows about the heroic age of human history and with more understanding than any, has described the epic hero as a man fighting with his back against a wall; and, I think we may add, fighting to the death.

Such heroism is usually associated with fighting in battle, and typical heroes are Brythnoth at the Battle of Malden in 991, or, to take a later example, Sir Richard Grenville in his little ship *Revenge* encountering and overwhelmed by the galleons of King

Philip II. And if most readers were asked to name instances of later date they might either cite those of Antarctic exploration or Alpine or Himalayan endeavour. I happened though to have been honoured by the friendship of two men who seem to me more typically epic than the last-named examples, since to them death itself was not the consequence of their heroism but the enemy they had to face from the early stages of their struggles. And these men were scholars, a business which to many must seem something remote from life, almost trivial. Yet whatever value you assign to scholarship, you could not deny that both men were supreme in their mastery of the particular line each pursued. Whether the two knew each other I am not sure. Both were professors with me at the University of Edinburgh, and both fell victim to diseases which though not, I believe, medically akin were strangely alike in their physical effects.

This is no place, except incidentally, to discuss the subjects of their studies, my object being merely to record my reverent admiration for two great spirits.

In an early chapter I mentioned the name of Bernard Pares (afterwards Sir Bernard), the unrivalled student of Russia in my time, with whom I attended meetings of the first Duma in 1907. I was able to renew my acquaintance with him at King's College, to which he became attached as Head of the School of Slavonic Studies at the University of London. It was therefore with keen pleasure that I heard of the appointment of his son Richard, whom I had never met, but who was already known as a rising historian, to the Chair of History in Edinburgh in 1945.

I had also heard of him during the war from my friend R. J. L. Kingsford, then London manager of the Cambridge University Press and president of the Publishers' Association. In his negotiations with the government he had found, as his opposite number in the Board of Trade, Richard Pares who was the official detailed for dealing with the book trade of the country. This situation led to a battle of wits which must have been wonderful, for Pares's mind was like a knife.

My anticipations were more than fulfilled when I came to hear his brilliant inaugural lecture. As history and the meaning

of history have always been among my chief interests, coming to
know Richard Pares was an event of first importance. My mind
went back to another inaugural lecture, that of Bury at Cambridge
in 1902, which led Trevelyan to proclaim Clio a Muse; for
though Pares would hardly have subscribed to Bury's creed, he
was leading a retreat from the school of Trevelyan in which I
had grown up. In this he seemed to belong to the school of Lewis
Namier; but this was not so. Certainly he was no disciple (as
Professor Rowse has misleadingly described him) or even a
follower. And though I often heard him refer to Namier as
'Uncle Lewis', it is unlikely that he got to know him personally
until they met at All Souls. He was brought face to face with
Namier almost accidentally when he began his career as an
historian by selecting the West Indies, and in particular the sugar
industry, as his special subject; and his unique reputation as a
'colonial historian' rests upon his work in this field.[1] But he is
best known among the general public for his Ford lectures
entitled *George III and the Politicians*.

Between them, and by quite different approaches, Pares and
Namier revolutionized our ideas of George III's reign and so
rendered out of date most of what my master Trevelyan had
written on that period. Furthermore, they seemed to be bringing
to an end that 'Whig' conception of modern English history
which Macaulay, Trevelyan's uncle, had inaugurated by writing
the history of England beginning with William III and the Great
Revolution of 1688.

Pares himself wrote, 'There is a perennial dialectic between
each generation of historians and its predecessor, not only
because new information is brought into use, but still more
because new emphases and new patterns take the place of old.'[2]
It would, however, be a mistake to say that the new patterns
obliterate the old. We shall continue to read our Trevelyan
(except where he is demonstrably false in his facts, as he was
about George III). And Carlyle's *French Revolution* will always
continue to be one of the greatest books in the world, as is,

[1] *Proceedings of the British Academy*, 1962.
[2] *The Historian's Business*, 1961, p. 3.

of course, Gibbon's *Decline and Fall*. If Namier, in denouncing 'fine writing', was merely condemning popular historical biographies which are now the fashion, he was not therefore commending the wooden style of many history textbooks, and indeed the style of not a few professional historians also.

But enough to show what a stimulus friendship with Pares became for me, who soon declared myself as unofficially one of his post-graduate students. Soon after he came to Edinburgh I spent a memorable evening with him and his father at the New Club. But it was not long after that before he began to grow lame and to walk with a stick. He managed for some years to get to his lecture-room by the help of a wheelchair; but there came a time when he was more or less confined to a little room in Carlton Terrace, looking out on to the Queen's Park. And there I would call upon him in the afternoon to bring him bits of my own writing for criticism, or more often to discuss problems of interest to us both, and to learn from his wisdom.

One instance stands out in my memory. I had just returned from my second visit to Germany in the autumn of 1953—a visit which left me greatly depressed, since I felt that the Nazi disease was still latent and might break out again at any time. I poured forth these fears, relating the experiences on which they were grounded, and asked him what he felt about the matter. 'Well,' he said, 'the Germans have been overwhelmingly defeated twice. It should be enough. It took two such crushing defeats to expel *la gloire* from France. It's true,' he went on, 'that France had a Boulanger; Germany may need a Boulanger to get rid of *die Macht*. And there is Russia.'

Soon after this he resigned the Chair at Edinburgh, and, All Souls offering him a Special Research Fellowship, returned to Oxford. He had lost the use of his hands and could only turn over the pages of a book by a special device invented for the purpose, while he continued to dictate notes to his secretary or a student helper, right up to the end. Yet I never saw him in the least gloomy. On the contrary, the gaiety of his temperament seemed quite unaffected by the increasing paralysis of his body. But he displayed the full quality of his heroism in the Ford

Lectures delivered in the Examination Schools at Oxford in 1952, entitled 'George III and the Politicians', a task in which he was less hampered by his physical disability because his mind was full to overflowing with the thesis he was expounding, since it was in effect a substitute for the history of the reign of George III which he was prevented by his affliction from contributing to the Oxford History of England series. The room was packed for the lecture, and those present will not soon forget the sight of him being carried in as if in a triumphal chair, by four stalwart undergraduates, and planted on the desk facing the audience.

Both my scholar heroes had wives who shared their courage and supported them in their hopeless fight against death in ways that the onlooker could only guess at. And it is to Mrs. Pares that I owe the account of another side of Richard's genius—his critical faculty. I am also much indebted for the facts of Richard Pares's career to his sister Mrs. Humphreys and her husband Professor Humphreys, Professor of Latin-American History in the University of London.

Pares continued to edit the *English Historical Review* until the end, and even managed to prepare the number for July 1958 which appeared after his death. Meanwhile, in 1954, a very serious problem confronted the editor. Arnold Toynbee's enormous *Study of History* became complete in ten volumes. Pares felt that the task of reviewing it would lay so great a burden on any one of his contributors who might seem suitable that he could not ask him to spare the time for it. And yet Toynbee's vast work cried out for authoritative criticism. On the one hand, it had been accepted without question by the ordinary public; on the other, it was viewed with extreme scepticism, to say the least of it, by some of the leading historians in both Britain and America.

There was nothing for it; the editor must do it himself. The review appeared in 1956, in Vol. lxxi of the *English Historical Review*, having been written during a summer holiday previously. Indeed, it ruined the summer holiday, which was spent, as he and his family generally did, in their cottage at Boot in Eskdale.

Pares as usual had one or two students with him to help in any piece of writing he was engaged on. The volumes were read in turn, notes were dictated as volume followed volume, and the despatch of each through an open window onto the lawn (fortunately the weather was fine) was greeted with cries of joy from Pares's little daughters, which became louder as the pile of rejects grew.

I first read it in the collected volume of Pares's writings, *The Historian's Business*, which was given me in South Africa by my friend Leo Marquard; it occupied many hours during my sea-voyage home, for I read it more than once with increasing astonishment, in spite of the fact that I was still ignorant of the conditions under which it had been written. My admiration of the feat was all the greater that I had myself been a member of that general reading public which had accepted Toynbee's book with its accumulation of learning about extinct civilizations as one of the masterpieces of our time. I was just then editing Shakespeare's *Coriolanus*, and as I watched volume after volume of Toynbee being mown down by the young historian that I had known in Edinburgh, I recalled to mind Volumnia's vision (Act I, scene 3, lines 37 ff.) of her son at work among his enemies,

> 'His bloody brow
> With his mail'd fist then wiping, forth he goes,
> Like to a harvest-man that's task'd to mow
> Or all or lose his hire.'

I learned much from Pares but no less, and of a different kind, from John Butt. I first met him and his wife Margot in 1958 in Newcastle, where he was Professor of English Literature, the occasion being when King's College had invited me to open the new wing for the housing of the Arts Faculty known as the Percy Building, to honour the memory of Lord Eustace Percy. And after the ceremony I went on to spend a night with the Butts at their house in Corbridge, driving over there via Hexham for my first visit to the great abbey.

It so happened that at this time the Regius Chair of English at Edinburgh was vacant, my successor Professor William

Renwick having attained the age of retirement. And Professor
Butt told me as we walked up and down his garden that he had
been sounded about succession to the post. How well I remember
the scene as he and Mrs. Butt asked me whether I thought they
would be happy in Edinburgh. I had myself been so happy in
the Chair, despite the interruption by the war, and still remained
happy to go on living as a citizen of the Athens of the North,
albeit as an outlander at Balerno, that I could advise them
without hesitation to cross the Tweed. And when they did so,
at the royal command, I gained a friendship which I value above
most others of my later years. It was a friendship too which
embraced the whole family, especially little Hilary.

When I retired from the professorship in 1945, remembering
certain initial difficulties I had had with my own predecessor
Sir Herbert Grierson, I had been very careful to do nothing
that could possibly be misinterpreted by my successor as inter-
fering with the English Department or even enquiring about
what went on therein. With John Butt, however, there were
no longer any fears of this kind to be dispelled. He showed
himself quite interested in memories of the university and the
department a generation earlier, both of which had changed very
considerably in the interval.

When I ceased to be professor many friends said to me, 'Surely
you will go back to England.' Never for a moment did I think of
doing so. As long as I went on editing Shakespeare's plays I
could find among my late colleagues scholars of various kinds
whose brains I could pick for the purpose of my Introductions.
And now my work on Shakespeare was coming to an end, I was
fortunate enough to discover, first of all in Richard Pares and
later in John Butt, teachers under whom I could carry on my
own general education, in this second instance learning to fill up
gaps in my knowledge of English literature itself. For Butt came
to us as a recognized master in two very different periods and
especially on two very different writers—Alexander Pope on the
one hand and Charles Dickens on the other.

I had indeed given a few lectures on Pope to my large First
Ordinary Class. But these lectures were of a very superficial

character; and I was now blessed with a chance of intimate conversation with a man whose knowledge of Pope was deeper than that possessed by most other living students. He was also engaged upon Volume VIII of the *Oxford History of English Literature*, which embraced the mid-eighteenth century, of which I had hitherto known very little.

I was still less well seen in Dickens, having read very few of his novels except *Pickwick Papers* and *David Copperfield*; yet now I found myself launched on that vast sea of adventure involved in the reading of his works. And Butt's approach to Dickens was the more fascinating to me because it was distinguished by a study, in collaboration with Professor Kathleen Tillotson, of the textual side of the great novelist's creation, which meant a study of his manuscripts and a discussion of his methods of publication and so on—in a word, a bibliographical approach different in many ways and yet also comparable with the bibliographical approach to Shakespeare's plays.

Yet to appreciate the full stature of the man one had to hear him lecture. I have spoken above of the brilliance of Pares's inaugural lecture. Butt's was no less brilliant; his main theme, how Boswell produced Johnson, kept the audience in ripples of laughter from beginning to end, as they were led to observe instance after instance in which the young Scot lured the Great Cham on to show off his paces as a conversationalist. But this part of the lecture was prefaced by a scarcely less humorous paragraph in which the usual bow which a newly-appointed professor is expected to make to his predecessor was expanded into a little history of the Chair of Rhetoric and English Literature he was about to occupy. The audience left the room feeling very happy both in what they had just heard and what they could look forward to in the future.

Butt came to us in 1959, after thirteen years as professor at King's College, Newcastle, in other words as a man already well experienced in both the administrative and the teaching sides of a professor's duties, though ever ready to adapt his methods to the needs and traditions of a Scottish university. But on all this side of the man, the eloquent tribute to him by

Professor Denys Hay published in the University of Edinburgh *Bulletin* for January 1966 speaks with greater knowledge than can be commanded by one who has long ceased to be part of the university machine and wishes now to speak of Butt as a friend.

In this connection I am proud to remember that he and Mrs. Butt travelled all the way from Edinburgh to Cambridge to attend my second marriage in 1963. It is true that one reason why they did so was that they themselves had become engaged in Cambridge and wished to recall memories. My own memory of their appearance is immortalized in a delightful photograph taken by the official photographer after the ceremony of the two of them looking very happy and debonair, both with hats on, he carrying an umbrella—for there was thunder round the corner—and somehow giving one a sense of his great height and 'willowy bearing', as it was later described by a writer in *The Times*.

Nevertheless, the disease which was later to prove fatal had already at this date begun to lay its hand upon him. I first heard of it when lying in the Nuffield Nursing Home after an unsuccessful operation on my right eye for the removal of a cataract. Mrs. Butt, who visited me there nearly every day, generally in the morning over a mug of beer, told me that her husband had strained his leg getting out of the bath, that the doctors could not make out what was wrong and that he had gone for treatment to the orthopaedic hospital at Fairmilehead—an experience of which he later gave an amusing account, of the athletes of various kinds with various strains and dislocations, but all of them with enormous appetites, whom he found as his companions.

On another occasion, about the middle of June 1965, he went for a week or so into the Western General Hospital for treatment; and when I called on him there one day, he said to me with a twinkle in his eye, 'Dover, you're a bit of a historian, aren't you?' A bit of a historian *manqué* I confessed to being. 'Well then,' he said, 'what has Scotland to do with Magna Carta?' 'Nothing at all,' I replied. He then showed me in *The Scotsman* that the Scottish Education Department had decreed a school

holiday to celebrate the seven hundred and fiftieth anniversary of
Magna Carta on 19th June, when it was being formally celebrated
in England by the Queen and the President of the United States.
We agreed that things could not be left so. I hurried home and
drafted a letter pointing out that the Scottish Education Department had displayed a sad ignorance of their own history, since the
legal system of Scotland is totally different both in origin and
nature from that in England, being based on Roman Law derived
from Dutch Law; whereas English Law, as all English people
know, is based on precedent. I despatched the draft letter for
Butt's approval and signature; and so in *The Scotsman* for the
following day two Englishmen enjoyed combining to give the
Education Department a lesson in their own constitutional
history, and by so doing earned the approval if not gratitude of
the lawyers in Parliament House.

The progress of Butt's disease was gradual but inexorable,
seeming to be arrested in one part of the body for a time and
then later breaking out in another. But the scholar and teacher
continued his work unchecked. As time went on, the class of
advanced students had to meet in his bedroom, and it was not
long before the end that he interviewed a candidate for one of the
new chairs in English that was to be filled. The volume of the
Oxford History of English Literature continued to be written,
the writing always preceded by most careful reading and weighing
of the works to be dealt with. To quote from the tribute by
Professor Hay already mentioned, 'In the last months of his life,
when he was working on the chapter in his book dealing with
the eighteenth-century historians, he read—carefully and appre-
ciatively—Gibbon, Hume and the others. Often in pain, with
every excuse for haste, he did his work with a dignity, an honesty
and an application which I find almost overpowering. So many
would have taken short cuts; so many men would have felt they
had every right to take short cuts.' And then Hay goes on, 'But
habitual thoroughness is, I believe, only part of the answer. The
rest is humility. In John Butt's passing we salute the death of a
gentle and humble man. I cannot conceive of higher praise than
that.'

My wife and I went to see him in bed at least once a week, when he would tell me how he was getting on with his reading and the chapter he was engaged in writing—or even at times other work which was occupying him, for example an obituary notice of Blair Leishman whom I had come to know through him and who had recently met his death by an accident in the Alps. But our talk ranged at times far afield; I felt I was continuing my general education at every visit, while I know that the visits were a help to him. And as I look back, I specially recall the moment when I whispered in his ear that the wonderful courage which he was showing in his affliction helped me to endure my own lack of sight.

He slipped away one night so quietly that the family did not know he was going. Perhaps it was deliberate, wishing to spare them the agony of a deathbed scene.

There had sprung up a deep affection between us, and I felt I had lost a younger but wiser brother—wiser and more learned, as I have said, for he was quite conscious of being my teacher. And it was like his gracious spirit to have bequeathed me a tape recording he had made himself of a score of poems, most of which he was aware I knew very little about. And these poems—which I now list—have been transferred to records which I can sit and listen to at any time.

Milton	At a Solemn Music
Herrick	'When he would have his verses read'
	'Men mind no state in sickness'
Dryden	Epilogue to Tyrannick Love
	To the Memory of Mr. Oldham
Swift	Baucis and Philemon
	Dooms-Day
Pope	Epistle to Miss Blount, on her Leaving the Town, after the Coronation
	To Mrs. M. B. on her Birth-day
	From Epistle II: To a Lady
Collins	A Song from Shakespeare's *Cymbeline*
Johnson	A short Song of Congratulation

Portraits

13

Special Occasions

Of four occasions that rank high in my memory, three may rightly be called 'royal occasions'. The first came about during the last days of George V's reign, while Baldwin was Prime Minister. One morning I received a letter, dated 13th December 1935, informing me that the King was 'graciously pleased to approve' that I 'be appointed a Member of the Order of Companions of Honour'. My name had obviously been suggested by Baldwin himself, prompted (one may guess) by the three *Hamlet* books that had just appeared—the edition of *Hamlet* (1934), *The Manuscript of Shakespeare's Hamlet* (1934) and *What Happens in Hamlet* (1935)—though I suspect that what had first drawn his attention to me was *The Essential Shakespeare*, published three years earlier in 1932.

George V, however, died on 20th January 1936, his successor being the young Edward VIII. The court business with its investitures nevertheless continued, and I received a second letter, dated 29th January 1936, saying that the King would hold an investiture at Buckingham Palace on the 18th February, and that my attendance was required, not later than 10.30 a.m. I had, it said, to appear dressed as follows,

'Black evening dress coat, black or white evening dress waistcoat, breeches of plain black evening dress material or stockinet, with three small black cloth or silk buttons, and black buckles at the knee, black silk hose, plain court shoes with bows, no buckles, white evening dress tie and white gloves.'

I give these details because I believe this was the last occasion on which this kind of court-dress was required, an ordinary black morning coat, I understand, being now worn for investitures.

I, of course, resorted to the inevitable Moss Bros., and after being measured by him (or perhaps I mean them), ordered the costume to be delivered at the Athenaeum on the day before the investiture. I was staying there because I was alone, my wife being unhappily unwell and therefore unable to accompany me to London. When the costume arrived I found part of the apparatus consisted of a little toy rapier or sword, or at least a black scabbard suggesting such a sword, very small and suspended from the waist with a couple of hangers. This addition was of some use to me, as it enabled me to understand more fully what Osric meant in *Hamlet* by his affected talk about 'hangers' when carrying Hamlet the challenge for the duel with Laertes. But I was certainly not going to appear in public as such a guy; so, having breakfasted in the coffee-room I went upstairs to my bedroom, put on the evening dress plus breeches etc., and then, covering it all up with a long macintosh, stole downstairs, jumped into a taxi and whisked off down the Mall to the Palace.

I was greatly struck with the efficiency of all the arrangements there. There were a number of persons waiting to be invested, in a long room which opened into a larger one where the ceremony would take place. I noticed among them a number of women. The first to be called in, presumably because we were receiving the highest honours on this occasion, were a general, an admiral and myself; and we three were placed together near the door into the large room. I could not help noticing, and being rather naughtily amused in doing so, that my two men of war were pitiably nervous at the prospect of having to face not an army or a navy but Majesty itself.

Presently I was myself in the Presence and saw before me a young man with hollow eyes, looking dreadfully ill. Though his relations with the lady who was later to become his wife as the Duchess of Windsor were already the talk of continental newspapers, the British press had kept a complete silence on the subject, so that it was unknown to the British public generally, and to myself in particular, while the question of abdication had not yet arisen.

The course of negotiations that preceded the final act, which dragged on until the 11th December, is now a matter of history and need not be dwelt upon. Suffice it to say here that I am one of the few persons alive who have received a high order from an uncrowned king.

My next encounter with royalty came as a result of my professorship at Edinburgh. In Chapter Six I spoke of Queen Elizabeth II's visit on 4th July 1956 to open the new building for the National Library of Scotland of which I was at that time Vice-Chairman of the Trustees under the chairmanship of Lord Crawford and Balcarres. After she had delivered her speech opening the building and had made a tour of the various departments of the Library, I had the honour of showing her a few of the valuable books in the Bute Collection, the purchase of which she had announced in her speech. My meeting with Her Majesty took place in a small room and was attended by a few persons only, including the Duke of Edinburgh, Lord Crawford, the Librarian and my wife. It was, too, the last thing in the programme before the royal party moved off to the Meadows where the Queen was to have tea with the Royal Company of Archers, those tall men in green with long bows whom she delighted to watch. There was only time therefore to show her a very small selection. I began with the first quarto of the Second Part of *Henry IV*, published in 1600, which I explained was the most expensive book that we had bought, and had cost four thousand pounds. 'But,' I observed, 'Your Majesty will notice that in ink on the title page there is an entry some years later than the date of publication, "Price five pence", so that its value has considerably increased in the interval.' This seemed to amuse her, and she laughed. I then showed her two quartos of *Richard II*. One of them was published during the time of Queen Elizabeth I and omitted the deposition scene because the Queen would not allow it. It is clear indeed from many references that Elizabeth I regarded herself as in some way closely connected with Richard, possibly because of the red hair which was common to them both. And this resemblance helps to account for the fact that *Richard II*, including the deposition scene, was acted by Shakespeare's company the day before the rising of the Earl of Essex which embittered her last years. I briefly explained all this and then showed the Queen the other quarto of the play, printed under James; this contains the deposition scene, as the censor under his Scottish Majesty could see no cause for objection. Lastly I showed her a prompt-book of a much later play called *Single Life*, which it afterwards occurred to me was not a very suitable book to exhibit to a married lady. It was interleaved, and on the blank page the prompter had written, 'And he opened the window and called "Woman!".' Just before this, Lord Crawford had reminded the Duke about the Archers, whereupon the Duke moved up to stand behind Her Majesty and said, 'Archers!' She took no notice; I flatter myself that the lecture was too interesting. And then again, 'Archers!' And when in a louder voice still he reiterated what was now a command, she lifted the book in her hands, and turning round to the audience, read out the prompter's addition, 'And he opened the window and called "Woman!" '—and then in her queenly voice to me, 'I think we must go now.'

The latest, and in memory the most precious, of the three royal occasions in which I was involved took place on 26th November 1959, when I received the Honorary Degree of D.Lit. of the University of London from the hands of its Chancellor, Queen Elizabeth the Queen Mother.

The names of those receiving the degree of Doctor may here be placed on record: Sir Alexander Carr-Saunders (Principal of the London School of Economics), D.Sc.; Sir Hans Krebs (Professor of Biochemistry at the University of Oxford), D.Sc.; Field Marshal Lord Alexander of Tunis, LL.D.; Viscount Dunrossil (W. S. Morrison, recently Speaker of the House of Commons and then Governor-General of Australia), LL.D.; Sir (then Mr.) Isaac Wolfson (Managing Director of the Great Universal Stores and founder and trustee of the Wolfson Foundation for the Advancement of Health, Education and Youth Activities in the U.K. and Commonwealth), LL.D.; and J.D.W., D.Lit.

After the dinner and the conferring of degrees a reception was held in another room at which my wife and I were greeted by various friends connected with the University including, we were delighted to see, Nora Milnes in gown and hood, who had been head of the Social Science department at Edinburgh University and who had more than once spent a quiet weekend with us at Balerno, mostly resting in bed after an arduous week. For us and the other honorary graduates, as we now were, a crowning honour was still reserved, a tête-à-tête with the Queen Mother herself in a separate room in which she sat on a raised chair with lower chairs on either side of her, one for the graduate, the other for his wife.

The Queen Mother will be acknowledged by even those most indifferent to the charms of royalty to be a lovely creature. My wife had met her sister, Lady Elphinstone, at some A.R.P. affair during the war, and the two ladies talked for a while about this; after which the Queen Mother turned to me and gave utterance to what I am sure was her perfectly genuine delight in the whole ceremony as she said, 'It's been a lovely evening, hasn't it?' What could an Elizabethan student, in spirit a contemporary of Sir Walter Raleigh, reply to this twentieth-century Gloriana? I said, 'Yes, but the loveliest thing of the whole was the flower at the centre.' She blushed slightly; I don't think it was in anger.

It is not only precious for being one of the highest honours I possess, but because it was the last occasion when I could enjoy a ceremony with my beloved wife Dorothy. She was already in failing health but could manage to come with me and shared to the full every incident of the great evening in company with the Queen Mother. During the dinner I was of necessity separated from her; but her comfort was throughout in the tender and affectionate charge of Professor James Sutherland and his wife Helen; the latter looked after her beforehand, and the Professor sat next to her at the dinner, even helping her with exquisite courtesy in what had become for her at that stage the difficult task of eating. Indeed, it was to him that I owed the whole procedure, as he was at that time Public Orator to the University and had, I make no doubt at all, suggested my name as one of the small company of honorary graduands; while it was his duty as Public Orator to deliver the 'charges' before the seven presentations.

I shall conclude by quoting the 'charge' he delivered in my

honour. As well as being extremely witty, it is generous beyond words, and readers of this book must remember that the speaker was an affectionate friend, so that the portrait lacks any of the 'roughnesses' and 'warts' that its original possesses. But the account is that of a great scholar supreme in another field of English literature from my own and therefore above the battle, and I can claim it as a fair estimate of scholarly opinion of my work at the end of a long career. Incidentally, the passage which especially amused the Queen Mother, herself a Scot, was that referring to professors of English as 'one of Scotland's chief exports'—examples being not only the speaker himself but his famous predecessor in the Chair at University College, W. P. Ker.

'Your Majesty and Chancellor, I present Professor John Dover Wilson.

'In the long history of Shakespearean scholarship the name of Professor Dover Wilson will always hold an honoured place, and he will be remembered both for his textual criticism and for his elucidation of the plays. In 1919, with Sir Arthur Quiller-Couch, he began to edit the New Cambridge Shakespeare, and the first volume appeared, with what was to prove uncharacteristic promptitude, in 1921. We are told that when this notable venture was launched, Q. at the prow and Dover at the helm, the Cambridge University Press expected to publish seven volumes every year; but, in fact, such are the exacting standards of modern scholarship, it has taken almost twice as many years to edit the plays as it took Shakespeare to write them. After 1931 Professor Dover Wilson carried on this great task singlehanded, but in recent years he has had some help from a number of younger scholars who owe most of what they know to his example and his generous encouragement. Now, after forty years of devoted work, Love's Labours are all but won; two volumes are still delayed by the printers' strike and three are yet to come. Perhaps we should have waited for the last volume to appear; but after so many decades our honorary graduate is hardly in a position to chide us for our impatience to give public recognition to his great work.

Special Occasions

'If he has kept us waiting, he has never been idle. We can claim some part of him in our own University, where for some years he was a Lecturer in English Language and Literature at Goldsmiths' College, and later Professor of Education at King's College. In 1935 he was appointed to the Regius Chair of English and Rhetoric in the University of Edinburgh, and in view of the fact that one of Scotland's chief exports is Professors of English this must be taken as a reluctant tribute to his eminence in the field of literary scholarship. When he retired ten years later, it was to devote his ever-abundant energy to the completion of his edition of Shakespeare.

'In John Dover Wilson we salute one of the great scholars of our time. The evidence of his scholarship is to be found not only in the volumes of the New Cambridge Shakespeare, but in such brilliant and imaginative studies as *What Happens in 'Hamlet'* and *The Fortunes of Falstaff*. Few men have ever looked more closely at the text of Shakespeare, or have weighed more carefully its dramatic and poetic significance. As Socrates was said to have brought philosophy down from heaven to inhabit among men, so he has made the common reader aware of the meaning and significance of textual criticism, and has profoundly influenced those who now act and produce the plays of Shakespeare.

'I request you, Chancellor, by the authority of the Senate, to admit John Dover Wilson to the Degree of Doctor of Literature, *honoris causa*.'

The last occasion I wish to record was one in which I necessarily featured as the central figure, for on 13th July 1961 I came to my eightieth birthday, for which my friends and publisher prepared a surprise celebration. First of all the Cambridge University Press printed *A List of his Published Writings, Presented to John Dover Wilson*, prepared by John Butt and by J. C. Maxwell, who had collaborated with me in recent volumes of the New Shakespeare. When they began compiling their list it was not long before they found that they must turn to me for help. But it was not until later on that I received an unexpected invitation to attend a dinner party at Prestonfield House, to meet a number of friends, at which the book list would be presented

281

to me. The names of these friends I was not told until we all arrived at the dinner together, when I became aware for the first time that it was provided by the University of Edinburgh, with the principal, Sir Edward Appleton, in the Chair, and the Bedellus in attendance. Several speeches were delivered, the last and, some other guests informed me, the best of the evening coming from my grandson Francis, on the text, 'Not a bad old grandfather'. My eyesight was already dim and I was never given a list of those at the table, but as far as my recollection goes, they included:

Sir Edward Appleton (in the Chair)
Professor John Butt (at the opposite end of the table)
R. J. L. Kingsford (Secretary of the C.U.P.)
Richard David (Manager of the C.U.P.)
Stanley Bennett (Chairman of the C.U.P.)
Professor Geoffrey Bullough
Sir Sydney Roberts (who proposed the toast)
J. C. Maxwell
Professor James Sutherland
F. P. Wilson
Dr. E. H. Cameron
The Rev. David Stalker (who said the Grace)
Professor Sidney Newman
Sir James Learmonth
Professor A. J. Beattie
Professor W. L. Renwick
Professor Peter Alexander
G. I. Duthie

Epilogue

'What I aspired to be,
And was not, comforts me.'

'I am a part of all that I have met;
Yet all experience is an arch where through
Gleams that untravelled world whose margin fades
Forever and forever when I move.'

'Last night returning from my twilight walk
I met the grey mist Death, whose eyeless brow
Was bent on me, and from his hand of chalk
He reached me flowers as from a withered bough:
O Death, what bitter nosegays givest thou!

Death said, I gather, and pursued his way.
Another stood by me, a shape in stone,
Sword-hacked and iron-stained, with breasts of clay,
And metal veins that sometimes fiery shone:
O Life, how naked and how hard when known!

Life said, As thou has carved me, such am I.
Then memory, like the nightjar on the pine,
And sightless hope, a woodlark in night sky,
Joined notes of Death and Life till night's decline:
Of Death, of Life, those inwound notes are mine.'

Dorothy Mary Baldwin (1) = JOHN DOVER WILSON = (2) Elizabeth E. Wintringham
dau. Canon E. C. Baldwin   b. 1881   dau. Sir Joseph Arkwright
b. 1885 : d. 1961   b. 1894

Monica = Godfrey   Audrey = David M.   Caroline = Rev. Eric W. S.
Hunter   Baldwin   Helen   Lawson   Elizabeth   Jeffrey
         b. 1908   Margaret   b. 1927
         d. 1944   b. 1911

Lindy = Francis A. Timothy   Matthew = Janet   Dennis
Serrurier Hunter   Dover   Monica   b. 1947
           b. 1939 Dover   b. 1943 (adopted)
                    b. 1943

David Dover   David   Gordon   Peter   Richard Rachel   Janet
b. 1967   John   Dover   Godfrey Eric   Ann   Monica
                               Sinclair b. 1958 b. 1960 b. 1962 b. 1965 b. 1967
                               b. 1957   (adopted)(adopted)

TABLE OF THE DESCENDANTS OF JOHN DOVER WILSON

13 JULY 1961

✣

A LIST OF HIS

PUBLISHED WRITINGS

PRESENTED TO

JOHN DOVER WILSON

ON HIS

EIGHTIETH

BIRTHDAY

WITH LATER ADDITIONS

BY THE AUTHOR

✣

CAMBRIDGE
AT THE UNIVERSITY PRESS
1961

JOHN DOVER WILSON

English Lector in the University of Helsingfors, Finland, 1906–1909
Lecturer in English at Goldsmiths' College, University
of London, 1909–1912
H.M. Inspector of Adult Education and Continuation Schools under
the Board of Education, 1912–1924
Professor of Education in the University of London,
King's College, 1924–1935
Regius Professor of Rhetoric and English Literature
in the University of Edinburgh, 1935–1945
Trustee of Shakespeare's Birthplace, 1931; Life Trustee, 1951
Fellow of the British Academy, 1931
Honorary Fellow of Gonville and Caius College, Cambridge, 1936
Companion of Honour, 1936
Honorary Member of the Deutsche Shakespeare-Gesellschaft, 1939
Trustee of the National Library of Scotland, 1946;
vice-chairman, 1951–56
Honorary LL.D., University of Natal, 1949
Honorary D.Litt., University of Durham, 1950
Honorary LL.D., University of Edinburgh, 1950
D. ès L. hon., University of Lille, 1953
Honorary Member of I.A.U.P.E., 1958
Honorary D.Lit., University of Leicester, 1959
Honorary D.Lit., University of London, 1960
Foreign Member of the Finnish Academy of Science and Letters, 1963
Member of the Board of Electors to the Merton Professorship of
English Literature, 1948

ABBREVIATIONS

C.H.E.L.   Cambridge History of English Literature
M.L.R.   Modern Language Review
R.E.S.   Review of English Studies
T.L.S.   The Times Literary Supplement

I

ANONYMOUS ARTICLES ON
FINLAND AND RUSSIA

1. Articles written as Special Correspondent for the *Manchester Guardian*. [The most important was the earliest and fullest account of the 'execution' of Father Gapon early in 1906 by the Social Revolutionaries under the instruction of Rutenberg, who afterwards became one of the founders of Israel—an account which was confirmed six weeks later in all detail by a brochure issued from the Social Revolutionary Executive Committee sitting in Paris. These details were supplied, however, the day after the 'execution' by Konni Zilliacus, father of the Labour Party politician, who had himself got them from Rutenberg, flying from Russia through Finland.]

1906

2. 'The Aims and Methods of the Social Revolutionary Party in Russia.' *The Independent Review*, XI, 137–50, under the pseudonym Wildover Johnson.

1914–15

3. 'Russia and her Ideals.' *The Round Table*, V, 103–35.

II

CONCERNING EDUCATION

1921

4. HUMANISM IN THE CONTINUATION SCHOOL. Board of Education. Educational Pamphlets, no. 43. [An elaborate pamphlet written in preparation for the opening of compulsory part-time day continuation schools for all adolescents of 14 to 18, as prescribed in the Act of 1918, though owing to the 'Geddes Axe' never brought into being.]

5. *The Teaching if English in England*. Being the report of the departmental committee appointed . . . to inquire into the position of English in the educational system of England. [The committee sat

from May 1919 until 1921. J.D.W. wrote chapter v, 'English in Commerical and Industrial Life'; in chapter VIII ('Literature and Adult Education'), sections 232–8, 'Literature and the Nation', 249–252, 'Literature in Workers' Educational Association Classes'; and in chapter IX ('Some Particular Aspects of the Teaching of English'), sections 254–66, 'The Problem of Grammar'.]

1927

6. *The Mind*. By Various Authors. A series of lectures delivered in King's College, London, during the Lent Term, 1927. Edited by R. J. S. McDowall. [The object of the course was to present 'a general idea of the mind as viewed from several academic standpoints'. J.D.W. contributed a lecture on 'Education', i.e. 'the mind considered from the point of view of the study of education'.]

1928

7. THE SCHOOLS OF ENGLAND: A STUDY IN RENAISSANCE. Based on a series of lectures first delivered in King's College, London. Edited by J.D.W. London: Sidgwick & Jackson, Ltd. [Besides an editorial note, J.D.W. contributed 'The Schools and the Nation'.]

8. 'Adult Education in Yorkshire.' *The Journal of Adult Education*, III, no. I, October 1928. [This journal was founded by J.D.W., and edited by him from 1926 to 1928. For his account of its genesis, see *Adult Education*, 1952.]

1929

9. 'Adult Education in England.' *The Nineteenth Century and After*, CVI, 346–55.

1931

10. (14 February.) Review of *Harrow Lectures on Education*, ed. J. Coade, and of L. P. Jacks's *The Education of the Whole Man* in *The Spectator*.

11. (14 October; 11 November.) 'Education in a Changing World', five broadcasts printed in *The Listener*.

1932

12. CULTURE AND ANARCHY. BY MATTHEW ARNOLD. Edited with an introduction by J.D.W. Cambridge: at the University Press. [Paperback ed. 1960.]

1933

13. *The Social and Political Ideas of some Representative Thinkers of the Victorian Age.* A series of lectures delivered at King's College, University of London, during the session 1931–2. Edited by F. J. C. Hearnshaw. [J.D.W.'s contribution was a lecture on 'Matthew Arnold and the Educationists'.]

1935

14. *Education of To-day.* A series of addresses delivered at the third Young Public School Masters' Conference at Harrow School in January 1935. Edited by E. D. Laborde. [J.D.W.'s address was entitled 'The Writing of English at School and Elsewhere'.]

1937

15. *The Life of Winifred Mercier.* By Lynda Grier. [Contains an introduction by J.D.W.]

III

EARLY WORKS
(BIBLIOGRAPHICAL AND OTHER)
ON ENGLISH LITERATURE
AND PURITANISM

1905

16. JOHN LYLY. Cambridge: Macmillan and Bowes. Printed by John Clay at the University Press [reviewed by A. Feuillerat in *M.L.R.*, I].

1907

17. (October.) 'A date in the Marprelate Controversy.' *The Library* (2nd ser.), VIII, 337–59.

1908

18. 'The Missing Title of Thomas Lodge's Reply to Gosson's *School of Abuse.*' *M.L.R.*, III, 166–8.

1909

19. (4 February.) 'The Legend of Sir Veritas.' *The New Age*, n.s. IV, 202. [A Spenserian skit *à propos* of a lengthy discussion on the subject of Miracles in *The New Age*, Chesterton, Belloc, Shaw, and Belford Bax being the chief disputants.]

20. (Spring.) *The Cambridge History of English Literature*. Vol. III. Renascence and Reformation. [Contains 'The Marprelate Controversy' by J.D.W.]

21. (April.) Review of William Pierce's *An Historical Introduction to the Marprelate Tracts*. *The Library* (2nd ser.), X, 214–18.

22. (July.) 'A new tract from the Marprelate press' [*An exhortation vnto the gouernours, and the people of* . . . *Wales* 1588]. *Ibid*. X, 225–40.

23. (July.) 'Anthony Munday, Pamphleteer and Pursuivant.' *M.L.R.*, IV, 484–90.

24. (29 July.) 'The Marprelate Controversy.' Letter to the *T.L.S.* [a reply to the *T.L.S.* review of *C.H.E.L.*, III].

25. (October.) 'The Rev. W. H. Hutton and *The Cambridge History of English Literature* [misprinted *Cambridge Modern History*].' [A letter in *The Church Family Newspaper*, replying to Hutton's review.]

26. (October.) 'Euphues and the Prodigal Son.' *The Library* (2nd ser.), X, 337–61.

1910

27. *The Cambridge History of English Literature*. Vol. VI. The Drama to 1642 part II. [Contains 'The Puritan Attack upon the Stage' by J.D.W.]

28. THE WOUNDS OF CIVIL WAR. BY THOMAS LODGE (1594). [A Malone Society Reprint.]

29. (October.) 'Giles Fletcher and *The Faerie Queene*.' *M.L.R.*, V, 493–4.

30. (October.) 'John Lyly's Relations by Marriage.' *Ibid*. V, 495–7.

1911

31. LIFE IN SHAKESPEARE'S ENGLAND. A BOOK OF ELIZABETHAN PROSE compiled by J.D.W. Cambridge: at the University Press. 2nd ed., 1913; Penguin ed., 1944. [See also no. 148 below.]

32. Review of A. Feuillerat's *John Lyly: Contribution à l'Histoire de la Renaissance en Angleterre*. *M.L.R.*, VI, 103–14.

33. 'Richard Schilders and the English Puritans.' *Transactions of the Bibliographical Society*, XI, 65–134.

1912

34. THE RESURRECTION OF OUR LORD. [A Malone Society Reprint in which J.D.W. collaborated with Bertram Dobell.]
35. 'Martin Marprelate and Shakespeare's Fluellin. A new theory of the authorship of the Marprelate tracts' [the case for Sir Roger Williams's authorship]. *The Library* (3rd ser.), III, 113–76. [Reprinted from *The Library* and published by Alexander Moring Ltd. 1912.]

1913

36. 'Did Sir Roger Williams write the Marprelate tracts? A rejoinder' [to R. B. McKerrow and W. Pierce]. *Ibid.* IV, 92–104.

IV
WAR-TIME AND JUST AFTER

1914

37. Review of J. M. Robertson's *The Baconian Heresy: a Confutation*. *M.L.R.*, IX, 527–9.
38. THE WAR AND DEMOCRACY. By R. W. Seton-Watson, J.D.W., Alfred E. Zimmern, and Arthur Greenwood. London: Macmillan & Co., Ltd. [Planned and edited by A.E.Z. and J.D.W. as a study-book for W.E.A. classes. Translated into many European languages. J.D.W.'s contributions are chapters on 'The National Idea in Europe, 1789–1914', and 'Russia'.]
39. ['Russia and her Ideals.' See no. 3 above.]

1916

40. POETRY AND THE CHILD. Oxford: at the University Press. English Association Pamphlet, no. 34.

1917

41. 'Prospects in English Literature.' Four articles by 'Muezzin' in *The Athenæum*: I, 'Poetry and Shopkeeping' (February); II, 'Pessimism and Prophecy' (March); III, 'Looking Backwards' (May); IV, 'The Great Schism' (June).

1918

42. (April.) 'The Parallel Plots in *Hamlet*: a Reply to Dr. W. W. Greg.' *M.L.R.*, XIII, 129–56.

43. [*Humanism in the Continuation School*, written early in 1918. See no. 4 above.]
44. 'The Copy for *Hamlet*, 1603.' *The Library* (3rd ser.). IX, 153–85.
45. 'The *Hamlet* Transcript, 1593.' *Ibid.* IX, 217–47. [44 and 45 were reprinted as a single pamphlet by Alexander Moring Ltd.]
46. (16 May; 25 July.) 'Hamlet's Solid Flesh.' Letters to the *T.L.S.*
47. (4 July.) 'Shakespeare's Versification and the Early Texts.' *Ibid.*
48. (July; August.) 'The play-scene in "Hamlet" restored. I. Lock and Key.' *The Athenæum.*
49. (September; November.) 'The play-scene in "Hamlet" restored. II. The Multiple Mouse-Trap, and how it works.' [48 and 49 together form the first draft of *What Happens in Hamlet*, ch. v.]
50. (14 November; 2 January 1919.) 'Hatching the Cock's Egg of Polonius.' Letters to the *T.L.S.*

1919

51. (With A. W. Pollard) 'What follows if some of the good Quarto editions of Shakespeare's plays were printed from his autograph manuscripts.' *Transactions of the Bibliographical Society*, XV, 136–9. [Summary of paper read 16 December 1918.]
52. (9, 16 January; 13 March; 7, 14 August.) 'The "Stolne and surreptitious" Shakespearian Texts: Why some of Shakespeare's plays were pirated; How some of Shakespeare's plays were pirated; Henry V (1600); Merry Wives of Windsor (1602); Romeo and Juliet, 1597.' [Five articles, with A. W. Pollard, in the *T.L.S.*]
53. (8 May; 29 May.) 'Shakespeare's Hand in the Play of "Sir Thomas More".' Letters to the *T.L.S.*

1920

54. (22 January.) 'Sidelights on Shakespeare.' Letter to the *T.L.S.* [in defence of Dugdale Sykes].
55. (29 January; 19 February.) 'Early Touring Companies.' Letters to the *T.L.S.* [in controversy with W. J. Lawrence].
56. (April.) 'Dramatic and Bibliographical Problems in *Hamlet*.' *M.L.R.*, XV, 163–6 [a reply to W. W. Greg's article in *M.L.R.*, XIV, October 1919].
57. (30 September.) 'Elizabethan Printing.' Letter to the *T.L.S.* [in reply to Bayfield].
58. (October.) 'A Note on Elisions in *The Faerie Queene*.' *M.L.R.*, XV, 409–14.

59. (October.) Review of J. M. Robertson's *The Problem of 'Hamlet'*; Elmer Edgar Stoll's *Hamlet: An Historical and Comparative Study*; and V. Østerberg's *Studier over Hamlet-Teksterne*, I: *ibid.* xv, 343–40.

V

EDITING SHAKESPEARE, AND OTHER WORK MAINLY ELIZABETHAN

1921

60. THE WORKS OF SHAKESPEARE. Edited by Sir Arthur Quiller-Couch and J.D.W. [Quiller-Couch retired from the edition on the completion of the comedies in 1931. The texts alone, with enlarged glossaries, began to be reissued in 1957 as 'The Cambridge Pocket Shakespeare' and in 1968 were re-issued in paperback. The volumes are listed separately below.]

61. THE TEMPEST. Cambridge: at the University Press. [This, and each succeeding play up to *The Winter's Tale* (1931), was edited by Sir Arthur Quiller-Couch and J.D.W., with an account of its stage-history by Harold Child. H.C. continued to contribute until *II Henry IV* and his death (November 1945).]

62. THE TWO GENTLEMEN OF VERONA.

63. THE MERRY WIVES OF WINDSOR.

64. (7, 21 April.) 'Shakespeare: a standard text.' Letters to the *T.L.S.* [in controversy with G. Bernard Shaw].

1922

65. MEASURE FOR MEASURE.

66. THE COMEDY OF ERRORS.

1923

67. MUCH ADO ABOUT NOTHING.

68. LOVE'S LABOUR'S LOST. [2nd ed., revised throughout, 1961.]

69. *Two Elizabethan stage abridgements: the Battle of Alcazar and Orlando Furioso: An essay in critical bibliography*, by W. W. Greg, 1923. [Contains (pp. 361–4) speculations by J.D.W. on *Orlando* and its

congeners (*The Famous Victories* and *A Shrew*) communicated in a private letter.]

70. *Shakespeare's Hand in the Play of Sir Thomas More.* Papers by Alfred W. Pollard and others. Cambridge: at the University Press. [Contains 'Bibliographical Links between the Three Pages and the Good Quartos' by J.D.W.]

1924

71. *A History of English Literature*, edited by John Buchan: Nelson, 1923. [J.D.W. contributed chapters in Sections II and III, including that on Shakespeare.]

72. A MIDSUMMER NIGHT'S DREAM.

73. *Studies in the First Folio, written for the Shakespeare Association in celebration of the First Folio Tercentenary and read at meetings of the Association held at King's College, University of London, May–June 1923. With an Introduction by Sir Israel Gollancz, 1924.* [Contains 'The Task of Heminge and Condell': a paper read by J.D.W. on 18 May 1923. An interesting volume as containing papers by both Sidney Lee and W. W. Greg.]

74. (28 August.) 'Love's Labour's Lost' [IV. iii. 333]. Letter to the *T.L.S.*

75. (25 September; 16 October.) 'Shakespearian Elisions in *Sir Thomas More*.' Letters to the *T.L.S.*

76. (December.) 'Scilens.' Letter in the *London Mercury*, XI, 187 [reply to Grethe Hjort, in November issue].

77. *Essays and Studies by Members of the English Association*, vol. x, 1924. [Contains 'Spellings and Misprints in the Second Quarto of *Hamlet*' by J.D.W.]

1925

78. Review of J. A. Fort's *The Two Dated Sonnets of Shakespeare*, and *The Sonnets of Shakespeare*, edited by T. G. Tucker: *R.E.S.*, I, 353–9.

1926

79. THE MERCHANT OF VENICE.

80. AS YOU LIKE IT.

81. (2 April.) 'The Teacher's World and Shakespeare.' Article in the *Teacher's World*.

82. Review of Rudolf Fischer's *Shakespeares Sonette*: *R.E.S.*, II, 350–4.

83. Review of *Studies in Shakespeare, Milton and Donne* (University of

Michigan publications, Language and Literature, vol. i): *ibid.* ii, 475–9.

1927

84. (6 January.) 'Marlowe and *As You Like It*.' Letter to the *T.L.S.*
85. Review of J. M. Robertson's *The Problems of the Shakespeare Sonnets*: *Monthly Criterion*, vi, 162–7.
86. (October.) 'Act- and Scene-Divisions in the Plays of Shakespeare: a Rejoinder to Sir Mark Hunter' [art. in July 1926.] *R.E.S.*, iii, 385–97. [See W. W. Greg's art. in *R.E.S.*, iv, 152–8.]
87. THE POETRY OF THE AGE OF WORDSWORTH. AN ANTHOLOGY OF THE FIVE MAJOR POETS. Selected with an introduction by J.D.W. Cambridge: at the University Press.

1928

88. THE TAMING OF THE SHREW.
89. THE TEMPEST. BY WILLIAM SHAKESPEARE. A FACSIMILE OF THE FIRST FOLIO TEXT. With an Introduction by J.D.W. London: Faber and Gwyer.
90. TWELFTH NIGHT. BY WILLIAM SHAKESPEARE. A FACSIMILE OF THE FIRST FOLIO TEXT. With an Introduction by J.D.W. London: Faber and Gwyer.
91. CORIOLANUS. BY WILLIAM SHAKESPEARE. A FACSIMILE OF THE FIRST FOLIO TEXT. With an Introduction by J.D.W. London: Faber and Gwyer.
92. MACBETH. BY WILLIAM SHAKESPEARE. A FAC-SIMILE OF THE FIRST FOLIO TEXT. With an Introduction by J.D.W. London: Faber and Gwyer.
93. (18 October; 1 November.) 'The Text of *Hamlet* i. ii. 129.' Letters to the *T.L.S.*
94. ' "They Sleepe All the Act." ' *R.E.S.*, iv, 191–3.
95. Review of D. Nichol Smith's *Shakespeare in the Eighteenth Century*: *The Library* (4th ser.), ix, 223.

1929

96. ALL'S WELL THAT ENDS WELL.
97. ANTONY AND CLEOPATRA. BY WILLIAM SHAKE-SPEARE. A FACSIMILE OF THE FIRST FOLIO TEXT. With an Introduction by J.D.W. London: Faber and Gwyer.

98. THE WINTER'S TALE. BY WILLIAM SHAKESPEARE. A FACSIMILE OF THE FIRST FOLIO TEXT. With an Introduction by J.D.W. London: Faber and Gwyer.

99. AS YOU LIKE IT. BY WILLIAM SHAKESPEARE. A FACSIMILE OF THE FIRST FOLIO TEXT. With an Introduction by J.D.W. London: Faber and Gwyer.

100. JULIUS CAESAR. BY WILLIAM SHAKESPEARE. A FACSIMILE OF THE FIRST FOLIO TEXT. With an Introduction by J.D.W. London: Faber and Gwyer.

101. SIX TRAGEDIES OF SHAKESPEARE: AN INTRODUCTION FOR THE PLAIN MAN. London: Longmans, Green and Co.

102. OF GHOSTES AND SPIRITS WALKING BY NYGHT. BY LEWES LAVATER (1572). Edited with introduction and appendix by J.D.W. and May Yardley. London: Oxford University Press for the Shakespeare Association.

103. *Proceedings of the British Academy* 1929. Vol xv. [Contains 'The Elizabethan Shakespeare' by J.D.W.: the Annual Shakespeare Lecture.]

104. (3 October.) 'Shakespeare's Puns on "Bonds" ' [*Twelfth Night*, III. i. 24]. Letter to the *T.L.S.*

105. Review of *The Tragedie of Coriolanus*, edited by Horace Howard Furness, Jr.: *R.E.S.* v, 215–18.

106. Review of G. F. Bradby's *The Problems of Hamlet*: *M.L.R.*, xxiv, 373–4.

1930

107. TWELFTH NIGHT. [2nd ed., 1949.]

108. THE TRAGEDIE OF HAMLET PRINCE OF DENMARKE. BY WILLIAM SHAKESPEARE. Edited by J.D.W. from the text of the second quarto. Illustrated by eighty wood engravings designed and cut by Edward Gordon Craig. And printed by Count Harry Kessler at the Cranach Press, Weimar. [A sequel to the Cranach *Hamlet* of 1929, the text of which is a German adaptation by Hauptmann. The 1930 volume contains the same cuts by Craig, but prints as consecutive borders to Shakespeare's text the stories by Saxo Grammaticus and Belleforest each accompanied by an English translation, while the whole concludes with an essay on 'The Text of *Hamlet*' and (in a jacket at the end) textual notes by J.D.W.]

List of Published Writings

109. 'The Schoolmaster in Shakespeare's Plays'. *Essays by Divers Hands. Being the Transactions of the Royal Society of Literature*, n.s. IX, 9–34.

110. (17 April.) ' "Sound" or "South" ' [*Twelfth Night*, I. i. 5]. Letter to the *T.L.S.*

111 (19 June.) 'Textual Points in *As You Like It* and *Twelfth Night*.' Letter to the *T.L.S.*

112. Review of *Much Ado About Nothing*, Parallel Passage Edition, edited by Alphonso Gerald Newcomer, completed by Henry David Gray: *M.L.R.*, XXV, 203–6.

113. 'Thirteen Volumes of Shakespeare: a Retrospect.' *Ibid.* XXV, 397–414.

114. Review of Thomas Middleton's *A Game of* [sic for *at*] *Chesse*, edited by R. C. Bald: *The Library* (4th ser.), XI, 105–16.

1931

115. THE WINTER'S TALE.

116. HENRY V. BY WILLIAM SHAKESPEARE. A FAC-SIMILE OF THE FIRST FOLIO TEXT. With an Introduction by J.D.W. London: Faber and Faber.

117. KING LEAR. BY WILLIAM SHAKESPEARE. A FAC-SIMILE OF THE FIRST FOLIO TEXT. With an Introduction by J.D.W. London: Faber and Faber.

118. FIRST STEPS IN SHAKESPEARE. [Scenes from *A Midsummer Night's Dream, The Merchant of Venice, Julius Caesar, Macbeth*. Each issued separately.] Arranged and edited by J.D.W. Cambridge: at the University Press.

119. (April.) Review of E. K. Chambers's *William Shakespeare: a Study of Facts and Problems: M.L.R.*, XXVI, 189–98.

120. (23 May.) 'Sir Philip Sidney', by Mona Wilson. Review in *The Spectator*.

121. (24 September; 29 October.) '*Hamlet*: a suggestion' [punctuation of *Hamlet*, II. ii. 307–14). Letters to the *T.L.S.*

1932

122. THE ESSENTIAL SHAKESPEARE: A BIOGRAPHICAL ADVENTURE. Cambridge: at the University Press. [German trans., by Fromziska Meister, 1953; Serbo-Croat trans., 1960; Paperback ed., 1960.]

List of Published Writings

1933

123. PARADOXES OF DEFENCE. BY GEORGE SILVER (1599). A Shakespeare Association Facsimile, with an introduction by J.D.W.
124. (8 June; 31 August.) 'Shakespeare Emendations.' Letters to the *T.L.S.*
125. (6, 20 July.) 'The Nook-shotten isle of Albion' [*Henry V*, III. v. 14]. Letters to the *T.L.S.*

1934

126. HAMLET. [2nd ed., 1936; with 20 pages of 'Corrections and additional notes'.]
127. THE MANUSCRIPT OF SHAKESPEARE'S *HAMLET* AND THE PROBLEMS OF ITS TRANSMISSION. 2 vols. Cambridge: at the University Press. [An expansion of lectures delivered as Sandars Reader in Bibliography, 1932.]
128. (18 January.) 'The Duel in *Hamlet*.' Letter to the *T.L.S.*
129. (20 September.) 'The Manuscript of *Hamlet*.' Letter to the *T.L.S.*

1935

130. WHAT HAPPENS IN *HAMLET*. Cambridge: at the University Press. [The second edition (1937) contains a new preface and seven pages of notes. The third edition (1951) contains a new preface and a reprint (Appendix F) of a review of S. de Madariaga's *On Hamlet* (no. 178 below). Paperback ed., 1960.]
131. *The Great Tudors*, edited by Katharine Garvin. [Contains a chapter on 'William Shakespeare' by A. W. Pollard and J.D.W. Readers, if any, are challenged to disintegrate authorship. Reprinted 1956.]
132. (3, 24 January.) 'Too too sullied flesh.' Letters to the *T.L.S.*
133. (16, 30 May; 13 June.) ' "The Genuine Text" ' [the case for the entire *Hamlet*]. Letters to the *T.L.S.*
134. Review of Frances A. Yates's *John Florio, the life of an Italian in Shakespeare's England: M.L.R.*, xxx, 522–4.

1936

135. KING JOHN.
136. THE MEANING OF *THE TEMPEST*. Newcastle upon Tyne: The Literary and Philosophical Society. The Robert Spence Watson Memorial Lecture, 1936.

137. (II, 25 January.) 'Was King Claudius a Usurper?' Letters to the *T.L.S.*

138. (14 April.) 'Shakespeare.' By Middleton Murry. Review in the *Manchester Guardian.*

139. (26 September; 17 October.) 'Prince Fortinbras.' Letters to the *T.L.S.*

140. (24 October; 7 November.) 'Perttaunt' [*Love's Labour's Lost*, v. ii. 67]. Letters to the *T.L.S.*

141. 'The Study of Shakespeare.' *University of Edinburgh Journal*, VIII, 3–13. [Inaugural Lecture.]

1937

142. (16 January.) 'Shakespeare, Milton, and Congreve [descriptions of Cleopatra, Dalila, and Millamant]. Letter to the *T.L.S.*

143. (17 March.) 'Shakespeare: the Scholar's Contribution'; a broadcast printed in *The Listener.*

1938

144. *Seventeenth Century Studies Presented to Sir Herbert Grierson.* [Contains a preface by J.D.W.]

145. (7 May.) '*Love's Labour's Lost*' [II. i. 222]. Letter to the *T.L.S.*

1939

146. RICHARD II.

147. LESLIE STEPHEN AND MATTHEW ARNOLD AS CRITICS OF WORDSWORTH. Cambridge: at the University Press. The Leslie Stephen Lecture, 1939.

148. THROUGH ELIZABETHAN EYES. An Abridgement of *Life in Shakespeare's England* for Junior Readers. [Contains a short preface and a glossary by J.D.W.]

149. 'The Political Background of Shakespeare's *Richard II* and *Henry IV*. A Lecture delivered before the German Shakespeare Society at Weimar': *Shakespeare-Jahrbuch*, LXXV, 36–51.

1940

150. *The Cambridge Bibliography of English Literature.* [Articles in vol. 1 on 'The Puritan Attack upon the Stage' and 'The Marprelate Controversy' are by J.D.W. with the help, respectively, of E. N. S. Thompson and A. F. S. Pearson.]

151. A Review of Oliver Elton's *Essays and Addresses*, *M.L.R.* XXXV, 532–3.

1942

152. Paraphrase of 'Nashe's "Kid in Æsop"': a Danish Interpretation by V. Østerberg'. *R.E.S.*, XVIII, 385–94.
153. 'Shakespeare's Universe.' *University of Edinburgh Journal*, XI, 216–33.

1943

154. THE FORTUNES OF FALSTAFF. Cambridge: at the University Press. The Clark Lectures, 1942–3.
155. (5 June.) 'Treasure in an old Book.' *Edinburgh Evening News.* [An account of the 'Shakespeare signature' discovered by the librarian of the Folger Memorial Library, Washington, in a copy of William Lambarde's Αρχαιονομία, *sive de priscis anglorum legibus libri*, 1568.]

1944

156. Review of Oliffe Richmond's *Challenge to Faith*: *University of Edinburgh Journal*, XIII, 134–6.

1945

157. (14 June.) Review of *Political Characters of Shakespeare*, by John Palmer, in *The Listener*.
158. (July.) Review of *Political Characters of Shakespeare*, by John Palmer, in *Britain To-day*.
159. 'The Origins and Development of Shakespeare's *Henry IV*.' *The Library* (4th ser.), XXVI, 2–16.

1946

160. I HENRY IV.
161. II HENRY IV.
162. 'A note on the Porter in "Macbeth".' *Edinburgh Bibliographical Society Transactions*, II, 413–16.

1947

163. HENRY V. [The stage-history of this and of all succeeding plays was written by C. B. Young.]
164. MACBETH.
165. *Shakespeare on the Soviet Stage.* By Mikhail M. Morozov. Translated by David Magarshack. With an introduction by J.D.W.
166. Review of Peter Alexander's *Shakespeare's Punctuation*: *R.E.S.*, XXIII, 70–8.

167. (With R. W. Hunt) 'The Authenticity of Simon Forman's *Bocke of Plaies.*' *Ibid.* XXIII, 193–200 [193–7 by J.D.W.].
168. (26 July.) 'Twelfth Night.' Letter to the *T.L.S.* [On Feste's song.]
169. 'New Ideas and Discoveries about Shakespeare.' *The Virginia Quarterly Review*, XXIII, 537–42.
170. 'The Joy of Editing Shakespeare', a ten-minute talk by J.D.W. printed in *The Listener*, 27 November [not J.D.W.'s title!]. Followed by a long discussion with William Bliss (letters on 4, 11, 18, 25 December, 1, 8 January, 5, 12 February) on the character of the First Folio.

1948

171. TITUS ANDRONICUS.
172. Tribute to Walter de la Mare on his Seventy-fifth Birthday [25 April 1948]. Contains 'Variations on the theme of *A Midsummer Night's Dream*' by J.D.W. [an elaboration of de la Mare's essay in disintegration, the introduction to his edition of *A Midsummer Night's Dream* (The Scholar's Library, Macmillan), 1935, reprinted in his *Pleasures and Speculations*, 1940].
173. *Shakespeare Survey* 1. [Contains '*Titus Andronicus* on the Stage in 1595', by J.D.W.]

1949

174. JULIUS CAESAR.
175. *Shakespeare Survey* 2. [Contains 'Ben Jonson and *Julius Caesar*', by J.D.W.]
176. POEMS | Printed by several Hands. | OXFORD | AT THE BODLEIAN LIBRARY | OVER AGAINST *THE KINGS ARMS* | 1949. [Contains a sonnet by Drayton first set up by J.D.W. and later distributed and reset by F. P. Wilson.]
177. (24 June.) 'Titus Andronicus.' Letter to the *T.L.S.* [On Peacham illustration.]
178. (18 August.) 'The Text of the Plays', a broadcast printed in *The Listener.*
179. (30 September.) 'Rebellious Dead.' Letter to the *T.L.S.* [On *Macbeth*, IV. i. 97.]
180. Review of Salvador de Madariaga's *On Hamlet: M.L.R.*, XLIV, 390–7.

1950

181. ANTONY AND CLEOPATRA.
182. (17 February.) 'The Wooing of Nerissa.' Letter to the *T.L.S.* [*Merchant of Venice*, III. ii. 199.]
183. (10 March.) 'Text Corruptions.' Letter to the *T.L.S.* [Reply to C. S. Lewis, 3 March, on verse 'fossils'.]

1951

184. *Shakespeare Survey* 4. [Contains 'Malone and the Upstart Crow', by J.D.W.]
185. *The Development of Shakespeare's Imagery.* By W. H. Clemen, with a preface by J.D.W.
186. (29 June.) 'The Upstart Crow.' Letter to the *T.L.S.* [Reply to Janet Spens.]
187. '*Titus and Vespasian* and Professor Alexander.' *M.L.R.*, XLVI, 250.

1952

188. I HENRY VI.
189. II HENRY VI.
190. III HENRY VI.
191. SHAKESPEARE'S HISTORIES AT STRATFORD 1951. By J.D.W. and T. C. Worsley. London: Max Reinhardt. J.D.W. contributed 'Shakespeare and English History as the Elizabethans understood it'.
192. Review of *Macbeth*, edited by Kenneth Muir: *R.E.S.*, n.s. III, 71–5.
193. Review of H. N. Paul's *The Royal Play of Macbeth: When, why, and how it was written by Shakespeare: ibid.* n.s. III, 386–8.
194. 'Shakespeare's *Richard III* and *The True Tragedy of Richard the Third*, 1594.' *Shakespeare Quarterly*, III, 299–306.
195. Rejoinder to R. Flatter's review of *Macbeth: Modern Philology*, XLIX, 274–5.

1954

196. RICHARD III.
197. *Talking of Shakespeare.* Edited by John Garrett. [A selection of twelve lectures from the annual courses for teachers delivered at Stratford between 1948 and 1953. J.D.W.'s is entitled 'On editing Shakespeare, with special reference to the problems of *Richard III*'.]

198. *Shakespeare Survey* 7. [Contains 'The New Way with Shakespeare's Texts: An Introduction for Lay Readers. I. The Foundations', by J.D.W.]

1955

199. (With G. I. Duthie) ROMEO AND JULIET.
200. *Shakespeare Survey* 8. [Contains 'The New Way with Shakespeare's Texts: An Introduction for Lay Readers. II. Recent work on the text of *Romeo and Juliet*', by J.D.W.]
201. Review of D. Hay's *Polydore Vergil: Renaissance Historian, and man of letters: M.L.R.*, L, 66–8.

1956

202. PERICLES. [Edited by J. C. Maxwell, with a prefatory note by J.D.W.]
203. *Shakespeare Survey* 9. [Contains 'The New Way with Shakespeare's Texts: An Introduction for Lay Readers. III. In sight of Shakespeare's Manuscripts', by J.D.W.]
204. Review of *William Shakespeare, the complete Works*, edited by C. J. Sisson, *M.L.R.*, LI, 240–2.
205. Review of Percy Simpson's *Studies in Elizabethan Drama: R.E.S.*, n.s. VII, 423–4.

1957

206. (With Alice Walker) OTHELLO.
207. TROILUS AND CRESSIDA. [Edited by Alice Walker, with a prefatory note by J.D.W.]
208. TIMON OF ATHENS. [Edited by J. C. Maxwell, with a prefatory note by J.D.W.]
209. *Shakespeare Survey* 10. [Contains 'Shakespeare's "small Latin"—how much?' by J.D.W.]
210. (2 September.) 'The Shakespeare Paradox'. *The Times.*
211. Review of *Essays by Divers Hands, being the Transactions of the Royal Society of Literature*, New Series, vol. XXVII, edited by Sir George Rostrevor Hamilton: *R.E.S.*, n.s. VIII, 336–9.
212. (October.) 'A Note on *Richard III*: the Bishop of Ely's Strawberries.' *M.L.R.*, LII, 563–4.

1958

213. *Shakespeare Survey* 11. (Contains 'The New Way with Shakespeare's

Texts: An Introduction for Lay Readers. IV. Towards the High Road', by J.D.W.]

214. 'The Composition of the Clarence Scenes in *Richard III.*' *M.L.R.*, LIII, 211–14.

215. Brief introductions to *Hamlet, King Lear, Othello,* and *Macbeth* written for the British Council to be translated in various languages and dialects of India, mainly for women readers.

1960

216. CYMBELINE. [Edited by J. C. Maxwell, with a prefatory note by J.D.W.]

217. (With G. I. Duthie) KING LEAR.

218. *The Living Shakespeare.* Edited by Robert Gittings. London: Heinemann. [Contains 'The Texts' by J.D.W. 'Closely based' on a series of broadcasts for the B.B.C.]

1961

219. CORIOLANUS.

220. (25 May.) 'The Works of William Shakespeare . . . recorded by Argo for the Marlowe Society', in *The Guardian.*

VI

PERSONALIA

1944

221. *Proceedings of the British Academy* 1944. Vol. xxx. [Contains 'George Charles Moore Smith', by J.D.W.: an obituary.]

1945

222. *Proceedings of the British Academy* 1945. Vol. xxxi. [Contains 'Alfred William Pollard', by J.D.W.: an obituary.]

1956

223. *Proceedings of the British Academy* 1956. Vol. xlii. [Contains an obituary of Sir Edmund Chambers by F. P. Wilson, to which J.D.W. contributed.]

1959

224. *Elizabethan and Jacobean Studies Presented to Frank Percy Wilson in*

List of Published Writings

Honour of his Seventieth Birthday. [Contains 'Memories of Harley Granville-Barker and Two of his Friends', by J.D.W.]

225. Part of 'Walter Wilson Greg, 9 July 1875–4 March 1959'. *The Library* (5th ser.), XIV, 151–74. [J.D.W.'s contribution, pp. 153–7.]

226. 'The Presentation of Finnish Runos', by T. J. Mustanoja. *Neuphilologische Mitteilungen*, LX, 1–11. [Contains (pp. 9–10) a memory by J.D.W. of runo-singing by two Finnish bards, 1907.]

1963

227. *An Introduction to the Sonnets of Shakespeare, for the use of historians and others*.

1964

228. *Times Lit. Sup.*, April.

229. *The Glasgow Herald*, 23 April.

230. An exhibition of printed books drawn from the resources of the National Library of Scotland and the library of the University of Edinburgh to mark the Quatercentenary of Shakespeare's birth. Introduction by J.D.W.

231. An article by J.D.W. in *The Guardian*.

232. 'A Scholar at Work' by J.D.W. in *Viewpoint Magazine* (last no. of a govt. periodical), April.

233. *Review of English Literature*, April. 'The Malone Society Records' by J.D.W.

234. *Modern Language Review* 1964. Vol. LIX. [Contains 'C. B. Young' by J.D.W.: an obituary note.]

1966

235. THE SONNETS.

236. THE POEMS. [Edited by J. C. Maxwell, with a prefatory note by J.D.W.]

237. *The Times*—letter on Laurence Olivier's Othello.

Index

Abercrombie, Lascelles, *Sale of St. Thomas*, 253
Aberdeen University, 126
'Activists' in Finland, 51–2
Acton, Lord, Professor of Modern History, Cambridge, 28, 30; *History of Freedom*, 32
Adam Smith, Sir George, and his wife Lilian, 147–8; *Geography of the Holy Land*, 147
Adamson, J. W. (King's College, London), his *Pioneers of Education* and *Short History of Education*, 106
'Adult Education in England' (J.D.W.), 113; *for* Adult education *see* Chambers, Morant, Pullinger, Spencer
Advisory Council on Scottish Education, 125
Advocates' Library, Scotland, 1682, 139
Akerman, Dr. and Mrs. (Pietermaritzburg), 229
Alexander, Field Marshal Lord (of Tunis), 278
Alexander, Professor Peter, 175, 283; *Shakespeare's Henry V,* and *Richard III*, 168
Allan, Julian (sculptor), 137
Allenby, Lord, 147
Alty, Thomas, and Mrs. (Rhodes University), 233, 234
Anderson, Mrs. Jock, of Balerno, 146
Andrew, S. O., and Mrs. S. O., 45–6, 67, 86, 100
Anglican Fellowship, 244, 248
Anglo-Saxon, teaching of, 98, 99
Appleton, Sir Edward, 103, 282
d'Aranyi, Jelly, 136
Archangel project, 53–4
Arnold, Matthew, 30, 148; as Board Schools Inspector, 69; *Culture and Anarchy*, 20, 113; *Empedocles on Etna*, 240
Ascroft, W., Edwin Wilson's lithographs after, 18
Asquith as successor to Lloyd George, 84, 85
Aston Stanford, Bucks., 21–2, 26
Atkinson, Mabel (Mrs. M. Palmer), 230
Attlee, Clement, and 1945 Labour Government, 259

Austro–Hungarian Empire, breakup of, 81
Aveling, Professor (King's College, London), 112
Azev, of Social Revolutionary Party, 56–8; and death of Gapon, 57–8; and Dournovo, 57

Bailey, John, English Association, 96, 99
Bald, R. C., editor of Middleton's *Game at Chesse*, 176
Baldwin, Dorothy, later Mrs. John Dover Wilson, 41–2
Baldwin, the Rev. E. C. and Mrs. E. C., 40–2
Baldwin, Godfrey Theodore, 40, 41, 42; poem in memory of, 43
Baldwin, Stanley, 275; and Lord Eustace Percy, 117
Balerno, life at, 145–52
Balerno, Lord, 147, 261
Balfour, A. J., 18, 68
Balfour, Francis Maitland, 18
Ballard, Dr., on use of compositions, 100
Barbirolli, Sir John, 137
Bards of old Finland, 61–3
Barker, Ernest (King's College, London), 103, 104, 113, 114; as Professor at Cambridge, 105
Barker, Felix, on the Oliviers, 210
Barlow, Alan, son-in-law of Horace Darwin, 86
Barlow, Erasmus, grandson of Charles Darwin, 17
Barrie, Sir James, 127–8; *The Boy David*, 196; Granville-Barker's funeral oration for, 196
Battle of Malden, The, 65, 122–3
Beales, A. C. F., 116
Beattie, Professor A., 282
Beattie, Dr. William, National Librarian of Scotland, 139, 141
Bennett, Stanley, Chairman of Cambridge University Press, 186, 282
Benson, Sir Frank, as Henry V, 200
Bentham, Jeremy, founder of University of London, Gower Street, 103–4, 107
Beowulf, 122
Bergner, Elizabeth, as Boy David, 196

Coulsdon Parish Church, 23
Coulton, G. G., *Fourscore Years*, 131
County Colleges of 1944 Act, 94
Craig, Gordon, 178
Cranage, Dean (of Norwich), 44, 45
Crawford, Lord, 140, 277, 278
Crawley, Ernest (*Mystic Rose, Tree of Life*), 25
Crichton-Stuart, Major, and the Bute Collection, 140–2, 263
Crowther Report of 1959, 94
Crutchley, Brooke, on Edwin Wilson, 20
Crystal Palace School of Engineering (founded by J.D.W's grandfather), 20
Cunningham, Archdeacon, 28, 31
Czechoslovakia, creation of, 81

Darwin, Charles, 17
Darwin, Erasmus, killed in First World War, 18
Darwin, Horace, 17, 18, 19, 86
David, Richard, of C.U.P., 186, 212, 282
Davie, Vice-Chancellor and Mrs., Cape Town, 232
Day continuation schools, 67 seqq., 87–91; compulsory, 88; in decline, 91–4
'Day release scheme', 94–5
Dearmer, Percy, 248
De la Mare, Richard, 174, 175
De la Mare, Walter, 177; tribute to, on 75th birthday, 175; wife and sons of, 47
Delhi, Baptist College in, 186
Derby, Earl of, 205
De Selincourt, Professor Ernest, 205
Deutschbein, Professor (Marburg), 220
Deutsche Shakespeare Gesellschaft, Weimar, 215, 216, 217, 221–2, 224
Dew-Smith, photographer, 17, 18
Dickens, Charles, 269, 270
Dickinson, Professor Croft, 129
Dickinson, Lowes, 29, 31, 33–4; *Greek View of Life*, 33; *The Meaning of Good*, 33, 35
Donner, Mr. and Mrs. Ossian and son Patrick, 58–9
Douglas, David C., *English Scholars*, 131
Douie, Charles, and education in prisons, 78
Dournovo, Prefect of Police, Moscow, 57
Dover family, present representatives of, 22; John Dover, J.D.W's maternal grandfather, 21–2
Drever, James, 126
Dryden, 123; *Absalom and Achitophel*, 133–4
Duff Coopers in Paris, 223
Dunrossil, Viscount, 278
Duthie, G. I., 282; editorial work by (Cambridge New Shakespeare), 187; *The Bad Quartos of Hamlet*, 168

Edelfelt, Albert, Finnish artist, 59
Edinburgh, the Duke of, 143, 277
Edinburgh University, J.D.W. as Professor at, 119–44
Education Act of 1902, 68
Education Act of 1918, 82, 87
Education Act of 1944, 87, 88, 94
Edward VIII, and J.D.W's decoration (C.H.), 276
Eliot, T. S., 127; lecturing at Edinburgh, 131–2; *The Family Reunion*, 132–3
Elizabeth II, Queen, 143, 277–8
Elizabeth, the Queen Mother, 138, 139, 278–9
Elphinstone, Lady, 279
Elton, Oliver, translator (Kessler *Hamlet*), 178
Elton, Professor (Liverpool), 65
Endorf, near Munich, 224
English Association, 96, 101, 125, 160; Report of English Committee (role of English studies in education), 97–100, 110
Enright, Miss, on English Studies Committee (1919), 96
Evans, Dame Edith: in Congreve's *Way of the World*, 212; in *Othello*, 212

Fabian Society, 48, 52
Fairgrieve, King's College, London, 107
Falkland Place, source of Bute Collection, 140, 141
Farinelli, Professor Arturo, 216, 221
Farrow, Betsy, King's College, London, 114
Fergusson, Bernard, 260
Ferrier, Kathleen, 136, 137
Festival of Britain, London 1951, 135
Fifoot, Mr., librarian (Edinburgh), 144
Figgis, Neville, 29, 31–3; at Marnhall and Mirfield, 32–3; *Churches in the Modern State*, 32; *Civilization at the Cross-Roads*, 32; *Studies of Political Thought, from Gerson to Grotius*, 32; *Theory of the Divine Right of Kings*, 31
Finland, 45–61; in 19th–20th centuries, 48–9; Academy of Science and Letters, 61; Literary Society, 61, 62
Firth, Sir Charles, on May 1919 English Studies committee, 96
Fisher, H. A. L., 33; *A History of Europe*, 33; as President of Board of Education, 84, 87, 91, 92, 94; Fisher Act, *see* Education Act of 1918
Fiske, John, philosopher, 241
Fleam Dyke, George Trevelyan's 'Sunday tramps' to, 29
Flecker, James Elroy, *Hassan*, 252

Henderson, Arthur, 217
Hetherington, Sir Hector, 115, 183
Hill, J. C., King's College, London, 107
Hirn, Yrjo, 49–50; *The Sacred Shrine*, 50
Hitler, 216–22, 226
Hjort, Greta, 'bad quarto', theory of, 165–166
Hoare, Sir Samuel, and the Holmes Circular, 70
Holland, Sir Thomas, 183–4; and J.D.W's Edinburgh appointment, 120, 121, 124 Lady Holland, 121
Holmes, E. G. A., and Holmes Circular (on school inspectorate), 69–70
Holtby, Winifred, *South Riding*, 131
Home Guard, 148–50
Homerton Training College, 44, 45
Housman, A. E., 238; friendship with Pollard, 239–42, *A Shropshire Lad*, 240, 241
Hull, as 'escape port' for Russians, 53
Humphreys, Professor and Mrs. (University of London), 267
Hunter, David, 226, 227, 235–6; daughter of (J.D.W's daughter-in-law), *see* Wilson, Godfrey and Monica
Hunterstoun 235–6
Huntington, Helen (Mrs. H. Granville-Barker), 190, 199
Hutchinson, F. E., 127
Huxley, Aldous: *After Many a Summer*, 131; *Brave New World*, 220
Huxley, Julian, King's College, London, 103, 112

Ice yachting in Helsinki, 59–60
Inchbald, Mrs. Elizabeth, quoted (on Falstaff), 254
Industrial democracy, *see* Morant (esp. 90)
Industrial Training Act of 1964, 95; Industrial Training Boards of Ministry of Labour, 95

Jackson, Barry (later Sir Barry), 175; Birmingham Repertory production by, of *Hamlet* in modern dress, 207; Malvern festivals of, 197–8, 207
Jackson, Professor Kenneth, 46
Jackson, Moses, St. John's College, Oxford, 239, 242
Jaggard and his compositors, 167, 176
James Tait Black prizes, 129–31
James, William, *Varieties of Religious Experience*, 156
Jeffrey, Eric, husband of J.D.W's daughter Caroline, 235
Jena, Edwin Wilson, studies in, 18
Johnston, Edward, and the Kessler *Hamlet*, 178
Jones, Daniel, phonetician, 99, 100

Jonson, Ben, *Bartholomew Fair*, 210
Journal of Adult Education, 117
Judges, A. V., King's College, London, 116
Jung, C., 108
'Jung Fennomans' (Young Finns), 48–50

Kaiser Wilhelm Gesellschaft, 216, 218
Kaiser Wilhelm Institut, Dalheim, 219–220
Kalevala tales of Finland, 61
Kantele (musical instrument), 62
Keller, Professor Wolfgang, 215, 216, 222
Kenley, Surrey, J.D.W's grandparents at, 22–3, 41
Kenyatta, Jomo, 226
Kenyon, Sir Frederick, on Pollard, 238
Ker, Professor W. P., 65, 238, 263, 280; on May 1919 English Teaching Committee, 97–8, 99
Kessler, Count Harry, Weimar Press of, 178–9
Keynes, Margaret, grand-daughter of Charles Darwin, 17
Keynes, Maynard, 36
Khan, Mr., of 'T' inspectorate, 70
King's College, Cambridge, 27, 35, 36
King's College, London, J.D.W. as Professor of Education at, 93–104; and King's College School, 239
King's College, Newcastle, 270; Lord Eustace Percy as Rector of, 117–18
Kingsford, R. J. L., of Cambridge University Press, 186, 264, 282
Kipling, Rudyard, 252
Kitchen, P. I., of Rugby Day Continuation School (*From Learning to Earning*), 91, 94
Kitchin, G., 126
Kittredge, Professor G. L., 205–6
Krakatoa eruption of 1883, 18
Krebs, Sir Hans, 278
Kropotkin Circle, 48, 58

Labour Colleges (Marxist rivals of W.E.A.), 80
Lambert, Mrs. (Balerno), 152
Lancing College, 40, 42; Ambrose Wilson as headmaster of, 23–4; J.D.W. as pupil at, 24
Laski, Harold, 117
Lavater: *Of Ghostes and Spirites walking by Nyght* (1572), 158
Lavin, Mary, *Tales from Bective Bridge*, 131
Learmonth, Sir James, 138–9, 282
Leeds University, J.D.W. at, 32–3, 83, 156

Leigh, Vivien, 135, 209
Leishman, Blair, 273
Le Loyer, Pierre, 1111 *Livres des Spectres* (1586), 158
Lenin, in 1917, 81
Leverhulme, Lord, 183
Lewis, C. S., 127
Library, The, articles in on the 'bad quartos', 160–6
Lincoln Gaol, J.D.W. lectures at, on Shakespeare, 78–9
Lindelöf, Professor Uno (Helsingfors), 50, 51, 61, 62
Listener, The, Edwin Muir reviewing for, 136
Lloyd George, David, 84; Health Service of, 68–9
Lodge, Thomas, pamphleteer, J.D.W. on, 155
London School of Economics, 114, 115
London Society for the Study of Religion, 247
Longfellow's *Hiawatha,* linked with Finnish *Kalevala,* 62
Longton, Staffs., early experimental University Tutorial classes at, 75; R. H. Tawney at, 77
Lönnrot, compiler of *Kalevala,* 62
Loring, William, Warden of Goldsmiths' College, 65
Love, John, of Balerno, 151
Lyly, J., 153, 155; *Sappho and Phao,* 141. *See also* Harness Prize

Macarthy, Lillah, 190
MacColl, D. S., *Wilson Steer,* 131
McDowall, Professor R. J. S., at King's College, London, 112
Macgregor, D. H., University Tutorial lecturer, 79–80
McKerrow, Professor, 154, 168, 172, 173, 174, 181–2; edits *Works of Thomas Nashe,* 155
McKillop, Professor Alan, 142
Maitland, Sir Alexander and Lady, 131, 136, 137, 147
Maitland, Professor (*Domesday Book and Beyond*), 28, 32
Malherbe, Professor (Pietermaritzburg), 229, 230
Malinowski, Professor, 226, 227
Malone Society reprints, 167
Manchester Grammar School, 46
Manchester Guardian, 54; publishes the Gapon story, 56
Mannerheim (Marshal), 59
Mansbridge, Albert: and the National Central Library, 75, 244–5; and the Workers' Educational Association, 69,

73, 74, 93; secures Chambers and Zimmern, 74; and University Tutorial Class Movement, 84
Marlowe Society's production of *Comus,* Rupert Brooke in, 39; *Dr. Faustus* with Brooke, Francis Cornford, 40
Marquard, Mr. and Mrs. Leo, 232, 268
Marshall, Alfred, 28, 31
Martin, L. C., 127
Martin Marprelate tracts (thesis on by J.D.W.), 44, 45, 153–4, 156, 173
Marvin, F. S., 78
Masaryk, J., 81
Masefield, John, on Granville-Barker's *Twelfth Night,* 189, 190
Masson, Professor, 127, 128
Matthews, Professor, of Fort Hare, 234
Matthews, W. R., of King's College, London, later Dean of St. Paul's, 103
Mawer, Professor Allen, 114, 115
Maxwell, J. C., 132, 281, 282; as an editor of New Cambridge Shakespeare, 187; of *Poems* of Shakespeare, 187; *List of his Published Writings Presented to John Dover Wilson,* 281, 287, seqq.
Medium Aevum (journal), 46
Meikle, Dr. (Institute of Historical Research and National Library of Scotland), 139
Melrose, Mr., of Balerno, 152
Meredith, George, 29, 41, 66, 128
Meredith, H. O., 36
Mill, James, on education, 113
Mill, John Stuart, 113
Milnes, Nora, 278–9
Milton, John, 123, 138
Milyonkof, head of Russian Constitutional Democrats, 52
Modern Language Review, 155, 156, 157, 158, 171–2, 177, 180
Monstrelet, *Chronique* (1400–44), 256
Montagu, Lady Mary Wortley, and the Bute Collection, 142–3
Montefiore, Claude, 247
Moore, G. E., *Principia Ethica,* 35
Moore Smith, G. C., 155
Moorman, F. W., 'Shakespeare's Ghosts', 158
Morant, Robert (Perm. Sec. to Board of Education), 87, 116–17; and the day continuation schools, 67–8, 70, 72, 83, 88, 90; and the Holmes Circular, 70; as constructor of first English State system of education, 68; as Secretary to Lloyd George's Health Service, 68–9
Morgan, Charles, *The Voyage,* 131
Mountbatten, Louis (Lord Mountbatten) replaces Wavell in India, 259
Mozley, Kenneth, 248

Muir, Edwin, 130, 136
Muirfield Golf Course, 129
Munday, Anthony, pamphleteer: J.D.W. on, 155
Munitions Area Recruiting Office, Munitions Area Dilution Office, J.D.W's work with, 85–6
Mussolini, 217
Mustanoja, Professor (Helsinki), 61

Namier, Lewis, 265
Nashe, Thomas, 45
Natal University, inauguration of, 228
National Liberal Club, 75
National Library (Central), origins of, 75
Newbolt, Sir Henry, chairman of May 1919 Committee (Teaching of English), 97, 98
New Cambridge Shakespeare (Cambridge Pocket Shakespeare), 30, 93, 112, 170–187; *for details see* 'Editing Shakespeare', 297 seqq.
Newcastle University, the Percy Building at, 118
New College, Oxford, 73
Newman, Cardinal: *Apologia* of, and Bishop Daniel Wilson, 21; *The Idea of a University*, 113
Newman, Professor Sidney, 137–8, 282
New Place, Stratford-on-Avon, 202
Nicholas II, Tsar, 49; *see also* St. Petersburg
Nietzsche (in Common's translations), 31–32, 109; *AntiChrist*, 31, 37; *Thus Spake Zarathustra*, 37
Normand, Lord (Lord Justice General of Scotland), and Lady Normand, 133, 134; Lord Normand on Wavell, 250
'Notes on the Copy' in the Cambridge Shakespeare series, 168, 169, 178, 179, 181
Nunn, Percy, King's College, London, 106, 107, 108, 109
Nyakyusa tribe, Godfrey and Monica Wilson among, 227

Oakeshott, Walter, 261
Oban, 135
Olivier, (Sir) Laurence and Lady (Vivien Leigh), 208–9, 263; in *Antony and Cleopatra*, 208–9; in *Titus Andronicus*, 210; in Shaw's *Caesar and Cleopatra*, 208–9; Laurence, 135, 192; in *Hamlet* (film), 211; in *Henry V* (film), 208; in *The Entertainer*, 211
Owen, Joseph, and the W.E.A., 82, 86
Oxford History of English Literature, 270, 272

Pares, Sir Bernard, 264; at meeting of Russian Duma, May 1906, 52

Pares, Professor Richard, 264–8, 269, 270; edits *English Historical Review*, 267; *George III and the Politicians*, 265, 266–7; *The Historian's Business*, 265, 268
Pares, Mrs. Richard, 267
Paris trip described, 223–4
Partridge, Professor (Witwatersrand), 234
Paterson, W. D., 126
Paton, Alan, *Cry the Beloved Country*, 261
'Payment by results' system in schools, 69
Percy, Lord Eustace: as Minister of Education, 117; contrib. to Zimmern's *War and Democracy*, 81, 117; *Education at the Crossroads*, 117; *John Knox*, 131; *Some Memories*, 117; at inauguration of Natal University, receives honorary degree, 228–9, 231–2; *see also* Newcastle University
Perkins, W. H., Director of Education for Warwickshire, 71, 94–5
Perry-Keane, Joanna, later Mrs. F. P. Wilson, 86
Perse School, Cambridge, J.D.W. at, 23
Petersen, Professor and Mrs. (Jena), 218
Philip, Sir Randall, and his son, 134–5, 136, 140
Phonetics, study of, 99, 100, 101
Piaget, 111
Pilgrim Trust, and purchase of Bute Collection, 142
Plato's *Republic*, for students of education, 109, 110–11, 112
Pollard, Alfred, 168, 186, 212; and Cambridge Shakespeare, 171, 173; description and appreciation of, 181–2, 237–249; children of, 156, 243, 244, 245, 246, 247, 248; and J.D.W's 'Marprelate' work, 154; edits *The Library*, 153–154; with J.D.W. at Malvern Festival, 197; introduces Peter Alexander's book, 168; *King Richard II: a New Quarto*, 244; *Life, Love and Light: Practical Morality*, 246, 247; Sandars Lectures for 1915, 'Shakespeare's Fight with the Pirates, 244; Shakespeare's Folios and Quartos, 158, 159, 164, 173; *Shakespeare's Hand in the Play of Sir Thomas More*, 161; *Short Title Catalogue*, 244; with J.D.W., 'The Stolne and Surreptitious Texts' (T.L.S.), 167, 170; J.D.W's British Academy obituary of, 147–8
Pollard and Bartlett, *A Census of Shakespeare's Quartos*, 141
Ponsonby, Lord, *Henry Ponsonby*, 131
Pope, Alexander, 123, 269–70
Porteous, A. J. D., 126
Praz, Mario, 127

Prescott, Hilda F., *Spanish Tudor*, 131
Priestley, Sir Raymond, in Natal, 228, 229, 231, 232
Primrose, Lord, 250
Proceedings of the Royal Society of Edinburgh, Edwin Wilson's work for, 19
Pullinger, Dorothy, 86
Pullinger, Frank, brother of Mrs. S. O. Andrew, Inspector and Administrator, 67–9, 82, 86; J.D.W. as H.M.I. under, 67 seqq.; death of, 91–3; and the 'Technical Branch', 69, 70
Purdom, C. B., 191
Purley home of J.D.W., 86, 137, 145, 207

Quartos, 'good' and 'bad', 159 seqq.; Pollard on, 164–5
Quartermaine, Leon, 192
Quiller-Couch, Sir Arthur, 36–7; and the Cambridge Shakespeare, 36–7, 170–1, 173, 177; on the May 1919 Teaching of English Committee, 95–7; *Oxford Book of English Prose*, 37; *Shakespeare's Workmanship*, 173; *Studies in Literature*, 36

Raleigh, Walter, as a 'born teacher', 238
Rankine, Harry, of Balerno, 150–1
Ravelrig, Balerno, 149
Raymont, Mr., Goldsmiths' College, 64
Read, Forrest, *Young Tom*, 131
Redgrave, (Sir) Michael, 192, 207, 208
Reid Orchestra, 136, 137
Renwick, Professor W., 282
Rhodes, R. Crompton, 175
Rhodes-Livingstone Institute, Northern Rhodesia, 227
Ridgeway, William, 38, 39; *The Origin of Tragedy*, 38; *The Horse*, 38
Ripman, Professor, in English Association debate with Robert Bridges, 101
Roberts, S. C. (later Sir Sydney), 212, 282; and the Cambridge Shakespeare, 172, 183, 184, 186; becomes Master of Pembroke, 185; *Adventures with Authors*, 212
Robeson, Mrs. Paul, 226
Rochdale, early experimental university tutorial classes at, 75
Rogers, Bruce, 170
Rosebery, Lord, 250
Rossetti, D. G., 41
Roundhay, Leeds, 78
Rowe, Nicholas, as Shakespeare's first biographer, 203
Rowse, Professor A. L., 265
Royal Court Theatre, 188–9; *see also* Granville-Barker, Shaw, G. B.
Royal Institute, later Royal Society, J.D.W. lectures at, 204

Runeberg, Finnish poet, 61
Rutenberg, friend of Gapon, 55, 56
Rutherford's High-mastership, Manchester Grammar School, 46
Rylands, George, speaking Shakespeare verse (in Marlowe Society records), 192

Sackville-West, V., *A Flame in the Sunlight*, 131
Sadler, Sir Michael, at Leeds University, 32–3
St. Augustine, *De Civitate Dei*, 32
St. Clair family, and Roslin Chapel, 138
St. Giles, Edinburgh, 1953 ceremonies at, 135
St. Petersburg, 'Bloody Sunday' in, 47–8, 52, 54, 55, 57; St. Peter and St. Paul fortress, 58
Saintsbury, George, 38; on learning Anglo-Saxon, 98–9
Sampson, George, on May 1919 English Teaching Committee, 96–7; *English for the English*, 97
Sandars Lectures at Cambridge: J.D.W's, 168, 179; Pollard's, 244
Sayle, Charles, 154
Schilders's press (Dutch), 154, 173
'Schmidt, Professor' (Tschaikowsky of Kropotkin Circle), 48
Schneider, G., lithographer, 18
Schonland, Sir Basil, 228
School leaving age, 88, 94–5
Schools of England: a Study in Renaissance (J.D.W. and others), 113
Schücking, Professor (Leipzig), 225
Scotsman, The, 271, 272
Scott, C. P., as editor of *Manchester Guardian*, 56
Scott, Thomas, 21
Secondary schools, 68, 88
Selby-Bigge, Sir Amherst, 82, 87–8, 92, 93, 94
Seton-Watson, Professor, part-author of *War and Democracy*, 81
'Seventeenth-century Studies' as tribute to Professor Grierson, 126–7
Shakespeare, the acting of, 188–212
Shakespeare Association, 158, 192, 193
Shakespeare Birthplace Trust, 201, 205
Shakespeare's plays, poems, sonnets, *see named authors and editors*
Shaw, George Bernard; and Granville-Barker, and Court Theatre productions, 45, 51, 188, 190; at Bridges–Ripman debate on phonetics, 101; at Malvern, 197–8; J.D.W. lectures on, in Finland, 51
Shaw, Mrs. G. B., 198
Sheffield University, and the University Tutorial classes, 84

Sheppard, J. T., 36
Shipley, Professor, Edwin Wilson's work for, 19
Shuttleworth, James Kay, 107
Sibelius, conducting his *Second Symphony*, 59; *Finlandia*, 59
Simpson, Percy, Shakespearian studies of, 158
Smith, Alick Buchanan, later Lord Balerno, 147
Smith, J. C., at Grierson's 70th birthday celebration, 126
Smith, N. Kemp, at same, 126
Smuts, General, 226, 228, 230, 231
Snow, C. P., 86
Social Revolutionary Party in Russia, 48, 51, 55, 56, 57, 81
Society for Pure English, 100
Soskice, P., 56
South Africa, J.D.W. in, 228–35; second visit, 235–6
South Kensington, Natural History Museum, Edwin Wilson's work at, 17
Spelling reformers (Robert Bridges, Daniel Jones), 99, 101
Spencer, Frederick, of 'T' inspectorate, 70, 71, 75, 113; as research assistant to B. and S. Webb, 71; *An Inspector's Testament*, 71
Spenser, Edmund, 123
Stalker, the Rev. David, 133–4, 282
Stapleton, Olaf, 79
Stephen, Sir Leslie, 36
Stewart, Dr., of Currie, 146–7
Stolypin's oppressions, under Tsar, 48, 52
Strachey, Lytton, 29, 34–7; and 'Q', 177; death of, 37; *Eminent Victorians*, 36; *Landmarks in French Literature*, 36; *Queen Victoria*, 36, 37
Strand Magazine, 54
Stratton, 'Chubby', 44
Strong, L. A. G., *Travellers*, 131
Suomi, 50
Sutherland, Professor James (and Mrs. James), 279, 280, 282
Sykes, Professor Norman, later Dean of Winchester, 114
Sweet's works, J.D.W's interest in, 65, 99
Swinburne, A. C., 41

'T' inspectorate after 1911, 70
Tawney, R. H., in early University Tutorial Classes, 75, 77–8; *The Agrarian Problem in the 16th Century*, 77; *Religion and the Rise of Capitalism*, 77
Taylor, A. E., 126, 127
Teachers' Diploma Course at King's College, J.D.W's institution of, 108–12

Tedder, Air-Marshal, Lord, 45
Temple, William, as President of W.E.A., 77
Tennyson, Alfred, Lord, 41, 253
Thirkill, Sir Henry, Master of Clare College, 262
Thomas, Sir Henry (British Museum), 245
Thompson, Sir Edward Maunde. and the 'Three pages' of Shakespeare's hand, 158, 160–1, 162, 163, 164; *Shakespeare's England*, 164
Thompson, George, reviver of Yorkshire W.E.A. after First War, 83
Thomson, J. J., Master of Trinity, Cambridge, 30
Tillotson, Professor Kathleen, 270
Tillyard, H. J. W., 37
Titley, Dr., of King's College, London, 107
Tovey, Sir Donald, 126, 136
Townsend-Warner, *Outlines of Industrial History*, 76
Toynbee, Arnold, *Studies of History*, 267–8
Trevelyan, Sir George, 29–31, 115, 265; Janet, wife of, 30, 31
Tschaikowsky, Nicholas, leader of Social Revolutionaries (Kropotkin Circle), 48, 49, 51; at J.D.W's home in Helsingfors, 58; as President of 'North Russian Republic', 81
Turku to Stockholm journey, 61

Underwood, Professor and Mrs., Johannesburg, 228
University Extension classes, 1850 and after, 73
University Tutorial Class Movement, 1907, 73–6, 79, 82–4

Vedrenne-Barker productions, (Royal) Court Theatre, 45, 198; *see* Granville-Barker
Volkovsky, Felix, of Kropotkin Circle, 58
Von Hügel, Baron, 247
Von Neurath, 219

Waldegrave, printer to King James VI, 154
Waley, Arthur, '*Monkey*' by Wu Ch'eng-ên, 131
Walker, Dr. Alice, as a later Cambridge Shakespeare editor, 187
Wallas, Graham, 71
Waller, A. A., 155–6, 173; offers J.D.W. editorship of Cambridge Shakespeare, 170, 171; Greg's attitude to, 172
Walthamstow, family links with, 21
Ward, Adolphus, Master of Peterhouse, 44, 47, 54, 153; and the Cambridge Shakespeare, 170, 173, 186; (and